AF192368

Dr David Henry Kanyumi

Social INSECURITY among the Vulnerable Groups in TANZANIA

novum pro

w w w . n o v u m - p u b l i s h i n g . c o . u k

© 2024 novum publishing

ISBN 978-3-99146-145-6
Editing: Stephanie Marrie
Cover photo:
Catay Cagatay I Dreamstime.com
Cover design, layout & typesetting:
novum publishing
Author's photo:
Venart Photography, Glasgow

www.novum-publishing.co.uk

Print product with financial
climate contribution
ClimatePartner.com/16547-2311-1001

Acknowledgements

Without the support of many people, this book could not have been successful. Therefore, I would like to express my gratitude to those people who kindly provided me with invaluable assistance in many ways.

Special thanks go to all the brave participants in my original research, who willingly shared their precious time and experience-based knowledge related to research questions during interviews. Participants who took part in interview meetings included: older people, street children, women, and the disabled—also, employees within the local non-governmental welfare organisations.

I want to express my sincere gratitude to the leadership of the three local organisations – MAPERECE, Dogodogo Street Children Trust, and SMGEO. They graciously allowed the original research to be conducted within their organisations and facilitated the participation of their respective clients in the study.

I would also like to express my gratitude to my family members, Esther Mageni, Henry Kanyumi, Bless, Ethan, Lydia, Saskia, and Lily K, for their unwavering love, support, and motivation.

Table of Contents

1 Introduction

The Tanzanian government provides minimal welfare support to its citizens, leaving many without reliable means to address their well-being. This lack of full and effective governmental involvement in providing social welfare leaves people in disadvantaged areas vulnerable. As a result, they often rely on relatives, take out loans, beg, or seek assistance from charities. However, local non-governmental welfare organisations have stepped in to fill the gap, focusing on specific social issues and supporting individuals to address societal problems and reach their full potential. However, the work and contribution of local non-governmental welfare organisations towards social problem-solving is an under-researched topic. There is currently a limited understanding of how people who work in local non-governmental welfare organisations and people who use these organisations' social services understand social problems, how they experience them, and what impact these organisations have on their experiences.

The emergence and involvement of local non-governmental social welfare organisations in social problem-solving occurs amidst a prevalence of social problems that affect citizens' livelihood and wellbeing. Tanzania is currently witnessing a lot of changes. These changes include rapid urbanisation, industrialisation, and the movement of young adults from rural areas to cities. Additionally, globalisation impacts the labour market due to the high flow of goods from outside Tanzania, negatively impacting local businesses. Local businesses are being negatively impacted by the availability of cheaper goods, particularly in the food industry. This trend is making it increasingly challenging for homegrown products to remain sustainable. Mkenda (2005a:3) understood globalisation as 'the process of increasing economic, political, social, and cultural integration, whereby influences beyond national boundaries have a crucial impact on constraining and influencing all aspects of national wellbeing.' In Tanzania, this interaction manifests through an increased flow of goods, ideas, and services, raised capital, and the migration of people. This new economic model and a unique way of realising livelihood entices young adults to move away from farming activities. Migration to cities is not a straightforward process. These social and economic phenomena enormously impact family structures, changing how family support- networks function. During a crisis, people, in general, previously tended to rely on the extended family network for support in their attempt to secure some normality in life. Vulnerable people, such as people with health problems, older people, and orphans, were supposed to rely on the extended family network support model. However, this extended family network-support model is crumbling. This fast diminishing of the extended family supporting network model necessitates the development of other social structural support, including local non-governmental welfare organisations, to address the welfare concerns of the majority disadvantaged populations of Tanzania. This book underscores the importance of understanding the responsibilities and social activities that local organisations fulfil in response to social issues. It explores how they carry out their work and the impact they have on situations and individuals. This knowledge is crucial for recognising the significant and useful role these organisations play in Tanzanian society today.

The book discusses four socially significant issues: old age, gender, street children, and disability. While appealing to a broad audience, it delves into academic perspectives to clarify these social problems. Social science research has reflected and demonstrated numerous studies on social problems and welfare concerns, including the four areas discussed in the book. Chapter Two provides a detailed analysis of each of the aforementioned social problems.

2 Four social problems characterising contemporary Tanzania

This chapter discusses the four social issues that significantly impact the wellbeing of some citizens in contemporary Tanzania. The discussion follows the following order:

- The challenges that affect older people's welfare in rural areas.
- The issues affecting street children's wellbeing.
- Gender inequality and discrimination and the impact of this on women's wellbeing. Inequality and discrimination and their impact on the wellbeing of people with disabilities.

2.1 Problems Affecting Older People in Rural Areas

Growing old in rural Tanzanian environments remains a vulnerable state of affairs for many. Various studies have attempted to understand, explain, and perceive the issues behind the problems experienced by older people. Stark evidence indicates the existence of social problems in Tanzania. A study by HelpAge International (2002) in the Mwanza rural area found that older people's issues included:

- Food shortages.
- Problems with drinking water.
- Inadequate clothing.
- Difficulty obtaining firewood.
- Lack of financial support to pay for health services. (HelpAge International, 2002).

Other issues mentioned were a lack of governmental assistance when medical attention is needed, a lack of local government support towards older people regarding food and housing, and concerns surrounding security among older people due to accusations of witchcraft (HelpAge Tanzania, 2002). others see the lack of wide application of social protection coverage scheme in Tanzania leaves the majority disadvantaged population at risk and, in some cases, irreversible risks. Lerisse et al. (2007) investigated the necessity of social protection and identified 'Extremely Vulnerable Groups.' Social groups including children and street children; persons with disabilities, unemployed youths; older people; people living with a long-term illness, such as people with HIV/AIDS; women and widows, people with substance abuse and alcoholics, are considered the most vulnerable social group in the Tanzanian society (Lerisse et al., 2007:8; Chitereka 2009) According to Lerisse et al. (2007:8), these highly vulnerable groups include individuals and households with high risks and a low capacity to cope. The vulnerability level varies from group to group due to differences in access to assets, whether social or capital and the physical capability necessary to mitigate the effects of impoverishing forces. (Lerisse et al, 2007). The tremendous impact of social problems on people's well-being, especially the population in disadvantaged areas, including rural settings, is primarily caused by the Government's apparent lack of general welfare provisions and other protection schemes that could enhance living reality and benefit vulnerable groups, including older people. Kitoka (2011) studied the dilemmas faced by the older population in Tanzania and discovered two aspects he considered the root causes of the problems. One aspect was a lack of general socio-economic protection covering all older people in the country. "Older people like those in the category of fishermen, herdsmen, and peasants do not belong to any existing formal social security schemes from which they can enjoy old-age benefits." (Kitoka, 2011:4). Indeed, a more significant percentage of the elderly live in rural areas where the main economic activities are predominantly informal or subsistence farming. This group represents a substantial social deficit whose problems cannot simply be addressed through self-help calls (Kitoka, 2011). As other research has found, the existing social security and pension schemes in Tanzania provide some protection, but only to those who were or are still formally employed, most of whom are urban dwellers.

The Tanzanian Government provides no general social welfare to its citizens, except for a small part of the population, mainly in urban settings, covered by a protection system and pension plan. Evidence shows that only around five per cent of the older generation benefit from a pension in Tanzania. The existing pension scheme, characterised as a pay-as-you-earn system, excludes most older people in rural areas who depend mainly on subsistence farming and small businesses, which may not always be reliable. Hence, most rely on informal and non-state-regulated social protection, mainly provided through family and community support structures (Stiglitz 2011:18, cited by Spitzer & Mabeyo, 2011). Research by Kitoka (2011:5) explained that "the rural elderly, most of whom have never had a formal job in their lifetime, are either left to depend on their children and close relatives or provide for themselves a basis of survival through some petty and income-generating activities. These activities include mat making, basket making, brewing local alcohol, selling baked items, to mention a few." Indeed, petty income-generating activities help in the short term but not in the long term without other formal support, e.g., from the Government. Additionally, the lack of money circulation affects small businesses in rural areas, as few people can buy things. The traditional family network support structure has historically played a significant role in shaping people's lives. It was common for individuals from different generations to reside together under one roof. This system is predominantly the case in rural areas but also characterised urban communities to a small degree. This socio-cultural life practice reflects the Tanzania Ageing policy, which prioritises family as the primary institution of care and support for older people (The United Republic of Tanzania:

National Ageing Policy, 2003a:2). However, in today's Tanzania, dependence on children or close relatives as a reliable social protection system for older people is problematic. That traditional support structure is steadily diminishing, caused partly by the migration of young adults into cities and other places and, in doing so, leaving the rural lifestyle and their older family members alone. Kitoka (2011:5) observed, "the rural-urban migration is depriving the majority of the rural elderly, not just the social and economic support, but it also leaves them vulnerable to the vicissitudes in their livelihoods." Other studies have observed this notable social change related to the care of older people in different communities within sub-Saharan Africa (Mwanyangala et al., 2010; Theron, 2013).

For disadvantaged social groups, meeting their social welfare needs essential to their well-being is vital. Bruggencate et al. (2017:1745) wrote, "Social needs are important basic human needs. When social needs are not satisfied, this can lead to mental and physical health problems." This observation is correct. Indeed, the chances for older people to stay physically and mentally healthy without the availability of ways to satisfy their social needs are slim in Tanzania's rural areas. A lack of general social security provision is a reality in Tanzania. Rwegoshora (2014) stressed the need for the Government to provide social security to all, regardless of the social and economic status of the individual. Rwegoshora considered social security a basic human right and a fundamental means of social cohesion. A social security scheme is essential for workers' well-being, in addition to that of their families and other community members. Additionally, these schemes' benefits to their beneficiaries are purely based on pay-as-you-go arrangements (Spitzer and Mabeyo, 2011). Contributions to the schemes are made as earnings allow them. The absence of any social protection coverage by the state and others that encompass a range of public actions addressing risk, vulnerability, and poverty leaves older people in precarious situations and susceptible to a host of dangers in rural settings (Spitzer and Mabeyo, 2011). There are numerous reasons why older people in rural areas do not have formal social security and are severely affected by problems. One explanation is that these people may not have had the chance and ability to contribute sufficiently to public or private social security provision schemes during their youth and adult lives. Indeed, other research has attributed the struggle of meeting older people's social welfare needs in rural areas to the history of a life of poverty at a young age, citing this as a root cause of the difficulties a person experiences in old age. Mwanyangala et al., (2010:37) observed that:

"In Tanzania, many older people reach retirement age after a lifetime of poverty and deprivation, poor access to health care and poor diet. This situation can leave them with insufficient personal savings because of a fragile earning history."

This quote raises a valid point that weak earning history in a person's life plays a part in difficulties in old age. The economies of rural Tanzanian settings are predominantly subsistence agriculture, which provides little or no pension coverage and limited health care services.

Older people's means of living and livelihood depend on a good harvest and selling agricultural products such as maise, rice, beans, and sorghum. However, when the harvest is poor, securing a high earning and surplus income is complicated. Other factors, such as the amount of rain and the timing of the rainy season, contribute to a good or bad harvest and, therefore, a person's income. It is no wonder that in these context settings, a person can reach old age with little or no savings at all in these settings. Tanzania's social security schemes typically target public employment and are confined to urban areas. Efforts to encourage outside formal employment to secure social security for their lives are not apparent. Indeed, in the past, the total reliance on traditional family-network support structures has meant that the idea of contributing to social security schemes for the future might not have been deemed necessary. In the past, most people would see the possibility of living and maintaining their social well-being through their children and grandchildren. Reflecting on the existence and usage of the traditional support structure, Kibuga and Dianga (2000:30) wrote:

"In the past, older persons in Africa lived within an extended family system. This system ensured that they were supported as their strength decreased and that there would be numerous family members to take over the more arduous household tasks, such as fetching water, gathering firewood, and cultivating crops. If the older members fell ill, there would always be someone to look after them."

As this quote indicates, the traditional support structure has served as a social security model that encompasses sources of livelihood and general social security for older people, especially in rural settings. Mesaki (2016) observed that populations, especially those in disadvantaged areas, are susceptible to poverty, sickness, and social exclusion. Indeed, the impacts of social problems on an individual's lived experience and general societal conditions are severe, partly due to a lack of intervention from the Government (Spitzer and Mabeyo,2011; Spitzer, 2019).

Furthermore, new structures, such as formal social security systems, fail to compensate for this void left by the breaking up of traditional family structures to protect older people. The National Ageing Policy is the most recent policy for older adults. (The United Republic of Tanzania, Older People Policy 2003a:2) reads: "The Government realises that older people are a resource in the development of our nation. The existence of Tanzania as a nation is evidence of older people's contribution in [the] political, economic, cultural and social arena." (The National Ageing Policy, United Republic of Tanzania, 2003a:2)

Despite this complimentary view of its senior citizens, the central Government still does not sufficiently intervene and address older people's social welfare needs in rural areas. The extended family system practised by most African societies has been interrupted by the emergence of social factors. These factors include colonial rule intrusion in African communities, modernisation, urbanisation, and industrialisation. These social forces contribute to and weaken the family network of care for older people (HelpAge International, 2001; Oluwabamide, 2005; Oluwabamide et al., 2012). The idea that one day circumstances could change or socio-economic changes could alter social living reality among traditional African communities might not have been part of their thinking framework. The apparent declining phenomenon of conventional support structures in Tanzania and other parts of sub-Saharan has devastating consequences on older people's experience. This reality means that many older people in rural communities are on their own, vulnerable, and unprotected (Mabeyo et al., 2014; Spitzer and Mabeyo, 2011).

Other studies associate the lack of support for older people with a change in attitudes by the younger generation. Kaseke (1998:51) explained that:

"Most young adults see things differently, assuming new modern cultural attitudes, values, interests, and priorities. Some children no longer feel obliged to support their parents, and this undermines their roles as a source of social protection in old age. Others still recognise their obligations but are constrained by the harsh economic climate. The difficult financial situation makes it difficult for them to extend adequate support to their parents. Overall, the assistance rendered is too little to make a difference in the lives of older people."

Kaseke's perspective on the situation is that the new modern lifestyle young Africans adopt strains financial resources. Therefore, it becomes a challenge to balance meeting their immediate needs and the needs of their parents or grandparents who have remained in rural areas.

Other studies saw HIV/AIDS and its effects as a significant factor affecting and altering family structures in traditional African societies. The loss of able young adults to HIV/AIDS has consequences for the patterns of care and support and the social fabric of the family, directly affecting the security of older people (Van Staden and Weich, 2007; Fernandez-Castilla, 2008). The AIDS pandemic has significantly eroded the principal financial and material support sources for older people (Tati, 2009). Indeed, many families have lost young family members to HIV/AIDS; consequently, older people are left to care for themselves, and others are left with the burden of caring for grandchildren.

Other studies have revealed health-related issues as another challenge facing older people in Tanzania. Bujari (2004) surveyed three regions, Dar-es-Salaam, Kilimanjaro, and Morogoro. He found that older people in the selected regions suffered from various health-related problems. He observed that older people's health-related issues are exacerbated by Tanzania's weak health system that lacked a specific focus for the aged. Consequently, this means that older people continue to suffer silently. Bujari suggested that Tanzania's health sector should acknowledge that health care for older people is deficient, recommending that the Tanzania Public Health Association spearhead a healthy lifestyle and active ageing campaign. He suggested that there should be a range of services and facilities for older people. For example, health promotion education should target older people and focus on a healthy lifestyle and moderate exercise to maximise physical fitness and restore functions. Bujari (2004:1) asserted, "although ageing may be an inevitable and irreversible biological process, it often reflects the success in the history of public health policies and social, economic development in a society."

Although Bujari conducted his research sixteen years ago, his observations about the welfare of older people still bear relevance today. Older people, particularly those in rural communities, still lack proper health-related provision services that could improve older people's physical and mental well-being. Indeed, this is an issue the Tanzanian Government must tackle, and it is an essential gap that this research will seek to address. Other research noted other developments, such as the changing role and status of older people in a society. Studies conducted in 1999 and 2000 observed that older people participate less in family and community in Africa and Tanzania. In the past, older people played a significant role, including guiding the younger generation in understanding history and culture, often advising their communities (O'Donoghue, 1999; Heslop et al., 2000). After more than five years, subsequent research made a similar observation about social change impacting older people's position and participation in the current African societies, including Tanzania. Urbanisation and modernisation are noted as the social forces affecting contemporary African cultures by breeding a new cultural way of thinking and lifestyle in the minds of the younger generation. Consequently, older people are increasingly socially isolated and unable to fulfil their roles (Nyaundi, 2005; Theron, 2013).

Another problem that older people face in rural settings, according to the literature, is victimisation and mistreatment. Older activists in Tanzania are concerned about the number of older people murdered because of witchcraft beliefs. Incidents of victimisation, abuse, and killing of older people are prevalent in Tanzanian rural communities (HelpAge Tanzania: Sauti Ya Wazee, 2014). The Tanzania Legal and Human Rights Centre report showed that 765 people, 505 of whom were women, were killed following alleged witchcraft accusations in 2013. Sadly, women seem twice as likely to encounter these allegations than men. This rate is a stark increase from the murders of 630 older people reported in 2012. This image is disconcerting and challenges the commonly held belief that respect for elderly individuals is a deeply ingrained feature of African societies (HelpAge Tanzania: Sauti Ya Wazee, 2014). Advocates for the well-being and rights of older people stated, "Violence against older people is a global issue. We should be celebrating ageing, and the invaluable contribution older people make. Everyone has the right to life; no one should have to live in fear of growing older." (HelpAge Tanzania: Sauti Ya Wazee, 2014:1). A study by HelpAge International (2011) observed that witchcraft accusations are a critical factor in violating women's rights in Sukumaland and are often generated by broader problems in the community. For example, a limited understanding of the nature or cause of illnesses can result in believing that a family has been bewitched. In cases where husbands have died, widows are often blamed, providing a pretext for deceased relatives to deny them the right to inherit family assets (HelpAge International 2011). Older people in rural settings are an easy target because they are physically weak and cannot defend themselves. Allegations of witchcraft are often linked to hatred and personal jealousy among relatives, disputes between neighbours or family over land and inheritance. Additionally, beliefs in witchcraft are encouraged by those in the traditional healing business for their own material gain; in this way, traditional healers are a part of the problem (HelpAge International 2011). Some traditional healers use witchcraft claims to maximise their profits; hence, they cunningly manipulate and play with the vulnerability of those seeking help. Unfortunately, those who are influenced by these superstitious beliefs and base their existence on them will always look for the physical agency in which they believe witchcraft manifests itself. Thus, older people are labelled as that agency (HelpAge Tanzania, 2014; Miguel, 2005). Often, to help a client believed to have a problem, such as illness, the traditional healer points to an older, vulnerable woman in the village as a cause of the problem (HelpAge International 2011). A person's ageing process is complicated, and the physical manifestations of ageing, such as wrinkles and other features, have now been construed as signs or indicators of someone being a witch. Kibuga and Dianga (2000) studied the victimisation and killing of older women by looking at witchcraft in four village communities in the Magu District of Tanzania. They found that in desperation, many people in the Magu district who faced social and economic problems sought answers from traditional healers, some of whom promoted notions of witchcraft. They found that older women in rural communities around the Magu district were beaten or murdered following these accusations of witchcraft because they had wrinkles and red eyes. The study suggested some recommendations to help break out of this cycle of violence against older women. They recommended that the Government adopt appropriate measures to enable society to change its negative and hostile attitude toward older people. Many older women live alone, in isolation, leaving them exposed to danger. Kibuga and Dianga, (2000:30) wrote of one woman:

"If she is frail due to poor nutrition and illness, she may not have the strength to leave her house much and an air of mystery may grow around her, which may strongly contribute to accusations of her being an mchawi (*witch*). The poor conditions in which she lives and the smoky fuel with which she cooks help to cause twisted limbs and gnarled hands, wrinkles and red eyes—unmistakable signs within this culture of being a witch. Also, the dilapidated state of her house makes her an easy target for break-ins and attacks on suspicion that she is a witch... Since she lives alone, she has no support to ward off the accusations and no resources to fight off attacks."

The above quote shows how dangerous the influence of superstitious beliefs can be on a community's mindset and attitude towards older people, adding to the issues they face. However, another perspective on the social problems that affect older people's well-being views them as structurally caused or having the origin of their problems at a structural level. Related to this perspective of the source of the problem, Kitoka (2011:6) wrote: "The problems of the older people as it appears could be indicative of a rather bigger problem constructed and embedded in the socio-economic structures, processes and institutions of the national policy within the Tanzanian society. To address the problem of the rural poor is an attempt to look at the structures and institutions, both "modern and traditional" within which those problems are found and embedded."

According to Kitoka, older people's issues are part of issues on a broader scale, including poverty, vulnerability and deprivation (2011). When considering the early quote by Kibuga and Dianga, 2000:30, and this quote by Kitoka, the notion that the social structure underpins the problems which affect older people's well-being is emphasised. So, while the discussion revealed issues relating to older people's immediate needs, the debate has also indicated that these issues emanate from within the community and the broader social and political contexts and are rooted in social structure.

The second problem area considered is the one concerning the welfare needs of street children.

2.2 Problems Affecting Street Children

This section discusses some of the perspectives by scholars concerning street children's living situation issues affecting their well-being in the Tanzanian context and some possible suggestions for improvement.

The problem of street children is a significant issue that characterises most cities in contemporary Tanzania. Various studies shed light on problems affecting the well-being of street children. Street children experience a shortage of welfare provisions. Their lives are vulnerable because they live and operate in a hazardous environment (McAlpine et al., 2010). By leaving home and living on the streets at a young age, children expose themselves to a dangerous physical and social environment. They miss out on the care essential to their personal and social development. Some children as young as six years old find themselves in unfortunate, complex living situations on the streets due to the loss of parents, lack of care from extended kinship, and other reasons (Niboye (2013) ; Railway Children Organisation-Street Children,2014). Fulfilling individual needs is a critical human demand; however, it is incredibly challenging, if not impossible, for a child or young person living on the streets to meet their essential needs.

Street children experience stigmatisation. The implications of living on the streets cause street children to become trapped in a cycle of poverty and neglect that few can escape (Moncrieffe, 2006; Nolan et al., 2007; Nolan et al., 2011; Afolabi, 2013). A child's vulnerability in the street manifests itself in an insufficient living environment, characterised by a lack of food malnutrition, and emotional support and security (Hai, 2014; Tsoka-Gwegweni et al., 2016). This book does not highlight and address the underlying root causes or situations that influence children to live and work on the streets but understands and considers addressing the aftermath of living on the streets and the social problems children living on the streets experience. The discussion focuses on the availability of social services provided by a local non-governmental organisation that ensures the well-being and needs of children, particularly those living and working on the streets. Indeed, what can be done to ensure that children or young people receive their necessities while living on the street? What can be done to reverse child homelessness altogether in Tanzania? Other perspectives have suggested that the emphasis on research on street children should shift away from attempts to define street children and engage more in analysing street children's relationship with the street environment (Connolly and Ennew, 1996; Parveen, 2014).

In the last twenty or more years, Tanzanian cities have undergone rapid changes that have transformed the urban environment and the lives of the millions of people who live in these settings, as discussed above. These changes have affected almost everybody, particularly the urban poor. One of the growing social problems associated with these changes is the tremendous increase in unsupervised children and young people living alone and working in the urban streets, as Lugalla and Mbwambo in 1999 indicated. The street children problem has grown and is especially acute in big cities like Dar-es-Salaam, Arusha, Morogoro, Moshi, Tanga, Mbeya, and Mwanza, where urban population growth rates have exploded amidst the severe social and economic crisis (Lugalla and Kibassa, 2003). This trend is also confirmed in a recent report issued by the Government of the United Republic of Tanzania and USAID Kizazi Kipya Project (2018). Gracey (2002) attributed the high presence of children working and living on the streets to the high influx of people moving from rural areas to larger towns and cities to seek better-paid work. In doing so, they leave behind family, destabilising traditional communities and cultural structures in the process. Children can be seen living alone on urban streets or spending most of their day on the streets in their quest for survival. Growing up in a city or town can offer these children a brighter future—or condemn them to a life of poverty and social exclusion (Luena, 2011).

Research and various social bodies have tried to understand street children at a conceptual level. The United Nations definition quoted by Lusk, (1992:294) perceived 'a street child as any boy or girl… [under the age of eighteen] for whom the street (in the widest sense of the word, including unoccupied dwellings, wasteland) has become his or her habitual abode and/or source of livelihood, and who is inadequately protected, supervised, or directed by responsible adults.'

Various scholarly perspectives exist about street children. One view provides a better way of considering and engaging with street children's social position (McAlpine et al., 2010). They insist on the importance of considering street children and youth homelessness as a problem from a community mental health, human rights, and economic development perspective (McAlpine et al., 2010). Undoubtedly, approaching the street children's social situation in this manner holds some potential in engaging people and the social structure to seriously address these problems and offer practical support that could change the situation.

Researchers of the street children phenomenon have attempted to identify and explain the reasons behind the emergence of street children in Africa and Tanzania. Heggenhougen and Lugalla (2005) considered how social change impacts young people's physical health, including HIV/AIDS, and mental health. They considered the implications of poverty and social inequalities on health, observing that the poorest disproportionately suffer the adverse health effects of social change in Tanzania. Another perspective is that of Japhet (2017), who linked the emergence of young children living rough in the streets of cities in Tanzania also to the outbreak of HIV/AIDS in the 1980s and 1990s, which along with economic hardships and the challenges of urbanisation damaged social relationships and structures. This situation resulted in a rapid increase in the number of street children as children, and young people lost their parents and guardians. Equally, Sangale (2004) made the same observation about the impact of HIV/AIDS on older people. Additionally, Japhet (2017) pointed out that while HIV/AIDS was a driving factor in the 1980s, new infections did drop.

However, today other factors lead children to live on the street, including broken families, poverty and lack of education. Other studies have suggested that the causes of children migrating to live on the streets away from their families are rooted in poverty, hunger, family breakdown, physical and mental abuse in the family, and the breakdown of traditional supportive community structures or the absence of them (Gracey, 2002; McAlpine et al., 2010). Similarly, Kopoka (2000) suggested that children living in difficult circumstances are more likely to find themselves in the streets than those cared for by both parents and growing up in a conducive social environment.

Other studies have conceptually categorised street children to understand their needs and vulnerability due to their street-dwelling status. Accordingly, Lugalla and Mbwambo (1999; 2002) have identified two types of street children in Dar-es-Salaam. They observed that 'children of the street' were more vulnerable and at a higher risk than 'children on the street'. 'Children of the street' here refers to a category of children who live and work in the streets but have no parents or close family to go to at the end of the day; hence, the street is their home. In contrast, the phrase 'children on the street' refers to children and young people who come to the streets every day to work but have a family to go home to at the end of each day. In their observation, Lugalla and Mbwambo found that more boys and fewer girls live or work in the streets, attributing the lower number of girls to cultural factors. Girls in Tanzanian society, especially in rural areas, appear to be under supervision or monitoring by their families, reducing their chances of running away. However, the girls who live or work in the streets suffer abuse and sexual exploitation in cities and are very vulnerable to mental and physical mistreatment.

Equally, Lerisse et al. (2007) talked about the vulnerability of street children and the risk they experience as a result of activities such as begging, garbage rummaging and stealing, working as a houseboy or house girl, and receiving meagre pay or no pay. In addition to being subjected to exploitation, they do not attend school. Additionally, other studies observed that Tanzanian children struggle due to a lack of care, security, and protection. As a result, orphaned and vulnerable children are often pushed into critical discrimination, stigmatisation, exploitation, abuse, and general neglect (Yangwe 2014; Save the Children, 2013).

Another researcher, Thomas de Benitez (2003), focused on perceptions' role and how they potentially underpin the public reaction towards street children. One perspective regards street children as deviants: threats or potential threats to public order whose allegedly deficient characteristics differentiate them from other children. This perspective naturally invites a repressive response to individual children. With this perspective, society or individuals implement a corrective, reactive, or repression-oriented model in dealing with street children. Another view, according to Thomas de Benitez (2003), is that which sees street children as victims. This perspective prompts a response toward street children with a more rehabilitative or protection-oriented model. Individuals or a society that holds this view assume a human rights-based perspective in dealing with or supporting street children. Indeed, perceptions about street children play a significant role in shaping the public or individual attitude and response towards the concerns of street children.

Some research has uncovered how negative perceptions affect street children within Tanzanian society. An investigation into the public's perception of street children in Dar-es-Salaam found that the reactions of both the public and officials have been to consider the street children a problem. This is a view shared by municipal officials, the police, and politicians alike. Street children are considered hooligans and vagabonds, prone to commit crimes (Buske, 2011; Chingonikaya et al., 2019; Quarshie, 2011). Consequently, the negative perception of street children and youths as being a threat to civil order has often resulted in their harsh treatment, with forcible removal from towns a frequent response and general repressive response and harassment by municipal authorities and police a common practice in Tanzania (Luena, 2011; Buske, 2011).

Other studies made a similar observation. They maintained that politicians, policymakers, and urban planners seem to be helpless in their efforts to either resolve the problem or assist street children; they have failed to prescribe plausible solutions that are realistic, down-to-earth, and concrete (Lugalla and Kibassa, 2003). This failure stems from the fact that the Government and the public are ignorant regarding urban street children in Tanzania. There has been no attempt to understand who these children and young people are, which would be a significant step towards generating better methods to deal with the social issues affecting their lives.

The East African Community, a political-socio-economic federation made up of five countries in the East African region—Kenya, Uganda, Tanzania, Rwanda, and Burundi—has made a joint effort to investigate social problems in the East African area, including street children and their need for social support and protection. Their investigation observed that children constitute more than 50% of the population of the East African Community, though, of course, not all live on the streets. Most of these children's living reality within the region is alarming, and their lives as children are made worse by conflict situations. Many children are affected by abuse, neglect, child labour, child trafficking, and child prostitution (East African Community, EAC Strategic Plan, 2012–2016:22).

As this discussion illustrates, the challenges that affect the well-being of street children are significant. However, the response, or lack thereof, to the plight of street children is often influenced by our perception of who they are. It is crucial that we recognise and understand that a street child is a human being, just like any other citizen. They, too, deserve the right to access all the welfare assistance that society can provide.

2.3 Gender Inequality and Discrimination of Women

Another issue that is so relevant to the Tanzania context this book has looked at is gender inequality. The reason for examining this issue is because it is an issue that seems to cut across all three of the other problems. Gender inequality and discrimination against women in Tanzania have received much attention in recent literature. The mistreatment of women is apparent at the domestic and societal levels. In the African context, including Tanzania, gender inequality often manifests itself in a variety of ways, including experiencing mistreatment and violence at the domestic level, having no equal access to opportunities that harness personal, social, and economic development, encountering obstacles in their quest for justice and experiencing their rights (McCleary-Sills et al., 2013; Idris 2018; Fox, 2016). There are many explanations for why this issue is so perpetual and critical in that society. One key noticeable reason worth highlighting is that the widespread dominance of patriarchal culture in Tanzania has shaped the community's perception of women's societal roles and positions. At the heart of the patriarchal cultural frame's social outlook in life is that women are subservient to male members of society.

While the prevalence of this issue may vary from region to region due to the reality that Tanzania has 125 ethnic tribes, the consequence of gender discrimination on women's social function and well-being is equal across tribes. In many other parts of Africa, women's social position and influence, whether at the domestic or societal level, has always depended on the justification by men. The held cultural and traditional values and practices often influence the reality of life for women. (Hamel, 2016; Mbepera, 2017; Tanzania Media Women's Association, Tanzania Gender Networking Programme, 2012; Tanzania Gender Indicators

Booklet, 2010). when cultural preferences precede women's potential rights to welfare and how significant their contribution to social and economic progress can be, one realises how much society has and is depriving itself of utilising this pool of human capital. Studies on this issue have contemplated what could be the solution to gender inequalities that manifest in forms such as women's discrimination, women's lack of freedom of self-expression, and the pursuit of their dreams and aspirations as they see fit. One way to address gender inequality and its effects on women is to have a paradigm shift in understanding gender relations, the status attributed to women in society, and promoting women's rights (Tibaijuka, 1994; Shastri, 2014).

At a conceptual level, "inequality" "Is a violation of human dignity. It denies the possibility for everybody's human capabilities to develop. It takes many forms and has many effects: premature death, ill health, humiliation, subjection, discrimination, exclusion from knowledge, or mainstream social life. Other effects are poverty, powerlessness, stress, insecurity, anxiety, lack of self-confidence and pride in oneself, and exclusion from opportunities and life chances." Matotay (2014:2). Often, individuals guided by a traditional cultural lens may not completely construe inequality and how it affects women. Yet, as the definition above shows, women experience disadvantages in various aspects of their lives. One of the aspects is the possibility of the individual utilising their full potential and realising social and economic progress. This consequential reality is collaborated by various sources. For example, The United Republic of Tanzania and USAID (2008) report on gender inequality expressed that gender-based violence is often used interchangeably with violence against women. There is an understanding that the term gender-based violence points to the dimensions within which violence against women takes place: women's subordinate status (both economic and social) makes them more vulnerable to violence and 'contributes to an environment that accepts, excuses, and even expects violence against women' (Heise et al., 2002; cited in Betron and Doggett, 2006:7).

The Organisation for Economic Cooperation and Development-OECD (2010) produced a report on gender and economic development in African countries, including Tanzania, found that Tanzanian women's rights within the family are poorly protected. In the year 2012, a United Nations report on gender equality and women status in Tanzania estimated that 25% of girls between 15 and 19 years of age were married, divorced, or widowed. The minimum legal age for marriage is 15 years for women and 18 years for men. Still, the law allows exceptions for girls aged 14 years under 'justifiable' circumstances, revealing the power imbalance between women and men in this culture.

The report also revealed another reality, namely, the culture of male dominance that in many ways leads to the subordination and even repression of women's voice in critical decision making. This cultural system deprives girls of the opportunity to grow and realise their potential instead of being subjected to marriage at a young age without their consent (Organisation for Economic Cooperation and Development—OECD, 2010). The report went further. The Tanzanian law recognises two types of marriage: monogamous and polygamous. Almost one-quarter of Tanzanian women live in polygamous marriages. Although, by law, mothers and fathers in Tanzania have equal rights regarding parental authority, many traditional practices discriminate against women. Even in inheritance matters, the Government and the judicial system recognise customary and Islamic laws, both of which contain provisions that discriminate against women. The Law Reform Commission has drafted amendments to remove discriminatory measures from existing inheritance laws (OECD, 2010). While this report is now ten years old, many of the issues raised remain in society. The amendment drafted by the Law Reform Commission, 2010 had little effect on the situation. Like on many other social problems, adequate deliberations occur at the policy level; however, these efforts do not always result in a changing reality on the ground. The lack of impact of adopted policy and law can be down to a lack of effective strategies and practical push by both central Government and local governmental authorities that can affect the intended change.

Global Gender Inequality Index gap report provides ways in which to assess the reality of gender disparity on the ground in societies and therefore shed light to the way in which we can understand gender-based problems especially in relation to women discrimination, particularly women's social status in the Tanzania society. Global Gender Gap Report (2018) set benchmarks that assess countries worldwide on their progress towards gender parity across four thematic dimensions: economic participation and opportunity, educational attainment, health and survival, and political empowerment. The Global Gender Gap Report 2018 understands that Gender parity is fundamental to determining that economies and societies thrive. Ensuring the full development and appropriate deployment of half of the world's total talent pool has a considerable bearing on the growth, competitiveness and future-readiness of economies and businesses worldwide (The Global Gender Gap Report, 2018).

The Gender Inequality Index (GII) tool reflects gender-based inequalities in three dimensions—reproductive health, empowerment, and economic activity, shed light on Tanzania's social gender inequality situation. According to Gender Inequality Index-GII: Reproductive health is measured by maternal mortality and adolescent birth rates. Empowerment is measured by the share of women's parliamentary seats and attainment in secondary and higher education. Economic activity is measured by the labour market participation rate for women and men. The GII can be interpreted as the loss in human development because of the inequality between female and male achievements in the dimensions mentioned above (UNDP, 2019). Examining Tanzanian gender situation data through the Gender

Inequality Index (GII) lens, the Human Development Index shows that Tanzania has a GII value of 0.539, ranking it 130 out of 162 countries in the 2018 index. In Tanzania, 37.2% of parliamentary seats are held by women, and 11.9% of adult women have reached at least a secondary level of education, compared to 16.9% of their male counterparts. For every 100,000 live births, 398 women die from pregnancy-related causes; the adolescent birth rate is 118.4 births per 1,000 women aged 15–19. Female participation in the labour market is 79.4% compared to 87.2% for men (UNDP, 2019). Several scholars and research bodies have indicated that many women in Tanzania do not have the same opportunities as men for education and economic independence. For example, the 2004 Demographic and Health Survey found that 64% of men completed primary education, while only 58% of women did the same (National Bureau of Statistics and ORC Macro, 2005).

Cultural mindsets and traditional practices significantly impact women's experiences of life. Several studies have delved into and sought to comprehend aspects such as gender roles in these societies. Zambelli et al. (2017) investigated one aspect concerning women's social living experience in Tanzania. They looked at women balancing paid and unpaid care work in rural settings and how gender norms play a part in keeping women in unpaid work areas, preventing them from seizing other potential social and economic opportunities. The perception of unpaid care work as a predominantly female activity reflected a broader, gendered view of work. For example, most women perceive men to be naturally better at household repair and construction, agricultural activities or care for animals—all activities that require more energy and strength. Gender norms appear to be enforced from a young age, with girls doing more household chores than their brothers, who do more work outside the home; however, this allocation is not as rigid as in later life stages (Zambelli et al., 2017:15). The point emerging here is that held gender cultural norms serve as a benchmark to determine women's role in society. Consequently, such cultural perspectives on gender roles impact other dimensions of social life, particularly the interpersonal social relationship of men and women and how they engage with each other when building a family.

Similarly, the studies of TAMWA (2013) and Ahmed (2017) considered women's social position and attributed gender-based violence in society to African traditions, arguing that most traditions are oppressive. Ahmed (2017:7) explicitly states, "Most African traditions discriminate against women and favour men in different social, economic, and political aspects. African traditions see women as commodity and have no value, thus promote gender-based violence among members within the family." One aspect of social reality in this quote is the dominance of patriarchal culture—male members occupy a position of power and influence the community's way of life. In contrast, female members in the same community are seen as second-class citizens and do not receive dignified treatment. Male-oriented culture fuels violent attitudes against women, undermining women's voices on critical social matters. There can be no doubt that traditional beliefs in communities partly cause inequality and violence against women. These problems revolve around views regarding gender roles and women's social status. Therefore, understanding the cultural aspects that act as the foundation for men's violent behaviour and mistreatment of women in society is critical in the fight against violence and discrimination against women.

Other perspectives focus on cultural and social norms to explain inequality and gender-based violence. Violence is visible in actions and behaviour intended to cause harm, i.e., domestic abuse. Women's life experience varies from one tribe to another due to the existence of different norms, values, and attitudes of the communities (The United Republic of Tanzania-Ministry of Health, Community Development, Gender, Elderly and Children, 2017; Vyas & Jansen, 2018).

There are essential contextually based insights on gender ine-quality and gender-based violence in Tanzania. In Tanzanian cul-ture, factors associated with partner violence against women are often framed within gender inequality and power imbalances between husbands and wives (Vyas & Jansen, 2018). Inequalities are thus considered products of broader structural systems. For example, Vyas & Jansen (2018:1) explained that Tanzania had undergone rapid economic and social changes over the past two decades. Increasing numbers of women are seeking paid work, and men's ideals of manhood have been reshaped with evidence of extramarital relations and alcohol use. Nationally representative population-based data documents that 46.2% of ever-married women have experienced physical or sexual part-ner violence in their lifetime (Vyas & Jansen 2018).

The Tanzanian government's report on inequality has pointed out that gender inequality and gender-based violence start from cultural practices and gender-biased societal attitudes. (United Republic of Tanzania-Gender Indicators Booklet 2010). Similarly, the World Health Organisation (WHO) report (2009) recognised traditional beliefs that influence men to think they have a right to control or discipline women through physical means. The WHO report observed that victims of sexual vio-lence in many societies, including Tanzania, also feel stigma-tised, inhibiting reporting (World Health Organisation (WHO), 2009). Likewise, Hagues (2017) found that discrimination to-wards women and girls still exists within families, schools, and the community, leading to the devaluation of girls' wellbeing and often resulting in the normalisation of their exploitation. One proposed solution to combating abuse, exploitation, and discrimination of adolescent girls is to educate women and girls directly. Girls, female teachers, and female mentors in each district need more knowledge of how the law protects them. Raising awareness of women's rights and the law must happen at the micro and macro-community levels, e.g., the village level. Her suggestions focus on victim empowerment and risk mitigation strategies. However, she does not focus on the root causes of those problems.

Other sources share how violence against women occurs in society—gender-based violence as appearing in various forms of physical, psychological, and sexual violence. Since much of this happens in the family environment, these forms of abuse are not often recognised as violence (Heise et al., 2002). Indeed, the lack of understanding or confusion about what constitutes violence renders the gaining of women's rights and conducive social living environments complex. In order to maintain a level of social well-being for individuals and the community, society must identify the attitudes and actions that put people's well-being at risk and seek ways to facilitate change. Family and community must understand which activities and behaviours constitute violence. In clarifying what physical abuse entails, Heise et al. (2002) elucidated that physical abuse is the intentional use of physical force with the potential to cause death, injury, or harm. It includes slapping, hitting, biting, and using or threatening to use a gun, knife, or weapon against another person (Heise et al., 2002, quoted in Ahmed 2017:7). Also, violence against women can take the form of coercive control and language that demeans women's self-belief and self-esteem. Other studies, including Vuckovic et al., 2017 the United Republic of Tanzania and USAID, 2008 and Holt, 2008, have made a similar observation. Domestic violence covers abuse across genders, regardless of age, ethnicity or sexuality; generally, men are more likely to be perpetrators of violence. Women tend to suffer more frequent and severe physical, mental, and psychological assaults that consequently impact their lives over a longer period (Devaney, 2014; Stanley and Devaney, 2017).

In Tanzanian society, resolving gender-based violence has not been very effective for a long time due to the lack of commitment and practical strategies that identify the root causes of stigma and violence against women. In tackling violence against women, Tanzanian society must strategically place effective strategies and support female victims of violence. One category of strategic measures must aim at helping victims of violence feel protected, recover, and realise their fundamental human rights. Implementing an adequate legal criminal justice system-based action plan is also necessary to ensure that men who abuse women at the domestic and social levels are held accountable for their behaviour. The insight expressed in the strategic vision of the Council of Europe provides sound and practical guidance about tackling domestic abuse and supporting victims. Specifically, the Convention states that its purpose is to ensure that:

"all parties shall take the necessary measures to promote changes in the social and cultural patterns of behaviour of women and men with a view to eradicating prejudices, customs, traditions and all other practices which are based on the idea of the inferiority of women or on stereotype roles for women and men." (Council of Europe, Convention, Article 12.1, cited in Devaney 2014:481).

While there may be other factors for discrimination and violence against women, patriarchal Culture ranks first. The governmental and legal bodies responsible for ensuring each citizen's welfare and rights must fulfil their responsibilities in all spheres. The idea of 'private' or 'public' should not limit the involvement and extent of governmental legal and social intervention efforts to address this problem, especially when individuals' lives and well-being are threatened due to abuse. Other perspectives look at gender-based discrimination and violence against women from the perspective of policies and laws, arguing that they do not adequately address gender inequality-related issues in many African societies. Ndulo (2011) studied African Customary Law, Customs, and Women's Rights in sub-Saharan Africa and Tanzania societies. He observed that:

"In a typical African country, the great majority of the people conduct their personal activities in accordance with and subject to customary law. Customary law has great impact in the area of personal law in regard to matters such as marriage, inheritance, and traditional authority, and because it developed in an era dominated by patriarchy some of its norms conflict with human rights norms guaranteeing equality between men and women." (Ndulo, 2011:87)

We should remember that using the term "African customary law" does not indicate a single uniform set of customs prevailing in any given country. Instead, it is a blanket description covering many legal systems. These systems are primarily ethnic in origin. These laws usually operate only within the area occupied by the ethnic group and cover disputes in which at least one of the parties is a member of the ethnic group (Ndulo, 2011:88). Customary law sees women as adjuncts to the group they belong to, such as a clan or tribe, rather than as equals (Ndulo, 1985; Van Doren, 1988). The study has revealed the tension between human rights activists and traditionalists regarding whether customary norms in national bills of rights in federal constitutions are compatible with human rights in African societies. The African traditionalists favour the application of customary law. African activists for human rights and women's rights maintain a different stance.

In Tanzania, laws and policies that offer women legal protection from gender-based violence (GBV) are limited. The Law of Marriage Act prohibits a spouse from inflicting corporal punishment on their spouse. However, the law has little impact because it does not protect unmarried couples from domestic violence and does not define corporal punishment, thereby excluding many forms of domestic violence, such as economic deprivation

(Tanzanian Women Lawyers Association, 2004). There is an observation that the traditional customary laws upon which most people base their lives are outdated and require changes to realise women's rights and justice. Ndulo (2011:87) argued that:
"The courts have an important role in ensuring that customary law is reformed and developed to ensure that it conforms to human rights norms and contributes to promoting equality between men and women. The guiding principle should be that customary law is living law and cannot, therefore, be static. It must be interpreted to take account of the lived experiences of the people it serves."

Furthermore, Rugira (2015) researched the causes and effects of violence against women concerning social and economic empowerment in the Mbulu District. He learned that a lack of tolerance and patience, excessive alcohol consumption, jealousy on the part of husbands and broader economic conditions such as lack of food and other basic needs underpinned violent behaviours towards women in domestic settings. Rugira's study found that very few women subjected to violence report these incidents, contributing to the lack of effectiveness of applicable laws and policies at the district level (Rugira, 2015). Patriarchal Culture contributes to gender inequality and violence against women in Tanzanian society (Minde, 2015). Similarly, Ali et al. (2017:1) explained that violence against women occurs primarily because of gender norms that appear at the societal and familial levels. Patriarchal gender norms and values reinforce and sustain girls' and women's low status and increase the likelihood that men will perpetrate violence against women (Dillip et al., 2018; Tanzania Gender Networking Programme, 2006).

Many studies agree that Culture plays a massive role in promoting gender equality. Culture is primarily seen as the distinctive patterns of ideas, beliefs, and norms that characterise the way of life and relations in a society or group within a community (Reeves and Baden, 2000). I believe that women and men are responsible for ensuring they sanction cultural values, cultural practices and social-cultural ways of living that promote equality and human dignity for all in a society. However, one traditional practice in Tanzania and Africa that many researchers see as a contributory factor for men abusing their partners is paying a bride price or dowry during the wedding process. Ahmed (2017:8) stated "Bride price is a common cultural practice in many African countries. Typically, the bride price consists of a contract where the groom pays material items (often cattle or animals) or money to the bride's family in exchange for her labour and her capacity of producing children."

While bride-price practices are widely accepted and validate customary marriages, negative ramifications of this practice are noticeable, including violence against women (Tanzania Media Women's Association (TAMWA), 2013; Ahmed 2017). Some men in this Culture believe they own and control their wives because they paid a bride price. Adichie (2014:1) noted, "Culture does not make people. People make Culture. If it is true that the full humanity of women is not our Culture, then we can and must make it our Culture." Reiterating her point, Adichie seems to be saying that the Culture in existence has created an unfavourable living environment for women, treating women as less and denying their rights. It is true when she says that people make Culture and, therefore, can change it. Thus, a culture that perpetuates inequality and suppression of women's rights, freedom, and progress can be changed by the same people of that society. Researchers investigated gender inequality 15 years ago; they recommended that the Tanzanian government and society as a whole must continue learning different and new ways to challenge deep-rooted gender stereotypes in communities (McCloskey, Williams & Larsen, 2005; McCrann, Lalor & Katabaro, 2006). This suggestion is still relevant in fighting against gender inequality in Tanzania in 2020. Gender equality is a phrase or notion that describes the absence of apparent or hidden differences between people based on gender. These differences can include discrimination regarding opportunities, resources, services, benefits, decision-making, power, and influence (Heise, Greene, Opper, 2019). What lies behind the drive for gender equality globally is the aspiration to see women and men in every Culture enjoy the same rights and opportunities across all sectors of society, including economic participation and decision-making.

The other issue considered in this discussion is inequality, discrimination, and its impact on people with disabilities' well-being.

2.4 People with Disabilities

People with Disabilities are a social group that face many challenges in realising their welfare need. People with disabilities should experience a life characterised by respect, dignity, and equal access to all the social rights and life opportunities available in society. It is their right to participate in development personally and socially, and a person's social well-being must not suffer just because they are physically disabled. Yet, stories of the life experiences of people with disabilities in Tanzanian society reveal the opposite. Evidence shows people with disabilities in Tanzania face challenges regarding their social welfare needs. They experience discrimination in accessing social and job opportunities (Mostert, 2016; Stone-MacDonald and Butera, 2014). Scholars' opinions about the situations the disabled face oscillate between two elements: on the one hand, they highlight the actual living reality of a person with a disability.

On the other hand, they negatively highlight the perceptions that influence their existing condition. Misconceptions surrounding disability, including attributing disability to superstitions and witchcraft beliefs, consequently put disabled people, including children, in a risky position (Groce et al., 2013; Franklin et al., 2018; Aley, 2016). The suffering of this social group impacts society's whole image and social progress; therefore, it is vital to pay particular attention to the concerns of this social group.

2.4.1 Understanding disability at conceptual level

At a conceptual level, Tanzania's formal understanding of disability, according to the Government, has evolved over the past three decades, as reflected in various vital policies and legal texts. The Disabled Persons Employment Act of 1982 adopted a narrow 'medicalised' definition which focused on the employment consequences of disability, defining a "disabled person" as: "a person who on account of injury, old age, disease or congenital deformity, is substantially handicapped in obtaining employment, or in undertaking work on his own account, of a kind which apart from that injury, old age, disease or deformity would be suited to his age, experience and qualification." (The United Republic of Tanzania Employment Act-1982:3)

In subsequent years, there has been a transition in the definition of disability from a medically based focus on the perceived deficiencies of individuals to acknowledging that disability is a socially constructed phenomenon. Reflecting on this development, the Tanzania National Policy on Disability of 2004 defined disability as:

"the loss or limitation of opportunities to take part in the normal life of the community on an equal level with others due to the temporary or permanent physical, mental or social barriers. A community's perception of disabled people could aggravate such a loss or limitation." (The United Republic of Tanzania-National Policy on Disability of 2004:1)

Understanding disabilities as socially constructed is vital in addressing social challenges affecting the welfare of people with disabilities in the country. This is not to say that a medical-based understanding of disability is irrelevant to constructing the deliberation of possible solutions to issues impacting this group. Still, only that evidence shows the most significant level at which society plays an active role in creating problems that have a devastating impact and adverse outcomes in the lives of a person with a disability in Tanzania.

2.4.2 The government's commitment towards people with disabilities

The United Republic of Tanzania has demonstrated a commitment to disability rights by enacting national policies on disabilities. Tanzania has, in addition to being a signatory to the United Nations Convention on the Rights of Persons with Disabilities (CRPD), made a public commitment to the rights of persons with disabilities through several national policy mechanisms, such as the Persons with Disabilities Act of 2010 (Aldersey, 2012). This act contains the earlier definition of disability in the National Policy on Disability and a separate description of a person with a disability in line with the UNCRPD. A person with a disability is a "[person with a] physical, intellectual, sensory, or mental impairment and whose functional capacity is limited by encountering attitudinal, environmental, and institutional barriers." (UNCRPD, 2006:4).

Despite these efforts and acknowledgements by the Tanzanian Government, various studies show that the living reality for a person with a disability is still difficult. Aside from physical impairment, people with disabilities encounter many social challenges. This reality is revealed by a study conducted by Ntamanwa (2015). Ntamanwa's respondents in the study attributed the problems faced by persons with disabilities in society to the following factors:

"Social discrimination towards people with a disability, the so-cial stigmatisation of people with a disability, lack of working facilities for people with a disability, low level of education for most people with a disability. Misconceptions and myths toward disability and the disabled, and social exclusion towards people with a disability in the labour market." (Ntamanwa, 2015:4). On every front, people with disabilities encounter social barriers, are stigmatised, are denied their rights to employment opportunities, and find accessing education difficult, resulting in some missing out on school. Ntamanwa indicates that the disabled encounter many social barriers hamper their personal, social, and economic development. Indeed, other studies have identified similar issues affecting people with disabilities (Uromi and Mazagwa et al., 2014; World Health Organisation, 2011; Knapp and Midgley, 2010).

Another aspect Ntamanwa (2015) investigated in his study was to understand factors that cause the low employment rate of people with physical disabilities in the urban Temeke area in Dar-es-Salaam. He identified reasons, including poor implementation of the Policy of Special Education for People with Disability, social and environmental barriers, poor socioeconomic status, and inadequate efforts to implement the National Policy on Disability (Ntamanwa, 2015). Furthermore, other studies have revealed more problems the disabled face in Tanzania, such as the lack of support in the learning environment. Participants in a study by Sightsavers, ADD International, and HelpAge International (2016) explained that they experienced several challenges, including the poor infrastructure of teaching and learning environments. For example, an 18-year-old participant (with a hearing impairment) reported:

"When I came back from the hospital, I could not hear properly. I was bright but started to drop in the class. I left school because I could not hear what was being taught, so I saw no importance in school." (Sightsavers, ADD International, HelpAge International, 2016:11).

Discrimination against children with disabilities limited teacher training in disability and challenges a person with a disability may face in the education environment has also been reported as an obstacle to accessing education by a person with disability. A 25-year-old participant (with a visual impairment) explained: "When I was in primary school, I told the teacher I could not see". I would ask: "Can you please read to me?" But the teacher would say, "Why do you come to school then if you cannot see" (Sightsavers, ADD International, HelpAge International, 2016:11). These cases indicate how unfriendly and unsupportive learning environments can obstruct a person with a disability from accessing education. As shown in the above testimonials, many pupils' learning environments do not seem to take note of their interests and concerns of students' disabilities in the learning process. Nolan et al. (2006) saw stigma as attitudes, feelings, and behaviours towards a social group that devalues their identity in a particular social context. For stigmatisation to occur, power must be exercised (Link et al., 2001). Sightsavers, ADD International, and HelpAge International (2016) recommended the following actions to enable children with disabilities to have equal access to education and quality learning. Researchers suggested that the Tanzania government must invest in educating more teachers about disabilities and issues that impede students from succeeding in education. Having well-trained teachers in the education sector would bring about quality, inclusive education for children with disabilities. Primary school curricula should be flexible and adapt to diverse learners' needs so children with disabilities can benefit from quality education. Moreover, other findings from other bodies have demonstrated the social issues affecting the lives of people with disabilities. The East African Community (East Africa Community—Strategic Plan, 2012–2016:23) acknowledged that:

"Generally, persons with Disabilities are vulnerable by virtue of their impairment and negative societal attitudes arising from fear, ignorance, superstitions, neglect and lack of awareness. As a result, Persons with Disabilities have inadequate access to services, information, resources, and limited participation in the socioeconomic development process."

The East African Community (East Africa Community-Strategic Plan, 2012–2016) also admitted that there is a lack of input and support given towards people with disabilities in their respective countries, as the report says:

"Nevertheless, Persons with Disabilities (PWDs) are often of low priority in society. They receive less education, skill training and medical attention, which reduces their employment opportunity and may even result in secondary disabilities and sometimes early death. Consequently, this discrimination and neglect erode Persons with disability self-esteem and confidence to the extent that they cannot voice their needs."

The above quotes acknowledge two things: people with disabilities endure many social challenges. Secondly, the system fails them in their society. Munyi (2012:5) pointed out that in Africa, the general societal attitude and orientation toward disability are central to the positive or negative life experience for a disabled person. Societies' mentality is significant because it largely determines how to realise the personal, social, educational, and psychological needs of people with disabilities. Similarly, Al-Rossan (2003) stressed that the message that children with a disability receive about themselves from their environment determines, to a large extent, their feelings about who they are, what they can do, and how they should behave. Munyi and Al-Rossan seem to be making the point that society's beliefs, perceptions about disability, and attitudes toward a person with a disability play a significant part in how society interacts with the person with a disability. At the same time, these attitudes can influence the self-perception of a person with a disability.

3 Understanding issues affecting people in Tanzania through the lens of social constructionism

The social constructionism perspective's relevant usage is demonstrated by looking at four problem areas: the welfare of street children, older people, and discrimination against women and people with disabilities in Tanzania, and in this manner, emphasises the significance of social constructivism as a way of understanding problems.

One crucial aspect worth drawing our attention to is to describe the notion of a 'problem," particularly the differentiation between problems of private and social nature. Social science researchers continue to grapple with understanding what constitutes a "problem." Mainly, what makes some problems and not others worthy of public attention, anxiety, or action? (Clarke and Cochrane, 2005).

Categorising a problem into "private" and "social" has prompted researchers to explain and offer perspectives as to why such division exists. For example, Clarke and Cochrane (2005) suggested that one answer to what is "social" about a social problem is that such problems have gained a hold on the attention of a particular society at a specific time. There is a point in stressing the word 'particular' here. Other problems may preoccupy other societies: what commands public attention in Germany, the USA, or China is likely to be different in at least some respects from a current social problem in the United Kingdom (Clarke and Cochrane, 2005, cited by Saraga, 2005:4).

Using time to understand problems, scholars illustrate how these factors and the culture in a particular era play a part. For example, Clarke and Cochrane (2005:4) wrote:

"In the late nineteenth century, for example, we would find that poverty, the maltreatment of children and divorce were being discussed as social problems, but others on the list (homelessness, child abuse, disaffected young people and non-attendance at school, school discipline, the treatment of vulnerable people in institutional care, vandalism, road rage, and lone parenting) did not attract much attention. There are two possible explanations for such differences. One is that social problems change. If there were no homeless people in the late nineteenth century, then we would not expect homelessness to have been discussed as a social problem. The second reason is that what is perceived as a social problem may change. Thus, there may indeed have been people who were homeless in the late nineteenth century. Still, their situation was perceived not as a social problem, but rather as a "fact of life" or as the consequence of mere individual misfortune— neither of which would make it a social problem."

Thus, the consideration of a problem being "social" varies from society to society, but within the same society may be seen differently at different times. Clarke and Cochrane (2005) pointed out that scale or volume is one factor that may make a difference as to whether things are perceived as private or public issues. The idea of 'scale or volume' implies that the recognition of a problem is dependent on the number of people impacted or the extent of damage caused. Clarke and Cochrane (2005:5) construed private problems as issues to be handled within households, families, or even communities. Public or social problems that are to be handled through forms of social intervention or regulation.

Private problems can turn into public issues, too, as the following example by Clarke and Cochrane (2005:10) demonstrated: "In the early 1990s, large numbers of property owners in the UK (and particularly in southeast England) found that the market value of their houses and flats had fallen below the original purchase price. A private trouble emerged as a public issue. It was named and became the problem of "negative equity." This was identified as a widespread problem rather than a matter of individual misfortune: it was seen to have causes (in the state of the economy) that lay beyond the individual's reach. It was also identified as something that required a public response—from mortgage lenders and the government. The numbers involved provide only part of the explanation of why this trouble became a public issue.

This quotation clarifies the sort of problem. Clarke and Cochrane explained that negative equity had significant social and economic consequences. It was associated with mounting personal debt, a lack of social mobility and a fear of the future that prevented people from taking risks. It was seen as causing a consumer confidence problem: this reduced consumer spending patterns, further threatening economic growth prospects. The example provided here suggests that the scale of a 'trouble' is insufficient for understanding why the trouble becomes a public issue. We need to understand the social context in which it occurs—its links to other current issues and values.

Scholars suggest that there are two routes to troubles becoming public. The first route lies in this question: whose problem is this? Clarke and Cochrane (2005) explained that some troubles become social or public problems due to the actions of those who experience them (or those who speak on behalf of such people). Thus, campaigns aim to capture public attention, with negative equity being one example. Other examples include campaigns to draw attention to the widespread incidence of domestic violence, despite its relative public invisibility, to raise a concern about the abuse or maltreatment of vulnerable people in institutional care, or to reveal the scale of and suffering associated with homelessness. Such campaigns try to articulate the experience of a particular condition and demand public action to remedy it. This route is built around the argument that people have problems (Clarke and Cochrane, 2005).

Indeed, HelpAge International Tanzania and other civil society groups broke the news about the ongoing killing and mistreatment of older people in Tanzania in the late 1990s and 2000s, mounting campaigns to address the issue. These actions challenged the government to regard this as a public problem. As a result, a social policy to protect and support older people's welfare was formed in 2003.

According to Clarke and Cochrane (2005), the second route to troubles becoming public is built around the argument that some people are problems. For example, we might be able to identify groups of people who are seen to pose a threat or danger to society in some way: vandals, noisy neighbours, hooligans, prostitutes, the mentally ill, and so on. The demand here is that society does something about 'these people'—police them, lock them up, treat them, and so forth. We can also identify Problems through both these routes. For example, if we examine homelessness, it is possible to see this as defined as a problem that some people have and as a problem that some people are. In the first case, the problem is perceived as the lack of access to a basic human need—adequate accommodation—which results in homeless people experiencing deprivation, misery, and suffering. In the second case, homelessness is perceived as a threat to everyday life: homeless people clutter city streets, are a health risk, prevent 'normal' people from going about their daily business, and are associated with crime and other perceived threats to the rest of society (Clarke and Cochrane, 2005). It can be noted that there is an overlap between homelessness as a social problem and the living reality of street children, as lack of accommodation, deprivation, and suffering are among the problems street children face.

Whether social problems emerge as social justice or social order issues, they are usually associated with the idea that something must be done. Social problems represent conditions that should not be allowed to continue because they are perceived as problems for society, requiring society to remedy them. In contrast, private troubles are matters for the individuals involved to resolve. Public issues or social problems demand a public response.

There are varying possible public responses to a social problem. At one extreme is the use of interventions intended to suppress or control social problems—for example, locking people up, inflicting physical punishments or deprivations on them, even—in the most severe form—killing them. Such interventions are intended to stop social problems by controlling the people seen as problems (juvenile delinquents, drug takers, thieves, terrorists). Intervention measures that seek to suppress and prevent social problems are usually associated with the view that social problems are a challenge or threat to social order (Clarke and Cochrane, 2005). Other interventions are intended to remedy or improve the circumstances or social conditions that cause problems—bringing about greater social justice, enhancing social welfare, or providing a degree of social protection. This type of response is demonstrated by a government providing citizens with some collective protection from dangers to their economic and social well-being (Clarke and Cochrane, 2005).

The social constructivism perspective has been at the centre of social science research, underpinning many investigations of social issues and efforts to address problems (Burr, 2003; Watkins et al., 2011; Elder-Vass, 2012; Galbin, 2014). Social constructivism as a perspective on social reality and knowledge stands on the belief that a great deal of human life exists as it does due to social and interpersonal influences (Gergen, 1985:265, cited in Galbin, 2014:82). When considered with human problems, this perspective argues that significant aspects of the issues that affect human well-being and functioning are socially constructed, rather than inevitable consequences of human nature or essential characteristics of the natural world.

Social constructivists believe that reality is formed through human activity. As members of society, human beings invent the world's properties (Kukla, 2000). Accordingly, we cannot truly discover reality or understand a situation or experience because reality does not exist before its social invention (Kim, 2001). According to social constructivism, knowledge is also a human product and is socially and culturally constructed (Prawat and Floden, 1994; Ernest, 1998). Individuals create meaning through their interactions with each other and the environment in which they live (Kim, 2001).

It follows then that learning or acquiring knowledge, according to social constructivism, is a social process. Learning does not occur only within an individual, nor is it a passive development of behaviours shaped by external forces, but it occurs when individuals are engaged in social activities (McMahon, 1997; Kim, 2001). Also, social constructivism embraces the idea that learning is the intersubjectivity of social meanings. Intersubjectivity is a shared understanding among individuals whose interactions are based on shared interests and assumptions that form the ground for their communication (Rogoff, 1990). Communications and interactions entail socially agreed-upon ideas of the world and the social patterns and rules of language use (Ernest, 1998). Personal meanings shaped through these experiences are affected by the intersubjectivity of the community to which the people belong (Gredler, 1997; Kim, 2001).

To understand the actuality or existence of problems, I considered social constructivism. I actively engaged socially with the targeted sample research population, establishing knowledge related to the subject matter, which can be viewed as a human social activity. Other social scientist shed light on the relevant role social constructivism play in understanding social issues and, indeed, helped in clarifying social problems discussed in this book. According to May and Powell (1996:1), social theory is "core to establishing frameworks for understanding in social science' and for 'interpreting human action." To this end, the discussion here draws on some scholars' perspectives on understanding and engaging with social situations within the social constructivism paradigm. The discussion centres around scholars who focus on specific issues and their interpretations. It demonstrates how the social constructivism approach is useful in understanding disability and its impact on the well-being of disabled individuals. The traditional biological/medical model and the typical approach to disability only consider the physical aspects, limiting our understanding of the challenges faced by people with disabilities. Examining learning disabilities and the challenges faced by individuals with disabilities from a constructivist perspective is vital, as it reveals the social factors that can significantly impact personal well-being and social functioning. Evidence shows that social scientist researchers, using social constructivism, have explored issues that affect people with disabilities in society. For example, Oliver was a British social scientist who adopted a social constructivism approach to understanding disability. Oliver (1983) advocated using the social model of disability, which separates impairment (issues within the body) from disability (social or structural barriers experienced by people with impairments) to understand and address the challenges facing a person with a disability. In his methodological deliberation on the welfare matters of people with disabilities, Oliver highlighted the importance of identifying socio-cultural and environmental factors that marginalise disabled people. He insisted that the root of disability lies in a failure of the social environment to allow someone to function to their full capacity, affecting a person as much as any functional impairment they may have (Oliver, 1990). Indeed, looking at situations that affect people with disabilities using the social constructivism perspective reveals socio-cultural and environmental factors that underpin the problems that affect the social well-being of people with disabilities.

The understanding of disability through social constructivism is distinguished from the knowledge of disability from a medical or individual perspective, focusing on the impact of social challenges on a person with a disability in society. The difference highlighted is that the social model defines disability as a social creation—a relationship between people with impairment and a disabling society. In contrast, the medical model defines disability as an individual's deficit (Shakespeare, 2010:270). Thus, the social constructivist understanding of disability distinguishes between impairment and disability. Furthermore, Oliver stated that much of the inconvenience and difficulty of living with a disability is not an inherent feature of the disability itself but a failure of society to adapt to the needs of people with disabilities (Oliver, 1990). Equally, Perry (2019) saw problems affecting disabled people due to the interaction between a person's characteristics and their unsuitable environment—not their medical condition. Likewise, Shakespeare (2010:269) adds that thinking through the social constructivism model of disability mandates barrier removal, anti-discrimination legislation, and other social oppression responses.

In consideration of disability within the African context, and in particular Tanzania, Magesa (1997) observed that discrimination and abuse against people with disabilities in society originate from an understanding of disability rooted in superstition. This attitude puts the life of a person with a disability in danger. He found that indigenous African beliefs concerning disability depict disability and persons with impairments negatively. Additionally, most African ideas tend to characterise disability as an affliction and, as such, it is viewed as an abnormality that represents 'diminishment or destruction of the force of life, and something must be done to restore it' (Magesa, 1997:193). Such a diminished life force is unwelcome. The negative perception of disability and disabled people tend to welcome a negative response. For example, the reaction towards disability from religious leaders would be aggressive. Religious specialists commonly attribute all afflictions to the actions of various mystical or trans-imperial realities such as curses, witchcraft, the ancestors, and God the Creator (Magesa, 1997). Indeed, social factors play a significant and complicated role and can have far-reaching negative impacts on the lived experiences of a person with a disability in society.

There is a connection between how a particular society understands an aspect of a situation and how that understanding shapes how that aspect is experienced. Many other social studies in Africa and Tanzania illustrated this (Mtshali, 2004; Shoko, 2007; Makhubu, 2009). For example, Massie (2006) highlighted those negative attitudes can become institutionalised and expounded this idea, stating:

"We often see the impact of negative attitudes on how one person treats another. But negative attitudes are also the foundation stone on which disabling policies and services are built. Harmful attitudes that limit and restrict are institutionalised in policies and services and so maintain the historical disadvantage that disabled people have faced." (Massie, 2006:15).

This quote challenges a policy that potentially creates a discriminatory attitude and excludes people with disabilities from full participation in society. Systems that lock up disabled people, according to Massie, may be motivated by a negative attitude towards disability and people with disabilities. Societal attitudes toward disability are significant barriers to the full participation of disabled people. Attitudes range from pity, awkwardness, and fear to low expectations about what disabled people can contribute. If negative attitudes persist, the full rightful acceptance of the disabled is unlikely (Massie, 2006, cited in Enock et al., 2015:116).

Other studies focused on these general prevailing attitudes and their impact on a person's self-image and function (Franzen 1990; Al-Rossan 2003; Munyi 2012). For example, Al-Rossan (2003) stressed that the message disabled children receive about themselves from their environment determines, to a large extent, their feelings about who they are, what they can do, and how they should behave. Equally, Munyi (2012) explained that people with disabilities frequently find their opportunities limited because of social rejection, discriminatory employment practices, architectural barriers, and inaccessibility to transport. Furthermore, Munyi indicated that the general societal attitude and orientation toward disability and people with disabilities are central to their positive or adverse life experiences (Munyi, 2012). Similarly, Ndlovu (2016) observed that people have an ambivalent opinion about the ideas and attitudes concerning disabilities and people with disabilities. Some African beliefs promote the stigmatisation and marginalisation of people with disabilities. These realities happen through exclusion and depicting them as objects of pity or ridicule and as victims of evil forces. General society's negative attitudes towards disability create unfavourable living conditions for people with disabilities. Ndlovu (2016:30) revealed that:

"The real challenges and barriers faced by people with disabilities do not necessarily emanate from their different forms of impairment—physical, mental, intellectual, or sensory. On the contrary, the main challenges are a number of environmental barriers that prevent people with disabilities from full enjoyment of life and unconditional inclusion in society."

Here, social factors are a stumbling block to the full experience of life and dignity for people with disabilities in society. Ndlovu emphasised that what disabled people primarily seek within any community is the empowerment to become as self-reliant, independent, and dignified as any other ordinary people. Yet, that reality is always hampered by the different social factors: "Factors that impact disability include the attitudes of other individuals and of a society that perceives those who have a disability as being different persons. And do not see them as human beings with equal rights and responsibilities." (Deputy Prime Minister's Office, 2013:7, quoted in Ndlovu, 2016:30).

The above quote reinforces that socio-cultural and structural factors embedded within society play a central role in creating an unfavourable social living environment for people with disabilities. Hence, from a social constructivist perspective, people with disabilities are disabled by society rather than by their bodies. Uromi and Mazagwa (2014) indicated that some of the problematic conditions the disabled face in Tanzania are stigma and social marginalisation. The creation of the Tanzanian Persons with Disabilities Act of 2010 by the Tanzanian Government demonstrates an awareness and understanding of the issues impacting the social well-being of people with disabilities from a social constructivist perspective. This policy incriminates all forms of mistreatment and discrimination against people with disabilities, and at the same time, this Act provides for the rights and duties of people with disabilities (Uromi and Mazagwa, 2014).

What transpires here in this discussion about disability is that the social constructivism perspective on disability takes seriously the socio-cultural and social-environmental factors surrounding an individual with a disability. It revealed how this social perspective enables us to understand issues and circumstances within society and social structural factors that impede an individual's life experience and acquisition of essential welfare needs. The perspective and approach one adopts to understanding issues impact the response to that issue and influence changes on the ground. Indeed, service providers whose work is influenced by the social constructivist way of understanding disability vary significantly in how they address issues and support people with disabilities, compared with those controlled by a medical model of disability in their service provision.

At this point, I should also acknowledge that there are studies that levelled criticism at the social perspective on disability and issues that affect people with disabilities. The criticism is that the social attitude and approach to understanding disability do not acknowledge the individual experience level. For example, it does not recognise the personal pain and suffering that may accompany disability because it focuses on social, structural and socio-cultural issues (Morris, 1991; French, 1993). Critics stress the importance of acknowledging the individual experience of impairment. For example, in considering this aspect, Liz Crow (1992:7) stated:

"As individuals, most of us simply cannot pretend with any conviction that our impairments are irrelevant because they influence every aspect of our lives. We must find a way to integrate them into our whole experience and identity for the sake of our physical and emotional well-being, and, subsequently, for our capacity to work against disability."

It's correct to argue that while acknowledging these limitations, many of the challenges the disabled people face in African societies, including Tanzania, may arise from their social-environmental reality, characterised mainly by shortcomings. Thus, understanding the social factors underpinning social issues is of great significance. The social model perspective is an appropriate framework for social work professional practice and social work by non-governmental agencies involved in social problem-solving. While the social model of disability has considerable potential to bring about changes concerning the welfare of people with disabilities at the socio-structural level, relying only on the social model may only give a partial picture of reality regarding the challenges a person with a disability may face. One cannot ignore that the individual situation, such as physical impairment, can also create a limitation or cause challenges in an individual's life.

Another social issue I considered using social constructivism methodology in this discussion is the welfare of street children in Tanzania.

A child's development relies on the adequate functioning of the relationships between the child and the social environment

(Norozi et al., 2016; Brown, 1999). One of the beliefs behind the social constructivism approach is the idea that the factors that cause children and youth to live on the streets and the issues that subsequently affect their well-being. In contrast, the streets have their origins as a function of social interaction. One way to interpret this assertion is that a lack of a healthy functioning social environment that supports a child's personal and social development within a family and broader community puts a child in a vulnerable position. The likelihood of this child meeting their essential needs and maintaining their well-being is limited. Being on the streets means putting oneself in harm's way, with these children alone and vulnerable (Kopoka, 2000; Mooney et al., 2009; McFarlane et al., 1995; Lugalla and Mbwambo, 1999). The lack of a healthy social environment, good social interactions, and familial and societal support of children all play a part in pushing children onto the streets, as various studies indicate. A study by Afolabi (2013) attributed the emergence of street children to faulty upbringing, neglect, and poor welfare for a particular group of children. This deficiency exists in the function of social interaction and the lack of adequate interventions and social provisions for a child's social well-being and, therefore, accounts for children and youth living rough on the streets. Similarly, Nasir et al. (2014:3) wrote:

"If the problem of street children is explored at the inner level, it would not be incorrect to say that poverty and parental negligence lie in the background of the street children and their fundamental problem relates to their fulfilling basic needs for survival."

The issues and the circumstances that lead children to the streets are more complex than we can fathom. Some challenges include an inability to meet essential needs in family settings, poverty, and strained parental-children's social relationships. It could be the case that a family struggles to meet the needs of their children through no fault of their own. However, the lack of local community support or governmental structural support to intervene in the situation and help the family to ease their burden leaves the family vulnerable, and many children struggling physically and mentally due to a lack of basic needs (Afolabi, 2013; Nasir et al., 2014).

Thus, the street children phenomenon cannot simply be attributed or associated with a 'faulty upbringing' and 'parental negligence', as viewing issues surrounding parental responsibility in a purely individualistic way ignores several factors. For example, in some cases, children encounter other children living in the urban streets and are led to believe that a better life or something better lies elsewhere. Equally, Kopoka (2000) explained that for many children and youths, the perception that larger towns offer more significant economic opportunities makes the street a more attractive destination than a poverty-stricken rural economy (Kopoka, 2000). However, Alem et al. (2016) demonstrated that life in the city is often difficult. Children usually do not have the education and basic skills necessary to deal with risk factors and cope with adversity. The relationship between the social construction of disability and the social construction of a problem such as that of street children is that both find the root cause of their issues within the community and social structure. Other studies concentrate on the interventional mechanisms of service towards street children. For example, a Ferguson (2007) study criticised traditional outreach approaches that bring service into the streets yet do not adequately replace the youths' high-risk behaviours. Additionally, job training program interventions often fail to address the mental health issues that hinder their productive employment. Drawing on social development principles, Ferguson (2007) suggests new ways of positive intervention for the welfare of street children through what she calls the 'social enterprise intervention' (SEI) model. This alternative social intervention model has specific far-reaching implications, namely, the tripartite effects of employment, service-related implications, and mental health outcomes for street youths. Given their street-dwelling status, homeless children can acquire vocational and business skills, clinical mentorships, and linkages to services that otherwise would not be available to them through SEI.

Gender inequality and its effect on women is another subject matter that the social constructivism approach contributes to. Social science researchers have employed social constructivism to understand and identify the factors underpinning the prevalence of inequality and the discrimination of women in society. For example, gender roles are a social construct. The way society perceives men and women's roles plays a significant part in creating a positive or negative attitude towards, for example, women and their social status and life experience (Schneider, Gruman and Coutts, 2005).

Gender inequality and discrimination against women is a significant concern in society, especially in Tanzanian culture. Focusing on the noticeable biological and physical differences between men and women, some have treated gender inequality and discrimination against women as natural (Bisanda et al., 2019). However, scholars have shown that the disparity between men and women and the mistreatment of women are socially constructed rather than natural. Power (2011) sees that gender discrimination is another way to define sexism, which is associated with discrimination and stereotyped beliefs against women. Discrimination and lack of societal understanding about women's issues, such as inequity and violence against women in family and society, make it difficult for them to succeed in their careers and see progress in areas they wish (Bisanda et al., 2019). Other studies focus on the role stereotypes play in gender discrimination. Stereotypes are beliefs about the characteristics, attributes, and behaviours of members of certain groups, and most of them are socio-cultural (Schneider, Gruman and Coutts, 2005; Henslin, 2006).

Many of the problems experienced by women in Tanzanian society originate not from the person herself but from issues embedded in the culture, cultural practice, and social structure. For example, Reeves and Baden (2000) believed that social and economic inequality and the mistreatment of women originate from patriarchal culture, which tends to dominate and dictate social relationships and women's participation in life. According to Reeves and Baden (2000:2), patriarchy is "systemic societal structures that institutionalise male physical, social, and economic power over women."' Similarly, the then Government minister, Asha-Rose Migiro (2012), maintained that Tanzania recognises that gender inequality is a significant obstacle to socio-economic and political development. She argues that gender inequality is one of the underlying causes of low productivity as, among other things, it hampers the participation of at least half of the country's population. However, others interpret the existence of gender imbalance and the neglect of women in Tanzania to indicate that government policies have not seriously challenged the basic structure of gender relations by creating awareness (Mbepera, 2015). Tanzania is a country that is dominated by a patriarchal system, with culture and values varying from one tribe to another. In patriarchal societies such as Tanzania, women are inferior, and so they are discriminated against concerning their access to various opportunities, regardless of their experiences and qualifications (Mbepera, 2015; Bhalalusesa and Mboya, 2003). There have not been enough efforts to raise awareness about women's rights, their participation, their due place in the socio-economic and political arena, and their safety and protection. Research attributes this problem to individuals and institutions' failure (Boughelaf, 2012). Another area where inequality is visible is the lack of equal access to education for girls and boys. In this culture, girls are discriminated against in accessing education (McCloskey et al., 2005).

Older people in rural Tanzania are another social group that formed part of this study. A lack of basic needs and social protection coverage is the reality that characterises many older people's lived experiences in rural communities in Tanzania. Eisikovits et al. (2013:1) contended from a social constructivism perspective that "abuse and neglect are products of complex social and psychological practices that reflect broader social arrangements." The quote indicates a framework in which social constructivism signifies phenomena relative to social contexts. Social science researchers observe that older people's abuse and neglect are shaped and influenced by social, interpersonal, and social-structural factors (Lowenstein et al., 2009). Cultural factors prevailing in society are also influential (Cohen, 2003). Indeed, interpersonal factors are sources of abuse and neglect, extending to intergenerational relationships in the family and community; older people experiencing life problems in Tanzania's rural communities emanates from issues embedded within the social-cultural structure. Loneliness, social isolation, social disengagement, a lack of social support, a lack of reliable means of livelihood, and health-related issues are factors that cause problems affecting older people's social well-being, having mental, psychological, and physical impacts. We, as researchers, must learn about the type of social support that can intervene in these situations.

As indicated in this discussion, using social constructivism as a general framework to understand issues that affect people's reality related to the highlighted social groups can provide a researcher with specific social knowledge of their situations. While the social group selected for this study may be distinct, the social constructivism framework helps us understand their lived experience concerning their problems and identifies some common aspects across the groups. In particular, socio-cultural values, attitudes, and social-structural factors create social situations that affect people's lives and social well-being. One can say that there are three different layers in understanding issues from the understanding of social constructionism perspective: A problem can be private or public; the reasons why particular personal circumstances become viewed as problematic; and how society interprets issues and attributes responsibility for them. From the perspective of social constructivism, I wanted to understand people's lived experiences regarding social issues and service. For example, if I were investigating the biological or medical nature of disabilities, I would have studied the work or services carried out by medical institutions for people with disabilities. However, because this is a social science qualitative research study, I considered social factors that potentially create a complex living environment for a person with a disability in society, including inequality, discrimination, and stigma. Hence, choose the organisations accordingly.

As part of this project, another subject matter that formed a case study looked at older people's lived experience in rural areas, particularly examining issues affecting their well-being in Tanzania's rural areas. To accomplish this investigation on a practical level, I selected and involved an organisation that addresses and supports older people affected by issues to solve their situations from a social constructivist perspective.

The research did not involve hospitals focusing solely on medical conditions or fixing issues such as physical conditions: cardiovascular issues, dementia, arthritis, or other health-related issues. Instead, I involved a local social organisation that addresses various issues and supports older people in solving their situations, including those with health-related concerns in rural areas, in this study. By involving the selected organisation, I sought to understand how it addresses social issues and provides interventional social support to clients to help them solve their problems.

Using the social constructivism perspective to learn about a social situation(s) point to behaviours, events, and entities impacting people's social well-being influenced by culture, history, social structure, and social context. Therefore, a social constructivism perspective helps us understand ideas and attitudes shaping people's lived experience of problems and service provision within a social community context.

4 Application of Dominelli's Social work practice model to understand the Local non-governmental Welfare Organisations' Response to social problems in Tanzania

The original study from which this book emanated used Dominelli's model in analysing and making sense of the empirical data and information relating to organisations' involvement and response to problems in their community settings. Dominelli (1997/2009), an author and social work educator, offers a model for thinking about different approaches that those involved in social work-related responsibilities may apply in their response to problems. The model comprises three methods: the maintenance, therapeutic, and emancipatory approaches, providing three ways of thinking about different social work types. Dominelli's Model: A General Framework The previous sections' discussion of social constructivism has shown that problems have individual and social dimensions.

I should add that the value of Dominelli's model in this study resides in how it covers immediate problems and social aspects. Dominelli (2009:12) asserts that "social workers' responses to requests for services are embedded in the three types of professional intervention: maintenance, therapeutic, and emancipatory." The first approach to social work practice specified by Dominelli is the 'maintenance approach'. According to Dominelli (1997/2009), maintenance is one way to consider the social work response to a problem, focusing on an individual's needs. This approach presumes that the nature of the service-user problem is rooted in individual actions and decisions rather than being more generally related to injustices inherent in our organisations, society, and institutions. Consequently, those who cannot or do not fit within the system are seen as responsible or at fault for their situation. In this context, the worker's role is to enable service users to cope with or adopt more 'acceptable' forms of behaviour so that both they and society can benefit from the professional intervention offered. Responses of this type will often be a technical activity that sees the workers' actions as pragmatic and provides information about resources and possibilities to the individual concerned (Dominelli, 1998).

Consequently, social workers using this approach would not prioritise concerns about social justice and anti-oppressive practice in addressing problems (West and Watson, 2006). Instead, the focus is on helping an individual without being concerned about the immediate broader social situation or more significant social problems beyond the client. Therefore, a social support system devised with this approach does not seek to offer the total transformation of an individual's circumstances, aside from providing the precise and necessary support required for an individual to function again. Assistance is provided based on clearly defined, often bureaucratic, criteria (Dominelli, 2009). To illustrate the maintenance approach, Dominelli gave this case as an example:

"An example is assessing an older person's need for aid and adaptations strictly in terms of current physical health and eligibility for services. There is no attempt to ascertain whether the lack of provisions now might cause deterioration later that would require even more public resources like health care. Nor does it ask a practitioner to consider the impact of policies on resource availability for certain needs or the appropriateness of eligibility criteria for groups of people who might be routinely excluded. Maintenance social workers are more likely to focus on individual (and family relationships) without noticing that many individuals with similar problems expose larger social issues." (Dominelli, 2009:12).

Social work, from this perspective, assists a client based on clearly defined, often bureaucratic criteria (Dominelli 1997). The debate on the maintenance approach focuses on the tension between care and control. For example, Dominelli (1997) argued that the maintenance-approach functions of social work have more emphasis on monitoring and controlling than caring. She pointedly remarked that:

"While I am not advocating that there is or should not be any degree of control in social work, I would like to see a shift towards the care side so that human needs are given primacy in reaching decisions about the kind of social work society should endorse." (Dominelli, 1997:52).

One of the essential factors here is that this model is re-source-driven. This way of addressing issues through trying to fit the person into society corresponds well with the medical model of disability discussed earlier, which seeks to fix a person without considering that other underlying social issues might complicate the individual's life. Social work undertaken with the maintenance approach is managerial in orientation, as it fits into clearly defined procedures. For example, for front-line workers, trying to achieve what works may mean meeting agency standards and government targets rather than responding to individual service users' needs (West and Watson, 2006:7).

The case for the maintenance approach argues that those who approach social work from the maintenance perspective believe that it is unrealistic in everyday practice to change societies to make them more equal or to create personal and social fulfilment through individual and community growth. This is because most practice objectives of social work activity refer to a small-scale change, which cannot lead to significant social and personal differences (Adams et al., 2009). Additionally, the argument for not seeking to transform society is made by social service stakeholders who finance and approve social work activities and want a better fit between society and individuals. The second way of responding to issues through social work, according to Dominelli (2009:12), is the 'therapeutic approach.' In therapeutic interventions, the prime focal point is improvement through interpersonal relationships. This approach focuses primarily on how an individual can improve their position through targeted professional interventions. A principal aim is to enhance a person's psychological and emotional functioning so that they can handle their affairs (Dominelli, 2009). Therapists working in one-to-one relationships form narratives that either draw upon or seek to resist dominant discourses to make sense of clients' experiences. In working with individuals therapeutically, the social worker's task is to open discursive spaces where clients can develop their own interpretive stories, giving meaning to their experiences and enabling them to understand how dominant discourses operate to suppress this story. In other words, it is about validating the clients' entitlement to explain their lives in their own way, and, in doing so, assist in their empowerment (Dominelli, 2002:86). Through listening and counselling, a social worker can explore a client's difficulty, any distress they may be experiencing, or their dissatisfaction with life or the loss of a sense of direction and purpose. According to Davies (2008:159), "By listening attentively and patiently, the social worker can begin to perceive the difficulties from the client's point of view and can help them to see things more clearly, possibly from a different perspective." To illustrate the therapeutic approach's point of view, Dominelli (2009) provided an example:

"This is instanced by an older woman who cannot form friendships with strangers because she fears they might attack her. She has caught burglars in her home and been seriously beaten. This experience left her suspicious of people she does not know and disinclined to interact with them as a form of self-protection. A therapeutic approach to her situation offers her trauma counselling to help re-establish her equilibrium and learn how to relate to other people as possible friends rather than merely as foes. Addressing the causes of criminal behaviour would be left for other professionals." (Dominelli, 2009:12).

Indeed, as indicated by this quote, the therapeutic approach takes the form of counselling as a way of enabling choice or change or reducing confusion (McLeod, 2003). Carl Rogers, who was the originator of client-centred therapy, believed that people have a 'self-actualising tendency' and, with the proper support, can trust their own feelings and thoughts to make their own decisions and life choices. The therapist's role is to create the conditions that allow growth to occur (Carl Rogers, cited in Davies, 2008:160). Supporting individuals through a therapeutic approach can also mean providing them with 'tools' that might aid the desired change in their lives. The word 'tool' is not restricted to an item; it can also include 'knowledge' or the right action and way to recovery. Additionally, through this approach, an individual may learn about programmes or assistance relevant to their situation and needs.

The third approach to social work practice, according to Dominelli (2009:13), is the "'emancipatory approach."' Emancipatory approaches cover a spectrum of practices broader than the maintenance or therapeutic approaches (Adams et al., 2009). This approach is associated with radical social work and questions the balance of power in society and the distribution of resources. It identifies the oppressive nature of social relations and argues that social workers are responsible for doing something about these while helping people as individuals (Dominelli, 2002). In clarifying the usage of an emancipatory approach from a practical point of view, Dominelli (2002:85) wrote:

"Practitioners who follow emancipatory approaches seek to achieve anti-oppressive practice by focusing on the specifics of a situation in a holistic manner and mediating between its personal and structural components. To obtain this impact, social workers and their clients develop clear goals to pursue and use networking and negotiation techniques to secure change. Change usually occurs at the micro-level, where interpersonal relationships are the target of the intervention(s). But sometimes success in these requires change at either meso- or macro-levels or both."

Dominelli gave an example illustrating the emancipatory way of responding to an issue. For example, "if poverty is causing personal hardship, institutional (meso-level) and/or societal (macro-level) changes may be required alongside endeavours aimed at helping the individual to control its deleterious effect on his or her life." (Dominelli, 2002:86). Social work with an emancipatory approach sees service users as victims of unjust social relations while acknowledging their strength and vital role in influencing social change in their contexts that could benefit individual situations (Collins, 2000; Adams et al., 2009). The emancipatory approach corresponds well with the social model of disability discussed earlier. Both methods endeavour to unravel underlying social factors that play a part in problem creation and affect people in society. Furthermore, social work undertaken with an emancipatory view sees the root causes of problems as lying within the elite's existing social structures and interests. Thus, to address the issues their clients face, social work practitioners would holistically focus on the specifics of a situation and mediate between individual and structural components (Adams et al., 2009).

In this approach, social work's function is to enable those at the receiving end of oppression to challenge its sources, including the institution of social work and the state (Dominelli 2002a). This approach is not about fitting service users to the system but empowering them to gain greater awareness of their oppression and challenge systems. The responsibility of social workers with an emancipatory perspective and approach would be to enable those who experience oppression to understand and take more control over their lives (Dominelli, 2002). The emancipatory perspective argues that we must transform societies to benefit the most impoverished and oppressed. This approach has also been called an anti-oppressive practice because of its commitment to realising social justice. On top of the various approaches social workers could take to address social problems in Africa, the emancipatory approach is relevant and appropriate to many issues the majority of people face in the societies of Africa.

The emancipatory approach and response are suitable for addressing problems that involve multiple social divisions and social-cultural and social-structural entrenched issues in a community. This social work approach seeks to empower change, promote self-reliance, and serve the community (Jordan 2004). Jordan further explains that an emancipatory approach increases people's independence by enabling them to see options and make choices relevant to their needs. These choices have the potential to transform their lives. Emancipatory social work brings out technologies of the self. The phrase' technologies of the self' refers to knowledge and tools regarded as necessary, especially when working with poor and disadvantaged people. Hence, emancipatory social work would motivate, instruct, and equip them with needed knowledge and skills that could enable them to stand and address the issues they face (Jordan 2004). Payne, (2006) postulates that social work undertaken through the emancipatory perspective regards social work's role as seeking cooperation and mutual support in society so that the most oppressed and disadvantaged people can gain power over their lives. Dominelli (2002) called these endeavours emancipatory approaches because they aim to free people from oppression. Others call this the transformational approach because it seeks to transform societies to benefit the most impoverished and oppressed (Ferguson, 2008). The emancipatory approach reflects very well the social construction paradigm-perspective of social problems. Therefore, it has the potential to bring about a comprehensive understanding of what lies beneath the issues that affect the well-being of, for example, older people, street children, women, and people with disabilities in Tanzania.

The original work from which the information of this book was derived used Dominelli's social work model in understanding and analysing the local-nongovernmental organisations' activities in Tanzania. Accordingly, Dominelli's model provides a valuable tool for helping to frame and make sense of the activities taking place across the three local NGOs that have participated in the current study. Although Dominelli does not rank the three professional interventional techniques in order of importance, she emphasises that each approach is valid (Dominelli, 2009). That choice of method by a social worker or a social organisation reflects principles and values to tackle social problems. The approaches have certain similarities and differences. All three aim to equip individuals, groups or communities with coping mechanisms. One of the main differences is the impact on the broader community and society as a whole, with the emancipatory approach seeing "the removal of structural inequalities as essential to ensuring social justice at the individual level" (Dominelli, 2009:14).

5 The current focus of the debate surrounding the social work profession's role in Africa

As the origin work of this study was conducted in an African context—Tanzania—and therefore, it was essential to understand the debate surrounding the contribution of social work to the country's social welfare concerns. In exploring the literature and debate surrounding the role of social work, I found the discussion of social researchers and practitioners in Africa and Tanzania to be preoccupied with this question: what is the right approach to the role of social work in responding to social problems in this context? Consequently, the debate surrounding social work practice in the African region reveals an inclination toward a social developmental approach (or the 'developmental social work model' as it is also known) as a focus and response to problems. The paragraphs below explore the background of this and define what this method is all about.

5.1 Developmental Social Work Method: A Perspective from Tanzania

It is essential to know about the 'developmental social work model,' as the literature and scholars in Africa and Tanzania espouse it as the most appropriate approach in responding to problems in this context. Moreover, as the subsequent discussion indicates, the social developmental approach shares common themes with the third part of Dominelli's model, the emancipatory approach.

The current debates on social work practice in East Africa and Tanzania have provided a contextual-based perspective on the role of social work in Africa and Tanzania. The discussions surrounding this matter reveal scholars' preferred direction for social work in Africa. They argue that African social work must focus on social and economic developmental matters. Their thinking is captured by the term" developmental social work model" or the "social developmental model" (Midgley, 1995; Spitzer, 2019). The literature on social work practice in Africa indicates unique cultural-based thinking and perspectives concerning which methodology for social work practice is appropriate. Spitzer (2019:567) wrote, " Social work in East Africa is confronted with a myriad of social and structural problems. The heritage of imported theories and concepts from the West is still affecting education and practice. The profession lacks resources and has only limited influence on social policies." Some aspects of this quote are worth noting. Spitzer mentioned that social work in the East African zone is faced with numerous social and structural issues. He also, in this statement, emphasises 'the heritage of imported theories and concepts from the West." This phrase by Spitzer reflects on the reasons that lie behind the emergence of the current debate by academicians and social work experts in Tanzania. The discussions indicate factors that underlie their perspective and their orientation towards applying the social developmental model. These factors include the need for social work to target the whole population, including socio-cultural, structural, and economic factors, to demonstrate what they believe social work ought to represent in that region. Scholars in social work have observed the under-utilisation of the developmental social work model in social work practice. Critics acknowledge the effort of social work's propensity to promote empowering and radical social work practice. However, there are still concerns that social work has not wholeheartedly adopted the development paradigm as its praxis clings more to clinical 'psychosocial' and service-oriented approaches than to community interventions (Mayadas and Elliott, 2001). At this juncture, it is crucial to know the answer to this question: what does the "social developmental" or "developmental social work method" involve? In clarifying this question, Midgley (1995:25) perceived it as a "process of planned social change designed to promote the wellbeing of the population as a whole in conjunction with a dynamic process of economic development." Thus, Midgley saw social development and economic development as interdependent. In other words, social and economic development factors reinforce one another, and no meaningful progress can occur without due regard being given to both elements. Furthermore, Midgley's definition emphasises that social development is a process of change directed at the conditions that prevent groups and communities from realising their potential. Thus, although, as the description indicates, this method gives much attention to social factors, it is social progress that concerns the developmental social work approach and economic development. These definitions point to the fact that social development as a model of practice underscores the importance of macro-policies in changing the conditions or structures that undermine people's welfare or wellbeing in the context of Africa.

Midgley and Conley provided another interpretation of developmental social work (2010:20), writing, "developmental social work, which is also known as the social development approach to social work, emphasises the role of social investment in professional practice. These investments meet the material needs of social work clients and facilitate their full integration into the social and economic life of the community." Clarifying what social investment represents, Midgley and Conley (2010:152) wrote: "Social investment strategies derived from the social development approach seek to enhance the learning and earning capacities of individuals through strengthening human capital, building interpersonal skills, facilitating access to financial capital, and enhancing social networks. The underlying philosophy is that one's economic wellbeing influences all dimensions of personal wellbeing."

The aspect of understanding emerging from this quote is that social work with the social development approach seeks to enhance an individual's economic and personal wellbeing. Examples of social investment strategies can be drawn from the context of South Africa concerning their approach to homeless youths' welfare. In South Africa, the traditional service delivery for homeless youths consists of residential services and outreach and shelter services. These traditional services aim to mitigate homeless youths' physical health, mental health, and social problems (Midgley and Conley, 2010). However, a study by Ferguson (2007) examined the role of social work with homeless youths and observed that the traditional approach has not sufficiently produced effective outcomes in homeless youths' lives.

Drawing on social development principles, Ferguson articulated the need for social investment strategies. In her view, traditional service provision reflects the remedial approach to social work, failing to replace homeless youth's street-survival behaviours with other legal, income-generating activities. These approaches focus on meeting the youths' basic needs. Ferguson argued that in the case of homeless youths, successful strategies to move them from the informal to the formal economy require more than employment in low-paying positions since their formal labour-market participation is often hindered by the challenges inherent in living on the streets (Ferguson, 2007 cited in Midgley and Conley, 2010:146; Ferguson, 2007). Therefore, Ferguson suggested social investment strategies, including social enterprises, vocational cooperatives, affirmative businesses, and peer lending, as an alternative approach based on the developmental social work principles (Ferguson, 2007 quoted in Midgley and Conley, 2010:147; Ferguson, 2007). The activities mentioned here demonstrate an emancipatory response to a problem that considers factors beyond the individual and includes systematic social structural root causes to enhance individuals' social and economic well-being.

Another perspective on the social developmental model is given by Edwin Kaseke, who explored the role of social work in Zimbabwe. Kaseke (1991) emphasised that the social development model emphasises macro-level policies and intervention strategies, unlike the community development concept that focuses on the micro-level. Social development calls for active participation or government intervention, unlike community development, where the Government takes a passive role, expecting communities to determine and implement the changes they need to see at a local level without reference to the central issues. Kaseke seems to bring across the point that using the developmental social work method in problem-solving effectively means social workers should focus more on a macro level. However, only approaching the macro-level issues can easily overlook individual living circumstances and environmental factors directly impacting personal living circumstances. Additionally, solutions that could be directly beneficial to a client may not easily be realised, as effort could be lost in improving the system at the macro level, where we are less likely to experience gains in the short term. Commenting on the operationalising of the social developmental model in social work practice, Dominelli (1997:35) stressed that this 'requires social workers to reinterpret their professionalism—away from the detached bureaucrat or technician into the well-informed activist who cares about and for others.'

The earlier definitions of the developmental social work method by Midgley and Conley (2010) re-oriented social workers' responsibility to the community level and are structurally focused. The implication is that social work undertaken with the developmental social work approach concerns bringing social and economic change and social progress to the whole population.

Scholars and experts raise criticisms against using the individ-ualistic approach, be it maintenance or therapeutic. The argu-ment is that these approaches are irrelevant in the context of Africa. It may be the case that the relevance of the maintenance and therapeutic approaches and responses would depend on how one understands and uses them appropriately according to the problem at hand. These approaches have proved rele-vant elsewhere, in other societies, such as the United Kingdom. The philosophical approach to life is an issue here; the collec-tive and community outlook on life in sub-Saharan Africa could also explain the dislike and discouragement of methods focus-ing on the individual situation.

Scholars explain why this method might be relevant for social work practice and in social and economic problem-solving in Tanzania and Africa in general. One argument revealed by the literature is the dissatisfaction with using a remedial/curative approach by social workers in problem-solving in Africa. The argument levelled against using this approach in the African context is that it is generally reactive and deals with the symp-toms instead of the causes of social problems and is therefore seen to be an inadequate method (Ibrahima and Mattaini, 2019). Scholars and social work experts argue that the curative ap-proach on its own has proved a failure in curbing issues, such as poverty, unemployment, inadequate shelter, homelessness, illiteracy, diseases, and ignorance (Chitereka, 2009; Green, 2008; Mupedziswa, 2005). The assessment here reflects a social con-structivism perspective on understanding problems as dis-cussed earlier. The criticism levelled against using a curative or therapeutic approach to social problem-solving is that it does not go far enough to change the more significant issues (e.g., joblessness, illiteracy) that may underpin the social problems individuals might be experiencing.

Another criticism levelled against Tanzania's current social work practice is the gaps between social work interventions and community participation in the solution-finding process. This point is featured in Patel's observation. Patel (2005) saw one of the weaknesses of the intervention casework method is its inability to challenge the wider structures of marginalisation and impoverishment (Patel, 2005; cited in Manyama, 2018:49). Similarly, Kaseke (1991:44) pointed out that social workers used casework as the primary intervention method, focusing on enabling the individual to realise adequate social functioning. However, Kaseke argued that this type of response did not enhance proper social functioning as it assumes that the individual is to blame for their problems. Yet, the problem can be attributed to their environmental situation in many instances. From his point of view, it is important to have a balanced approach to problem-solving that considers the social structural root cause of issues while paying attention to the immediate impact of problems at an individual level.

Positive comments concerning the developmental social work model come from William Manyama, an assistant lecturer at the Institute of Social Work, Dar es Salaam, Tanzania. Manyama (2018) stressed that the principal value and strength of the developmental social work method is that it is centred on the hope that it can pull together community resources to address social and economic problems. He further pointed out that utilising the developmental social work method would enable practitioners to address the structural, institutional, and individual factors that underlie social problems. Manyama (2018:43) wrote, "The nature of economic and social problems facing vulnerable populations in Tanzania today requires a combination of different methods including that of developmental social work if sustainable development has to be realised." Correspondingly, another perspective contends that social workers should focus on individuals when providing services and play a stimulating role in the community to become aware of the problems facing them to act (Lombard, 2007) eventually.

Some authors claim that the developmental social work method, or social developmental model, has existed in Africa for a long time. Spitzer et al. (2014) argued that the casework-focused method replaced Africa's developmental social work method because of colonialism and globalisation. The developmental social work method was applied to ameliorate social and economic problems facing the continent before the emergence of modern social welfare and social work practice (Midgley, 1995; Mupedziswa, 2005; Mwansa, 2012). In this context, families, kinship, and neighbourhoods implemented this developmental thinking and practice to member groups through community participation and empowerment (Lombard and Wairire, 2010). It needs to be noted that the notion described here is unlike the community development concept propagated by Kaseke, as outlined earlier. The idea that the developmental social work model was a familiar method and was therefore used in the traditional African family to solve the socio-economic issue seems to be an overclaim as there is no evidence-based research can prove the existence and usage of this model as it is understood today in the traditional African society in Tanzania.

Even though this claim of the method is a historic part of Tanzanian society, others have observed that this method is not commonly or widely used in social work practice in the Tanzanian context. For example, the seminal work of Mabeyo et al. (2014) ranked the developmental social work method at the bottom of social work practice in Tanzania. Mabeyo et al.'s (2014) research depicted that most social workers (70%) were predominantly using a casework method and entrenched with counselling, while 18% dealt with developmental social work methods. However, this piece of literature did not state the reasons for the underutilisation of this method in Tanzania. It did not give alternative suggestions on making the developmental social work method work better.

Reflections from the Tanzanian social work point of view concerning using the developmental social work method, cited by

Manyama's study, tell us how this method is seen and understood on the ground. In his investigation, Manyama (2018:48-49) asked social workers about their knowledge and perceptions of the developmental social work method. Some of his findings and participants' responses are as follows:

"As a social worker, I do not use this method much as most of my activities are related to individuals' problems like matrimonial conflicts while community development concerns fall in the remit of community development officers." (Male social worker, 32 years, Government employee).

Another respondent said: "I think we need to have refresher courses to clear doubts surrounding developmental social work method (Government employee, 39 years)." (Manyama 2018:48). Another respondent explained, "There is no way I can think of doing activities related to the developmental social work method. Much of what we are doing is matrimonial, maintenance, foster care, and adoption issues, etc. (Male social worker, 42 years, Government employee)" (Manyama 2018:49).

In essence, the above quotes indicate two main points: first, the respondents prioritise immediate problems over long-term ones; second, the respondents seem unable to capture the relevance of the method because they see problems in their immediacy rather than their structural context.

As the discussion above shows, scholars and social workers in East Africa and Tanzania debate which functions of social work are most relevant to people's and societies' needs in this part of the world. Generally, the discussion reveals a preference for a social change or developmental function, and they advocate adopting developmental forms of social work. Furthermore, they emphasised that the focus of developmental social work must be on issues embedded within society and social structures that influence the population's social and economic development. However, as social workers focus on matters at the structural and societal level, they must not exclude or ignore the individual situation. Midgley (2014) laid down his reflection on this matter, saying:

"A commitment to developmental social work must not preclude concern for those with serious personal and family problems which require remedial interventions…I believe that the different types of social work practice are able to encompass multiple functions." (Midgley, 2014, cited in Spitzer et al., 2014: vii).

Supporting and utilising the social developmental or developmental social work model as the only method and ignoring other techniques presents only one focus of what the role of social work could encompass and accomplish in Africa. Under these circumstances, the role of social work would become more about fixing the entire social and economic system of a country and improving situations at a structural level, hoping that this endeavour could automatically improve grassroots situations and bring about the hopes for changes for individuals. However, one must acknowledge one point regarding the above assertion. There is a need to use a method that can comprehensively enable those involved in addressing problems and supporting those affected by issues to undertake a broader examination of situations and not just focus on fixing an individual concerned. The proponents of the developmental social work model emphasise that it is essential for social work in Tanzania to focus on longer-term structural change that might minimise the likelihood of specific problems emerging in the future. This focus on social structural change is indeed crucial in problem-solving in the long term. However, I would emphasise that individuals' concerns with immediacy impact on people's well-being and functioning must also receive the attention of social workers in society.

Criticism about the developmental social work method, or social developmental model, may be directed at the contextual socio-economic ground upon which the proponents justify using this method. This method seems to be starkly economy-oriented, demanding that social workers facilitate social and economic change for the whole community and move away from helping individuals with social problems.

The emphasis on using the 'developmental social work model' as the only appropriate method for social work practice and response to a social problem in Africa/Tanzania seems to imply a lack of appreciation that there may be a diverse range of issues. Hence, various issues may need different interventional responses. Therefore, one method may not suit all problems.

5.2 Conclusion on the debate of social work focus and method of practice in Africa

As the above discussion has demonstrated, the debate concerning social work's role in Africa has mainly focused on establishing the 'right' method of social work practice. As a result of this question, the answer became advocacy for the social developmental approach or the 'developmental social work model'. As the discussion has shown, this method is considered the only approach suitable for social work practice and response, and other forms are deemed irrelevant; however, as previously illustrated, people on the ground express that situations demand a different approach (study by Manyama, 2018). Hence, I believe that Dominelli's model enhances the social developmental model by broadening our focus to consider the alternative approaches that might also have a role to play in social problem-solving in Tanzania.

As the research uses Dominelli's model as a lens to look at the handling of social problems by local social welfare organisations, it is essential to reflect on the social developmental paradigm in light of that model. On the surface, the developmental social work model is predominantly emancipatory because the main focus seems to be economy-oriented and addressing issues of the society at large. However, examining the developmental social work model more closely indicates that it contains some therapeutic elements too. The developmental social work model has therapeutic features in its conceptualisation of issues and orientation to addressing problems. This is the case when scholars describe the focus on equipping individuals with the skills they need to improve their circumstances. Otherwise, the social developmental model is closely aligned with the emancipatory approach. The emancipatory approach of Dominelli and the social developmental model understand social and economic problems impacting individuals to originate in societal structure. So, to solve those problems, both models promote change at the societal and structural levels.

Though the developmental social work model encompasses some therapeutic features, the model focuses on economic and societal change. As a method to solving social problems, it is a shortfall because the model does not offer diverse ways of addressing issues. While I understand the argument for using the social developmental approach and see the value and impact of social work operating under this model at the societal level, I argue for diverse approaches that address issues of immediacy—problems of a personal nature—and a social-structural nature. Since the subject matter at the heart of this research was about understanding social service provisions by specific local organisations in Tanzanian society, it seemed essential to develop a historical understanding of social welfare provision. Therefore, the next section, Chapter Five, forms part of the strategy for answering research questions by examining historical knowledge of the social welfare provision in Tanzania. The chapter gives us a historical contextual understanding of the country and explains the place and role of non-governmental welfare organisations in Tanzania's social problem-solving.

6 History of the Development of Social Welfare in Tanzania

Understanding history is crucial for analysing how communities address social issues and people's welfare needs. This chapter is dedicated to understanding the unique welfare arrangements in Tanzania and their evolution. It examines specific historical developments that have shaped the country's social welfare provision efforts. The discussion of history here is in line with the overall focus of the original thesis, which aimed at exploring the role that local non-governmental welfare agencies play in addressing social problems in contemporary Tanzanian society. Therefore, the discussion in this chapter will cover the following points:

- Part one examines pre-colonial welfare arrangements in traditional communities in Tanzania.
- Part two examines the effect of colonialism on the economic and social welfare arrangements in Tanzania.
- Part three presents illustrative activities of more formalised welfare arrangements in the colonial period.
- Part four explains actions that have had some bearing on formal social welfare arrangements following Tanzanian independence.
- Part five discusses the role of voluntary-sector non-governmental organisations in social welfare service delivery.
- Part six highlights pressing issues in contemporary Tanzania.

Before diving into the history of social welfare arrangements, it must be clarified that today's country known as Tanzania (formal name: United Republic of Tanzania) was formed after independence in 1961 of the mainland Tanganyika and union with the archipelagos of Zanzibar. In this chapter concerning history, I used the name Tanganyika for anything occurring before 1961 and

Tanzania for anything happening in the post-independent era. Before independence, the account does not include Zanzibar as it focuses on mainland Tanganyika.

6.1 Pre-Colonial Welfare Arrangements in Africa and Tanzania

When looking back across history to learn about the practical living realities of traditional communities of Tanzania, certain features related to welfare provision practice become apparent. Social research into the functioning of traditional societies observes that voluntarism has cultural roots in the Tanzanian context and Africa in general. Pre-colonial communities in Africa and Tanzania had ways of solving social problems distinct to their held cultural values, relying on mutual aid, kinship, and community support to meet basic needs. Traditional cultural beliefs and practices encouraged collective responsibility, solidarity, and reciprocity (Patel et al., 2007; Ezedike, 2009). In the absence of collective social security systems from the state, pension schemes, and social welfare programmes run by voluntary organisations, the family carried responsibility for providing welfare and insurance, ensuring that the aged, children, infirm, and disabled people were all looked after. The family occupied a central position because of its ability to create a strong sense of social community grounded upon shared norms and interdependency (Larkin et al., 2012). The family institution in times past was a social and economic unit, and it was the context in which an individual who experienced social issues received mutual support, help, and care. Therefore, with this mindset and expectation, economic cooperation was critical to the family (Larkin et al., 2012). Though the family bore full responsibility for intervening and supporting individuals whose social well-being was threatened by diverse circumstances, the sense of collective belonging and identity shared by individuals increased collaboration and support in times of trouble between families and neighbourhoods. Circumstances such as losing a family member, famine, and people losing their habitats due to heavy rain would cause the rise of strong support beyond a concerned family to include support from others within the neighbourhood. Studies on African cultural values and life in traditional African society have indicated some cultural values and marks that draw people together practically under challenging times. These values include a sense of community life, hospitality and collective responsibility (Malunga, 2006; Mbiti, 1970; Davidson, 1969).

A life of interdependency and mutuality characterised traditional societies in Africa. These distinctive features are rooted in the African cultural philosophies of life. Literature on the way of life in Africa has indicated the perspective and belief underpinning the social living experience of people in traditional African societies. According to Mbiti (1970), most traditional African communities built their life on the idea of collective identity—' I am because we are, and since we are, therefore I am' (Mbiti, 1970:141). This belief greatly influences individuals' perceptions of life and significantly shapes their approach to life in most traditional societies.

One assumption one might draw from Mbiti's pronouncement is that, in the African context, the communal identity is more important than the individuals' interests. Of course, this strong sense of community may jeopardise individual creativity, meaning a person cannot retain their own identity if it does not align with the community's framework. However, Benjamin (1976:132) did not believe this was the case; he emphasised that "African views of man strike a balance between his collective identity as a member of society and his personal identity as a unique individual." This philosophy on life depicts an understanding that a person acquires selfhood through belonging, interaction, and experiences over time in a collective framework (Kunhiyop,

2008:21; Nyerere, 1967; Benjamin, 1976). Indeed, the sense of community's identity and philosophical outlook in life shaped and influenced the social structures, interpersonal relationships, and living experiences of African people.

One area which seems to clearly illustrate the sense of solidarity and mutuality within families and communities is in the practice of bringing up children. In many African societies, especially sub-Saharan African communities, children could spend a significant amount of time with relatives, such as aunts, uncles, or grandparents who lived far away from home. Through this practice, the family showed children the nature of kinship and the extent of familial and kinship relations (Nyaundi, 2005). There were some benefits associated with this way of child-rearing. Children learned that they were part of a vast network of relatives, who are as important as the immediate family of father, mother, and siblings. Such systems were helpful in calamities, for example, in the case of a child losing one or both parents and being forced to relocate to live with relatives who would be responsible for their upbringing (Mbiti, 1969; Diamond, 2012; Scottish Parenting Forum community, December 2002).

Another area that clearly illustrates the role family played in fulfilling welfare provisions for an individual in traditional societies in Tanzania was how individuals and communities cared for older people. Spitzer and Mabeyo (2011:4) observed that "Caring for the elderly has traditionally been the responsibility of the family. In Africa and some pre-literate cultures, the family (both nuclear and extended) deems it a divine responsibility to care for their elderly." A study by Kitoka made a similar observation concerning welfare arrangements in African culture. When individuals face specific contingent situations, such as sickness, the physical and psychological challenges of ageing, a shortage of food, homelessness, and loss of parents, the hope for recovery and sustenance is provided by the extended family networks (Kitoka, 2011). However, it must be noted that there were likely to be issues, too, in that era despite the strong community sense. Various studies contend that the patriarchal cultural system underpinned and influenced People's social living experience at both domestic and community levels, and consequently, life built around a patriarchal system would have undermined women's and children's roles in societies (Diamond, 2012; Mbepera, 2015). Superstitious beliefs and witchcraft may have had an impact on the living reality, too (Miguel, 2005).

However, like many parts of Africa, foreign powers occupied Tanzanian society. Colonial regime occupations, including those of the German and British, have profoundly impacted society's way of life, severely disrupting the features mentioned above of interdependency, mutual support, solidarity, and reliance on subsistence farming, which characterised life in the 1880s. Upon arrival in Tanzania, colonial invasion regimes made irreversible economic and social changes to the lives of the local native people. In line with the colonial master's demands, the colonial governments substituted a cash economy for the current subsistence economy. The activities and workforce created by colonial powers in Tanzania introduced formal social welfare programmes that were supposed to mitigate individual workers' situations. As some studies have rightly observed, in Africa, colonial regimes initially developed social welfare programmes in the 1950s and 1960s as a safety net for white workers (Dixon, 1987). Evidence also showed that there were some attempts to develop some services for non-white workers (Eckert, 2004).

One may ask, if the colonial era began in the 1880s and welfare programmes were only introduced in the 1950s and 1960s, what happened in between?

The answer is that before the colonial invasion and the subsequent introduction of social welfare systems, communities in Tanzania had their ways of intervening and assisting those whose social well-being was threatened. As indicated in the preceding discussion, families and communities with various economic and social means of livelihood and sustenance played significant roles. Additionally, churches were a leading source of social service provision, primarily through missionaries. Missionary-led social activities and international non-governmental organisations have led to the subsequent emergence of local non-governmental welfare organisations operating in Tanzania today.

The colonialist administration controlled and subjugated the Tanzanian native people during the colonial era. The native people were no longer free to organise their own lives and conduct their subsistence farming. Instead, the colonial master forced the local communities to get involved in cash-crop agricultural activities, not for their benefit but for the colonial regime's advantage. As a result, these changes to Tanzania meant the country had to develop more formalised welfare arrangements; however, these only received proper attention and further proper development following independence in the 1960s. Despite this development, the country had immense social problems, and the existing welfare provision arrangements faced many limitations. Vulnerable populations faced a social protection vacuum whereby both formal programmes and informal practices failed to provide the safety nets that individuals and families need to survive against disease or other shocks (Barrientos and DeJong, 2004; Skoufias et al., 2006). Existing social issues and a lack of sufficient interventions by the state created a need to develop and further the involvement of voluntary welfare agencies in social problem-solving. These non-governmental agencies both provide services and act as advocates for improving the well-being of the population, particularly marginalised and socially disadvantaged members of society.

The section that follows explores the social welfare provision in the society of Tanganyika while under colonial regimes. It explicitly highlights any activities, policy deliberations, and actions implemented by those in authority in realising welfare provision to the public during that colonial period.

6.2 Impact of Colonialism on Economic and Social Welfare Arrangements

Before political independence in 1961, Tanganyika's (Tanzania's name before union with Zanzibar in 1964) economy was under the control of its colonial masters, Germany and Great Britain, who were the colonial powers that occupied Tanzania from 1885 to 1961 (Ngowi, 2009). It needs to be noted that the archipelago of Zanzibar and Pemba became a British protectorate in 1891 after being under the control of the Sultan of Oman for centuries (Knappert, 1992). Due to the fact that all three case studies are located on mainland Tanganyika which covers the vast geographical area of Tanzania, this research focuses on Tanganyika. This section explores the impacts that the two colonial regimes (Germany and Great Britain) have had on three aspects of native people's lives: politics, economic, and social wellbeing (focusing on the element of social welfare policies) in their respective periods of occupation in Tanzania.

6.2.1 Tanganyika Under German Colonialists (1884–1918)

There were several political and economic reasons behind the German occupation of Tanganyika. The invasion seems to have been political in the sense that it happened because of political decisions that took place in Berlin in the year 1884 to colonise and subject other cultures, as Germany was seeking to expand its colonial empire at this point. To ensure political and administrative control in Tanganyika, Germany formed 'German East

Africa' (German: Deutsch-Ostafrika). Bridgman and Clarke (1965) perceived the establishment of German East Africa as a step towards creating a settler-dominated white man's country in the East African region. There is a perspective that the German colonial regime did not consider its presence in Tanganyika to be a temporary occupation but rather a permanent one, making itself the complete owner of Tanganyika and its people. Indeed, during the colonial era, many Western colonial regimes shared a similar motive and agenda; namely, they went into Africa to permanently occupy and subjugate the places and societies they encountered. Of course, as history tells us, this permanent or timeless physical occupation did not happen in the long-run. Economic motivations were at the forefront of Germany's invasion and occupation of the Tanganyika territory. Researchers investigating colonial history point out colonisation's general economic motives were acquiring raw materials for economic development in the regime's home countries (Sunseri, 1997; Ngowi, 2009). German rule established stations that served as administrative units, including in Dar es Salaam, Bagamoyo, Tanga, and Kilwa. Additionally, they laid down communication infrastructure to enable the networking of all activity areas regarded as necessary to their general operation in the country (Haupt, 1984).

One industrial area in which the German colonial regime was interested and became subsequently involved was gold mining activity from 1907 onwards. The colonial administration conducted gold mining activities at the underground Sekenke gold mining site located in the Singida Region of Tanzania. During World War I, the German regime used gold from the Sekenke mine to mint coins to pay German troops fighting against forces in the Belgian Congo (Currie Rose resource, Sekenke Gold mine-Wikipedia, accessed on 8th June 2020).

Another area in which German colonial occupation had an impact is in the agricultural and economic sector of native society.

The colonial regime brought with it a cash-crop economy model to the Tanganyika colony. Consequently, the cash economy system replaced the enduring subsistence farming-based economy that natives of the country practised for the generations past. History reveals that various sources described the type of cash crops that were part of the German agricultural scheme implemented in Tanganyika. The cash crops represented economic growth and commerce and included more than 100,000 acres (40,000 ha) set apart for sisal cultivation, which was the largest cash crop. There were large cotton plantations, two million coffee trees were planted, and rubber trees grew on 200,000 acres (81,000 ha) (Brode, 1969). Other efforts made by the colonial regime in supporting its economic endeavour included the construction of road infrastructure across the production areas. Railway infrastructures were constructed with the purpose of making remote agricultural areas more accessible in order to facilitate the transportation of raw materials to principal harbours, such as Kigoma and Dar es Salaam. This fact is reflected by Werner Haupt (1984), who highlighted that at the beginning of 1888 the Usambara Railway was built from Tanga to Moshi to bring these agricultural products to the market. This central railroad linked Dar es Salaam, Tabora, Morogoro, and Kigoma, and was about 775 miles long (1247 km) (Haupt, 1984, accessed at https://en.wikipedia.org/wiki/German_East_Africa#cite_note-Haupt-16, on 9th June 2020).

Historical records show intensified economic and agricultural efforts by the German regime in Tanganyika, which had the primary purpose of re-ordering the economies into a colonial pattern. In highlighting this, Iliffe (1969:127) wrote:

"The German rulers' objective was to foster valuable cash crops to the German market from Tanganyika in the 1890s. They distributed cottonseeds to the natives and village headmen and along the southern coast in the hope of liberating the German textile industries from American cotton supplies. They experimented with coffee, rubber, tea, tobacco, and cotton on various estates in the northeast, a region that recorded a high number of European settlements in the late 1890s. They introduced the sisal plantations in 1893, which turned out to be the major colony plantation cash-crop export over the next two decades." As shown in the above quotation, the real motivation behind these developments and their purpose fulfilled the interests and needs of the colonisers at that time. The natives were under intense pressure, forced to accept the cash-crop agricultural model and provide the labour force for the intended economic production. On top of that, the colonial regime required them to pay taxes to the colonial master. Koponen (1994) explained that the German administration started with a hut tax and then added head (the taxation of a person) taxation in 1905. These taxations took the form of 6–12 rupees for urban dwellings and 3 rupees for those in rural areas. Initially, in places where the cash nexus had scarcely penetrated, the levy was paid through labour or raised from whole communities rather than individuals. However, after a period, the colonial regime collected taxation solely in cash and from individual Africans.

The German administration used both German officials and African intermediaries, who received a percentage of the money raised, to ensure the smooth collection of taxes (Koponen, 1994; Burton, 2008).

One explanation for the introduction of taxation and hard labour by the colonial regime, according to literature, was to educate the Tanganyikan natives. Remarking on the purpose of taxation, Iliffe (1969) explained that the rationale behind the taxation system's establishment was 'educational.' It was supposed to oblige Africans to accustom themselves to European administrative discipline and accept payment-based labour (Iliffe, 1969). Similarly, Maduga (2015) pointed out that the colonial government used taxation to control and force the indigenous people to accept paid employment.

Consequently, Tanganyika black native people were now compelled to learn and embrace a new model of generating economy and accept a payment-based labour employment plan. For the colonial regime to succeed in its social and labour productivity goals, they put ruthless measures in place to subdue and control the natives. The pressing need for higher revenues outweighed the 'educational' objective. Following the introduction of sisal in 1893 into the then-German East African Tanganyika colony and the subsequent instituting of this industry by the turn of the century, sisal plantations became the colonial institution par excellence (Sabea, 2009). In the German colonial administration's eyes, these remarkable developments called for the strict supervision of those who worked on the farms. Commenting on the German colonial attitude of supervision, Sabea (2009:135) wrote:

"… the quest for controlling people and moulding them into manageable subjects on the part of the state and establishing a steady and disciplined labour force on the part of plantations never ceased to dominate the agenda of administrators and plantation managers. In the same vein, the attempt of workers to subvert and challenge these agenda in constituting their lives also never ceased to mark workers' social reality."

Another apparent aspect concerning the colonial regime's way of 'dealing' with the native population was its use of force and oppressive tactics. However, applying these tactics triggered an adverse reaction from the indigenous people. Many native Africans who resisted, opposing the taxes and heavy labour, were killed. Resistance in the form of evasion was widespread. A tax collector's appearance in an area often resulted in avoidance or an exodus of inhabitants (Koponen, 1988). The imposition of this process was a matter of significant irritation to Africans. Most colonial empires and regimes used brutal colonisation policies to enforce their rule in various territories across Africa. Other research has indicated that the German colonial administration in Tanganyika was probably the most violent regime (Pakenham, 1992). They killed chiefs who resisted colonisation, imposed high taxation, and used forced labour to produce resources and goods that were then sent to Germany to develop the economy and society there. Those who did not obey were tortured and imprisoned, and local people were forced to work on construction projects where they were beaten and exploited (Gellately and Kiernan, 2003; Asante, 2007).

The German occupation and activities in Tanganyika harmed the social, cultural, structural, and economic aspects of the natives' lives. People in these communities were forced to participate in cash-crop production (Bossert, 1987), disrupting the existing operations and social order. Tanganyika became the supplier of raw materials such as minerals and agricultural commodities, and in subsequent decades, Tanganyika became the buyer of processed, manufactured goods from Germany and Europe (Sunseri, 1997; Rodney, 1982). The economic structure established by the colonial powers has had many far-reaching implications almost fifty years after the independence of many African countries. In 'Development for Exploitation—German Colonial Policies in Tanzania,' Rodney (1982) pointed out that Africa progressed development in Europe at the same rate as Europe reversed development in Africa. With a combination of power politics, brutal control, and economic exploitation techniques, the German colonial regime subdued the Tanganyikan native communities for material gain. Rodney pointed out that colonialism was primarily intended to exploit the continent and send back profits to the imperialists' home country (Rodney, 1972:231). The long-term purpose of the German occupation of Tanganyika determined the general approach to dealing with indigenous African people under colonialism.

One piece of knowledge I wanted to obtain through this historical enquiry was whether any concern was shown for the welfare of native African people in the German regime's activities in the Tanganyika territory and to what extent. Other studies do shed light on this matter. For example, Taylor (1963) observed that the approach and way in which the German regime operated was not socially friendly and did not foster a healthy social relationship with Tanganyikan natives. Taylor (1963:20) wrote: "From the beginning of their administration, the Germans were to have difficulties with the attitude of the native population. The natives' antagonism and resistance to the Germans' operation were due to the German policies affecting the natives. Also, it was because the German administrators were not interested in the welfare of the people, but rather in the economic development of the area. Karl Peters, known to the natives as Mkono-wa damu (the man with the blood-stained hands), eventually had to be recalled in 1893 from the Mount Kilimanjaro area due to his harsh and oppressive policies."

Historical evidence, including the above quote, clearly indicates that the German regime in Tanganyika was not interested in the social welfare needs of Tanganyikan native people. How the colonial government involved itself with African native people and generally conducted its affairs in Tanganyika demonstrated the very essence of colonialism. Other histories about Germany's presence and operation in East Africa indicated that the regime did not intend to develop colonies themselves, whether economically or socially (Henderson, 1935).

Colonialism is the economic, social, political, and cultural domination of society over an extended period of time (understanding social and economic relationships. http://www.anthrocervone. org/development/ Accessed on Tuesday 1 Dec 2020). In elaborating further, domination is power, usually in the form of social power—that is, control over other people. The colonial regime took over the Tanganyikan territory, conquered the native people, utilised the natives as a labour force, and appropriated local resources for their own profit, using several methods and strategies to maintain their direct economies and their social and political domination of native Africans within their territories during the period of their colonial rule.

The devastating impact of the German colonial regime's brutality on indigenous people came into view and was demonstrated in the Majimaji rebellion. The hut and head taxation, forced labour, and difficult living conditions that local people were subjected to triggered this war. Vita vya Majimaji, the Majimaji rebellions, started in 1905 and ended in 1907 (also known as the water war) in the southern part of the country (Maduga, 2015), proving to be the most widespread revolt that East Africa had ever seen. It swept across the country, involving nearly 20 different ethnic groups (Gellately and Kiernan, 2003). The significant result of this social discontent was a tremendous loss of life and the great devastation and exhaustion of resources (Taylor, 1963). Studies on the effects of the Majimaji war indicate that indigenous groups, including the Ngoni, Matumbi, Uvivunda, Pangwa, Kilosa, and Mahenge, in the southern part of Tanzania were among the communities that suffered a high loss of life (Iliffe, 1979; Gellately and Kiernan, 2003).

Indeed, the attitudes and manner in which the German regime carried out their rule in Tanganyika indicate in various ways that the welfare needs of the indigenous population did not matter to them at all, as various studies have attested. For example, Iliffe (1979) recounted the famine that affected the native people and the subsequent response of the German regime. Iliffe explains that this famine was spurred on through institutional racism spearheaded by unremorseful officers of the German Army. Captain Richter, who administered the Songea area in the aftermath of the rebellion, prevented cultivation and appropriated all food for his troops, and was quoted as saying, 'the fellows can just starve' (Iliffe, 1979). This attitude resulted from imperialistic notions of African inferiority and the belief that the welfare of Africans did not matter. Indeed, certain activities of the colonial regime indicated high economic production. Still, such economic output did not seem to translate into the social development or social well-being of the native communities. Let's take a moment to remember the significance of social policy in people's everyday lives. Social policy concerns itself with the relations necessary for human well-being and the systems by which welfare may be promoted or, for that matter, impaired (Dean, 2012:1). Furthermore, Dean (2012:2) elucidated that 'social well-being focuses on the state of being, it pays attention to people's being and the essence of their lives.' The term' social welfare' is associated with the availability of things deemed essential to human well-being or things one needs to make life worth living, essential services such as healthcare, education, water, and food; means of livelihood, such as a job and money; vital but intangible things, such as love, acceptance, freedom to life and self-expression, and security. Some of these elements could fall into the government's social welfare provision and authorised bodies that represent the general population's interests, such as charities, local associations, and churches (Dean, 2012; Baggott, 2004). When examining the role of the German colonial administration in Tanganyika, it becomes apparent that the colonial regime positioned itself as the dominant authority, exerting control over the lives of the indigenous population for its own economic interests. As historical evidence has shown in this discussion, the longer the regime controlled the local communities, the worse their social situations became; people experienced physical, mental, psychological, economic and social trauma.

Studies indicate that the German colonial regime introduced some protective policy measures for its workers in Tanganyika during its tenure. However, as historians have discovered, these measures were biased against native Africans and did not cover native workers. Colonial government officials serving in Tanganyika who were injured in the line of duty received compensation payments, including pension schemes, education, and health service provision (Tetzlaff, 1970). History tells us that the Governor of German East Africa issued a 'rights of indigenous workers' decree in 1909, making it mandatory for employers to guarantee their employees' medical care. Still, German employers in Tanganyika refused to execute this policy measure (Tetzlaff, 1970).

The history of Germany's occupation, colonial activity, and domination of the native black people of Tanzania would not be complete without considering German missionaries' work in the Tanganyika territory. The increase in the presence of German missionaries occurred concurrently with the control of the colonial regime, with these missionaries working alongside the exploitative colonial power in Tanganyika, as was the case in other parts of Africa.

During the early days of the German colonial period, institutional social provision for people experiencing poverty came chiefly from missionaries. Missionary church organisations worked closely with local people, focusing on social welfare-related issues. German Christian missionaries established mission stations and settlements in various parts of Tanzania, becoming havens of security and centres of an entirely new way of life compared to much of what went on around them. German missionary activities focused on evangelisation and educational activities. Mushi (2009:62) observed that:

"When the Christian missionaries arrived in East Africa in the 19th century …they carried out their evangelical and educational activities in those areas whose populations were free from Islamic influence, and where the climatic conditions were conducive for crops such as coffee, tea and bananas. These areas included Kilimanjaro, Bukoba and Mbeya."

Missionaries of different Christian traditions opened their mission stations in Tanzania. For example, the Evangelical Missionary Society for German East Africa started work in Tanga and Dar es Salaam in 1887. It later moved to the Usambaras and started the Usambara Trade School. Missionaries from the Benedictine

Fathers (German Catholics) opened stations in Dar es Salaam in 1889. They also extended their work to Lukuledi by 1895 and Peramiho and Tosamaganga by 1898. Mushi (2009:61) observed that at Peramiho and Tosamaganga, trade training was established in various crafts, and today, these two areas remain important trade centres. People in these areas specialised in making local craft products, and missionaries interested in craft materials became involved in training and shaping these local craft businesses, enhancing local people's understanding of trading.

Furthermore, the Leipzig Lutherans established other missionary activities and stations in Moshi in 1894. It is believed that German Lutheran missionary work in Moshi replaced the British Church Missionary Society (CMS), which was accused of inciting the Chagga tribe, the native people of the Moshi area, against the German Administration (Mushi, 2009). There were missionaries from other countries during the German colonial administration. This situation indicates an early tension between the German regime and the British regime, especially with regard to their respective missionaries, who operated in East Africa before World War I.

Among other areas, the mission organisations involved with local people in Tanganyika focused on education. In different mission stations, missionaries set up schools. Some studies observed that missionaries' approach, attitude, and involvement with native people were influenced by their preconceived ideas about black African people's humanity. For example, Mushi (2009:58) wrote: "the type of education offered by missionaries was guided by their general view of the African social environment. The Christian missionaries viewed Africans as backward, uncivilised, and uncultured with no tradition or history, unintelligent and lazy."

Influenced by these assumptions and perceptions of indigenous black Africans' deficiency, the reasons behind the missionary offer of formal education, according to Mushi (2009:57), were three-fold:

"to reproduce the Christian religious culture, reproduce Western economy, as well as pacify and control the natives. The African native was conceived as heathenish and cruel. He was a 'fallen man' who had to be redeemed and with him his society, whose values and practices the missionaries found repugnant. The missionaries regarded themselves as bearers, not only of the Gospel but of a completely new way of life. Thus, the early mission schools not only propagated the Gospel, and in so doing taught the 3Rs (reading, writing, and numeracy), but also sought to inculcate the moral and social values of the civilisation they represented."

Christian missions were backed by big church organisations and governments back in Europe. Missionaries provided education, but this education was poor for African pupils. The type of education provided (basic literacy and simple mathematics) was not intended to liberate black Africans or make them innovative in various areas, such as industry and agriculture, or enhance their knowledge so that they could enter other professions, such as education, medicine, engineering, or technology. Missionaries saw education primarily as a means to convert Africans. The missionaries taught the scriptures or other religious instruction books, translated by the missions, in order to stabilise the faith of converts and assist in their character development. New converts had to learn to read in their vernacular languages (Berman, 1974; Bassey, 1999; Ayandele, 1966). Likewise, Zu Selhausen (2019:2) pointed out that "vast Christian missionary efforts facilitated the unique historical process of African mass-conversion during the long 20th century. Formal education was a key aspect in missionary conversion strategies and thus, education became firmly connected to Christian missions." Indeed, many of those who attended mission schools converted and helped spread the gospel of Jesus Christ in their local languages (Berman, 1974; Frankema, 2012). Thus, in the words of Ajayi (1965:134), "the nursery of the infant Church. In the absence of major investments in African education by European colonial states, mission schools provided the bulk of education for most colonial periods (c. 1880–1960). Missions did not just provide education where the colonial state did not invest in it, instead, the supply of mission schools primarily relieved the colonial governments from financing public education (De Haas and Frankema, 2018). Thus, Christian missionaries played a crucial role in laying a foundation for developing formal mass education in post-colonial Africa.

Despite the above roles, others have suggested that, for the most part, missions were essential tools for colonial governments. Missionaries' close friendly relation with local communities and their Africa and Tanganyika activities significantly helped the colonial regime have a stronghold. One of the missions' most important contributions to the colonial regimes was their role in educating the native Africans. Mission schools provided a steady stream of educated Africans to fill the lower colonial administration positions and operate vocational and agricultural schools (Ayandele, 1966; Foster, 1965; Sheffield, 1973). Equally, Mushi (2009:64) pointed out that Christianity was used to prepare Africans for colonisation; for example, early missionaries such as Johann Ludwig Krapf and Johannes Rebmann did much of the earliest penetration of East Africa, and their earliest African converts became their collaborators during the colonial domination.

German powers lost their grip on Tanganyika at the end of World War I. From 1918 and throughout the following four decades, Tanzanian territory found itself under another colonial power, this time, the British regime. Therefore, in the section below, we consider the impact of the British colonial rule on the social well-being of indigenous people and investigate any aspects of social welfare during this occupation period.

6.2.2 Tanganyika Under British Colonialists (1918–1961)

Britain occupied Tanganyika, East Africa, officially from 1920 onward, after the German defeat in World War I, with Low and Lonsdale (1976:12) labelling this period the 'Second Colonial Occupation.' Eckert (2004) explained that the British colonial move to Tanganyika was motivated by an effort to increase the output of African economies to compensate for Britain's economic weakness. Economic motivations were part of the reason for a dramatic expansion of British state intervention in African societies. Great Britain took over the territory of Tanganyika according to the mandate of the League of Nations in January 1920 and henceforth appointed Horace Byatt as Governor of Tanganyika (Dougherty, 1966). The Governorship of Sir Horace Byatt (1920–1924) marked the first phase of the British administration's activities in Tanganyika. Dougherty (1966) explained that the European Allied Powers agreed to the British colonial takeover of Tanganyika, signing the Treaty of Versailles, which confirmed that the area known as Tanganyika would be formally under British control. The fate of the African people in Tanganyika was decided in Europe by European superpowers. This whole state of affairs is one of great sadness. One can only imagine the vulnerability and powerlessness that Tanganyikan society must have felt on the realisation that colonialism would continue.

Following this Treaty and the subsequent entry of British officials into Tanganyika, all Germans were expelled from Tanganyikan territory, including all German missionaries (Dougherty, 1966). The complete removal of every German from Tanganyika may have signified two things: the end of an era and the beginning of a new one, and the free operation of the British regime in order for them to command total and undivided loyalty and submission from the native people. The British government explicitly declared their seated desire to own Tanganyika as their permanent territory. In 1925, Mr L. S. Amery, who was then Secretary of State for the Colonies, stated:

"We have got rid of that intrusive block of German territory which, under the name of Tanganyika, has now been permanently incorporated in the British Empire. I stress that—permanently. It is an entire delusion that it is any less British than any other colony. Though we have laid ourselves under the League it is not one whit less British, nor does it make our tenure there one whit less permanent." (Amery quoted in Chidzero, 1961:40).

The British intent in taking over the Tanganyika territory was not to offer temporary oversight or protect the region, but as the quote above clearly states, it was the ownership of Tanganyika. In declaring this intent of ownership, it is implied that the British state would conquer and control the country's native inhabitants and their resources.

World War I had a devastating social and economic impact on the Tanganyikan native people. The war caused a tremendous loss of life, great devastation, and exhaustion of resources (Marsh and Kingsnorth, 1957). In describing the challenges and precarious situations that affected local people, and the subsequent disruption of the British administration takeover, Marsh and Kingsnorth wrote:

"The British faced many problems in 1918. The war in East Africa, Tanganyika, was not fought on the green and grassy plains but rather in the swampy lowlands. In these areas, the disease was easily caught and easily communicated – dysentery and malaria developed not only among the troops but also in the native population. Thirty thousand natives were said to have died from the famine. Amongst those remaining great numbers had pawned their children for food, husbands had left their wives, and mothers had deserted their children, family life had very nearly ceased to exist." (Marsh and Kingsnorth, 1957:230).

This account seems to convey the devastating reality of war for social relationships, the livelihoods of native people, and the emergence of hunger and disease, which lead to the loss of lives. Thus, this description seems to reveal one reality: the British colonial government was taking control over a society that was already exhausted and beset with many social problems that needed humane and appropriate social interventional solutions. However, the opposite happened. African black native communities continued to be suppressed, humiliated, and owned by the British regime for more than four decades.

Dougherty (1966:204) emphasised two pressing issues that faced the British administration in Tanganyika: 'the reinforcement of an effective administration, and economic reconstruction in Tanganyika.' The British regime in Tanganyika faced various challenges of a social and infrastructural nature. Marsh and Kingsnorth (1957) pointed out that the general operational condition in Tanganyika was made worse by the German soldiers in their retreat, as they purposefully destroyed many of the existing railway lines. The war had wide-ranging impacts, including destroying road infrastructure, commercial activity, and any semblance of a functioning commercial system. Though the German colonial state was defeated in WWI, it never accepted the idea of giving up without resistance to its colonies and the agricultural and economic activities established there, including in Tanganyikan territory. The act of destroying infrastructure, including the roads and lines of communication, indicates two things. Firstly, the Germans could not bear the idea that the British administration was inheriting infrastructure built by German rule and, therefore, did not want to give them an easy start. Secondly, these infrastructures did not belong to and were not set up to benefit the indigenous community. Due to this severe destruction of infrastructures caused by war and by the actions of a reluctant German regime to relinquish the Tanganyika territory, the work of rebuilding, bringing back social normality, and mending infrastructure was an almost insurmountable task, and so the British were anxious to embark on a reconstruction programme (Dougherty, 1966). British officials took what they considered to be an important step to bring about some level of social normality and working relationship between the British administration and local communities. According to written reports, the British officers made trips to various districts in order to win the confidence of the natives. This social visitation evoked a good response from the native population. It resulted in native people building their houses and villages closer to the main roads and trails, indicative of a greater confidence in the Government (Great Britain. Parliamentary Papers, Report on Tanganyika, 1921; cited in Dougherty, 1966). Despite this apparent confidence and potentially blind hope for improvement, the natives complained to the British about the state of their economy; they experienced a lack of employment, scarcity of cash, and basic daily needs. These items cited by natives as part of their complaints are noteworthy. The mentioning of these specific items could be interpreted to represent a change in the general thinking regarding the economy and way of earning a livelihood. Before colonialism in Tanganyika, natives' communities focused on subsistence farming for food production. The idea of viewing livelihood in terms of money and income was uncommon back then; however, this Tanganyikan society had experienced a different model of economy and money under German rule, and notions of employment and salary were gradually becoming an integral part of the thinking. Thus, it appears correct to assume that the British colonial regime was taking control over a society that was already in the process of change. Natives were increasingly embracing a modern economic lifestyle and breaking away from traditional thinking and models of living.

In order to aid their administration efforts in Tanganyika, the British establishment back in London sent grants-in-aid to support expenditure costs between 1917 and 1927. Sayers (1930) explained that one of the main reasons for the necessity of grants was a deficit in railway expenditure, and problems of railroad development were a constant issue for the British in Tanganyika. Despite these grants, the high cost of railway expenditure meant that the budget showed a deficit until 1928 (Sayers, 1930).

Another issue the British colonial administrators encountered and had to address in Tanganyika was land distribution. Previously, the Germans had seized the best land for their settlers and divided it without paying much attention to the interests of natives, tribes, or boundaries (Dougherty, 1966). The question now was whether this existing land distribution should remain as it was or whether land should be given back to the indigenous people. The focus was on larger land areas, especially the formerly prosperous sisal estates. The prevailing solution seemed to be the idea that the sisal estates and large plantations should be sold, and the selling of this land was to begin in 1922 (Ingham, 1962; Dougherty, 1966). The subject of land alienation was included in the Report for Tanganyika of 1921, which pointed out that the British Government had bought northern plantations for restoration to the natives. When the land was finally re-sold, the main nationalities buying it were Greeks, Indians, and British citizens. The Tanganyikan natives did not receive any part of these prosperous areas (Sayers, 1930).

The decisions and actions of the British administration regarding the affairs of the land distribution indicated deep-seated prejudice and discrimination against black native Tanganyika. The regime denied the native people their fundamental right to ownership of valuable resources essential to their livelihood and social wellbeing. The German colonial Government had taken land by force from the natives, but now the current British colonial regime sold and distributed land properties amongst themselves, Greeks, and Indians. The way in which the British colonial administration acted and decided on this land distribution and the exclusion of the Tanganyikan indigenous people was actually in line with and supported by their colonial policy, as some studies have indicated. Ndjovu (2015) undertook a historical study into the British Colonial Land Expropriation in Tanganyika, and made this observation:

"The British took over Tanganyika from the Germans in 1919 after the First World War. In facilitating colonial economic policies, the British colonial Government enacted Land Ordinance Cap 113 of 1923 and Land Acquisition Ordinance Cap 118 of 1926. These laws facilitated the acquisition of native lands and considerably changed the way expropriation was handled leaving behind permanent marks on the later practice. The colonial practice exposed the innermost economic intents of the British Government—the use of legal phrases like 'for public purpose' embedded in the ordinance had multiple legal interpretations and a loose definition befitting the colonial economic cravings of the time." Ndjovu (2015:10)

Land was an asset of significant importance to the colonial regime's long-term gain. Therefore, it is no wonder that the colonial regime established a policy established to justify these acts, regardless of whether such actions were hurting the economy and social wellbeing of the native people. One crucial question worth examining at this juncture is whether the British colonial regime's activities in Tanganyika contributed to the development of the social welfare of native people and society in general and how.

Researchers acknowledge that, in the economic sphere, steps were taken, and a positive outcome was evident, as can be ascertained from the fact that after World War I, Tanganyika had considerably more revenue and trade than before the war (Buell, 1928). However, other studies indicate that this economic development was not without its costs. To realise economic development in Tanganyika the British establishment relied on financial assistance from the home government in London. Dougherty (1966) explained that, in the year 1922, financial aid was given to Tanganyika as loans upon which interest was to be paid. Exchequer loans totalled £3,315,446—the most signif-icant portion of which, £2,045,523, was provided for productive objects (Leubuscher, 1944).

In the sphere of social development, British rule was not highly successful. It is almost impossible to divorce the social and eco-nomic realms since many of the problems confronted encom-pass both areas. Records show that under the leadership of Governor Byatt, the British administration did not successfully bring about social development in the Tanganyikan territory, and studies point to some factors that contributed to the lack of impact in this area. One controversial idea that created debate amongst the British colonial officers in Tanganyika was using local African chiefs in leadership positions or acting as inter-mediaries between the colonial authority and the local popu-lation. Dougherty (1966) pointed out that in 1923, the Native Authority Ordinance was issued so that more power might be conferred upon the native rulers. The usage of local leaders as part of colonial governing is historically known as indirect rule. Colonial regimes applied the indirect rule model of leadership across Africa and Tanganyika. This leadership model was sup-posed to allow traditional African rulers to be involved in the administrative structures of their fellow Africans at the local level, while the colonial officials oversaw from above (Suleman, 2016). Researchers have considered why colonial regimes opted for the usage of indirect rule. One view is that the European ad-ministrators wanted their instructions or orders to appear as if they were emanating directly from the traditional African rul-ers. This approach aimed at reducing African resistance against European policies (Suleman, 2016). However, the idea of includ-ing local African leaders in the colonial administrative network did not please Europeans. In particular, the non-native settlers in the Tanganyikan territory were uneasy about the idea of na-tives being socially empowered or counted as part of the British administration. They questioned whether any sort of native administration might have been useful (Dougherty, 1966).

Nevertheless, it appears that this questioning, and some of the attitudes of the British regime in Tanganyika, was not always in line with their written operational conventions or treaties. The requirement to prioritise and consider the natives' interests in the Tanganyika colony by the British regime was supposed to be a question of principle as indicated in the Permanent Mandates Commission of the League of Nations. It stated that "the non-native is an incidental and not a principal factor." (Dougherty 1966:207). Equally, it was stipulated that non-native settlers should not dominate the agricultural scene. This idea was expressed in 1923 by the Duke of Devonshire, who was then Secretary of State for the Colonies:

"His Majesty's Government think it necessary definitely to record their considered opinion that the interests of the African natives must be paramount and that if and when those interests and the interests of the immigrant races should conflict, the former should prevail. His Majesty's Government regards themselves as exercising a trust, on behalf of the African population."(Chidzero, 1961:14)

The above paragraphs (including the indented quotation) cover three issues. One matter is the inclusion and usage of indigenous leaders as agents of colonial rule. The inclusion of representatives of native communities as part of the British line of leadership was meant to signify trust and a social working relationship. Another issue raised in the above quotation is the need for and importance of colonial administration to consider the different interests of indigenous and other populations as stipulated by the expectations of the official treaty. However, self-centredness and material gains dominated and characterised the British colonial regime in Tanganyika, making it impossible for the indigenous people's interests and social welfare needs to feature in the wider purposes of the colonial administration. Equally, Byatt stated in a speech to the London Chamber of Commerce (on 22nd May 1922) that the sole future of the Tanganyikan economy lay in the development of the native, and not non-native, cultivation; thus, he alienated the immigrant races of Tanganyika (Dougherty, 1966).

Both above accounts stress the official understanding of what was supposed to happen during colonisation. The native African people and their wellbeing were the first consideration accounted for in whatever the British colonial regime was doing or intending to do in Tanganyika. But this is a contradiction of what happened on the ground. As transpired, the implementation of these conventions received resistance on the ground, mainly from those who signed them in the first place. European businesspeople at the time were interested in economic growth and benefit, rather than seeing native black people standing on equal ground socially and their social wellbeing improved. Ingham (1962:25) wrote, "British businessmen interested in Tanganyika in the post-war years felt that social and economic growth could only be attained by the encouragement of larger-scale farming and European enterprises." Thus, the British administration made vast land plantation areas available to non-native settlers (Dougherty, 1966).

Another matter which was a source of discontent among the British colonial officials was the realisation that the Chagga people were growing Arabica coffee on Mount Kilimanjaro. The non-natives resented the fact that the native people were growing a "European crop" (Sayers, 1930). However, the idea that coffee is a European crop is untrue. This understanding was based on misinformation and a sense of cultural superiority. It was not Byatt who was primarily responsible for the encouragement of native cultivation. The scheme originated with Sir Charles Dundas, who had studied captured German records during the war. Dundas discovered that the soil upon which the Chagga people lived (in the higher slopes of Mount Kilimanjaro) could quickly be adopted for the growing of Arabica coffee (Sayers, 1930). Other historians interpret the British colonial officials' attitude towards the Chagga people as an indication of British desire to have total domination over local people. For example, Padmore (1949) argued that:

"the 'coffee controversy' was just another illustration of the degree to which the non-natives wanted the sole monopoly of the Tanganyika coffee market. Thus, the Dar-es-Salaam Times was but a mouthpiece for the capitalistic imperialism which hoped to run Tanganyika on the same economic, political, and racial principles as South Africa, that is, white capital and black labour … European political bosses and African helots." (Padmore, 1949:62).

The second phase of the British colonial administration of Tanganyika was under the Governorship of Sir Donald Cameron, 1925–1931. During his tenure in office, Sir Donald initiated and advanced the system of indirect (native) administration:

"The system of "Indirect Administration" [is] based on several principles and is designed to adapt for local Government the tribal institutions which the native people have evolved for themselves… so that the latter may develop constitutionally from their past, guided and restrained by the traditions and sanctions which they have inherited, moulded or modified as they may be on the advice of British officers. It is an essential feature of the system that the British Government rules through these native institutions which are an integral part of the machinery of Government, just as the administrative officers are an essential part of the Government with well-defined powers and functions recognised by the Government and by law." (Dougherty, 1966:205).

Sir Donald had a stepping-stone to assist him in advancing his programme of native administration. This development followed the Native Authority Ordinance passed during Byatt's governorship in 1923. The implementation of this ordinance was complex and met with resistance within the British administration, as different interests and priorities competed. Just as had been the case in the first phase of British rule under Governor Byatt, the British officials in Tanganyika could not agree on the idea of elevating local African leaders into colonial administration, and Governor Cameron faced resistance (Mair, 1936; Ingham, 1962). The idea of introducing a social welfare policy that focused on improving the social wellbeing of native society and intervening in individuals' social circumstances was a bone of contention among the British colonial administration, both in London and in Dar es Salaam, Tanganyika. Historians have provided various perspectives explaining why the British administration discouraged the idea of introducing a state-sponsored social security system for the wellbeing of the Tanganyikan natives. This idea was rejected vehemently by the British, and some of the reasons used as a basis for this rejection are explained below. One explanation for the British administration's avoiding introducing a standard social security welfare system was the fear of the costs it might incur. Cooper (1996) explained that the British colonial administration in Tanganyika was against introducing any social protection system, such as family allowances for native Tanganyikan workers and society in general. Setting up a general family allowance scheme for the whole population was also a contentious matter back in society in the UK during this time. The British Government was rejecting calls to introduce such a social scheme (Pedersen, 1993; Spicker, 2014). Thus, it is not surprising to find that they also resisted calls for its introduction elsewhere, including in the Tanganyika territory. The British establishment regarded the implementation of these standards in their African territories as "not realistic" (Cooper, 1996:83). Colonial officials mainly put forward political arguments against the idea. However, Eckert (2004) argued that the main reason behind this reluctance was because the cost of providing European scale benefits could not be borne by the colonial regime, especially not in a supposedly underdeveloped territory like Tanganyika. Equally, Molohan (1959), a provincial commissioner, argued against any move by the British administration to set up a social policy scheme that intended to benefit the natives. He emphasised that "any form of compulsory state-controlled provident fund scheme … is out of the question because of the high cost of administration that would be involved" (Molohan, 1959:67). Under the prevailing economic circumstances in Tanganyika, the British colonial regime argued that the price of a government-run social security system would have been high even if it were only to include a small number of African workers and employees.

Furthermore, another perspective emphasises that the introduction and management of a formal social security system was likely to be impossible because of the cost not only in Tanganyika but in the many colonies that Great Britain managed in Africa. It is estimated that there were twenty or more such colonies under British control in Africa alone (Kanyandago, 2002). It is undeniable that the British colonial empire had spread across Africa purposely to acquire maximum resource gains for the building up of the economy and social conditions back in the United Kingdom alone. However, the official position dictated that the British colonial regime in Tanganyika should prioritise the natives' interests.

The British administration in Tanganyika had a contradictory attitude towards the natives. On the one hand, the British colonial regime worried about the financial cost of setting up a social security system for the native society. However, on the other hand, this colonial regime was committed and vigorously involved in the continued looting of resources, forcing native people to work for the regime's interest while ignoring their welfare needs—an attitude nothing short of selfish and exploitative. It is also important to note that during this period, workers from non-African backgrounds, including the British colonial officials, received social security protection that was not extended to native African workers.

Studies in British colonial history indicate that the British Government adopted a 'laissez-faire' attitude towards the colonies' economic development. According to T.C. (1943), the reason for this approach appears to have been the maintenance of law and order in the colony so that the trading and mining companies could operate without interruption in their work, ensuring a steady flow of vital raw material to the country. Reflecting on this impact of this social plan on the ground, Perham, cited in T.C. (1943:140), has pungently remarked: "British colonial administrators, reflecting and indeed prolonging the attitude of their kin in Britain, lavished their attention upon political development, while the more powerful economic forces were allowed their free and devastating attack upon native society."

The general native welfare needs were not considered as a priority of the British colonial regime. Native societies experienced food shortages: among other reasons, this situation was caused mainly by the colonial regime's policy that introduced large plantations and demanded that native communities offer a labour force to realise the high production levels of cash-crops. Balancing colonial demands around massive cash-crop production and at the same time cultivating for one's own welfare needs was a challenging undertaking. In many circumstances, communities found themselves without sufficient food and without any external interventional support.

Another perspective that seemed to influence the lack of implementation of a social policy system in which the natives were beneficiaries was that the British officials regarded a formal social security system to be "non-African." Iliffe (1987) pointed out that until the Second World War, the colonial state and European private employers delegated the field of social security entirely to what they labelled "traditional African solidarity" and occasionally to the few individuals and church welfare institutions. Furthermore, in 1959, Gower, an acting governor, justified the lack of state-sponsored social security systems by linking this with African society's specific nature. Gower expressed this view: "The underlying philosophy that social security is not the responsibility of the individual or of his family is alien to Africa" (Gower 1959, quoted in Eckert, 2004:475). Gower's statement implies that the introduction of a state-sponsored social welfare scheme would not have been a notion familiar or known to local native African people. The expressed assumption was that the native Africans understood that the responsibility of providing social security rested with individuals and families and not with another body or government, as was the practice in the United Kingdom. Therefore, Gower's statement indicates that having such a system in place would be imposing something alien onto the native black people; hence, he did not see the necessity of a social security system provided by a government. Although this may align with how social security was ensured in line with the pre-colonial era, the time has now changed, and communities are influenced and controlled by the colonial regime. Evidence shows that there was no direct communication with native Africans or whether they were involved in discussions as to whether such a policy applied to them or not. It may be the case that the British colonial regime in Tanganyika, as in other parts of Africa, from the beginning made a conscious decision that the social welfare of native black people was not a main priority. Under no circumstances were they going to change their position on this matter. Herbert (1974:45) asserted that colonial powers had no desire to finance state welfare programmes for Africans. Manji and O'Coill (2002:569) wrote: "Government social services for the indigenous population were minimal. Social policy was geared towards ensuring the integrity of the structures of colonial rule. It was designed to secure a sufficient quality of labour to guarantee reasonably efficient exploitation of the colony. The goals of social development (such as they were) were defined in the metropolis. Within that framework, policy formulation and implementation were usually decentralised, being delegated to the colonial governor and administration." Other studies observe that the implementation of a social security system in Africa was coupled with many challenges as there was little urgency for the formalising of regulated labour markets and state-sponsored social security (Low and Lonsdale, 1976). However, other views direct blame towards native Africans who did not insist upon the meeting of their needs, rights, and social welfare. For example, Brennan (2002) pointed out that in the late 1940s, strikes spearheaded by railway workers and dockworkers mainly focused on demands for higher wages to meet high living costs. African trade unionists and nationalists in Tanganyika were not aggressive enough about social security issues (Friedland, 1969). The Tanganyika African Government Servants Association (TAGSA), an occupational group that preferred petitions rather than striking, complained about the high costs of newspapers, living spaces, cinema, books, and tickets several years after the Second World War (Tanzania National Archive, 1951 Cited in Eckert, 2004). The native African workers did not stress enough the need for social welfare provision but instead demanded higher wages over campaigning for a more general social security scheme. The lack of focus on rights and social welfare provision could have stemmed from a general lack of understanding regarding their rights and living circumstances. I suspect that they were deprived of both requirements but that they saw it necessary to request an increase in wages to at least to meet their daily needs.

Another social issue that created an unfavourable social working environment and tension for black African workers was the British colonial administration's attitude towards favouring Asian employees. The colonial government held back African recruitment for higher administrative posts that incorporated pension rights until the later years of occupation (Eckert, 2004). African workers' awareness of their rights grew, and they made demands for change, and more development concerning social security emerged. During his tenure from 1925–1931, the Governor of Tanganyika, Sir Donald Cameron, influenced the British regime to enact a policy called the 'Master and Servants Ordinance.' This policy offered small industrial compensation paid by employers to their employees in the case of industrial accidents (Bossert, 1985). However, initially, African workers who were government clerks were classified into lower administrative ranks that lacked both employer contributions and pension rights (Dougherty, 1966).

One matter in the above paragraph deserves further attention and deliberation. There is a connection between the policy of favouring 'Asian' employees and the demands for more significant social security provisions. An institution that operates following a policy of favouritism with regard to its employees—for example, treating some employees with high regard and giving them privileges while treating others in a discriminatory manner—contributes to furthering the social problems of those discriminated against. If an employer values all employees equally regardless of their cultural background, such an employer would assist them equally in every way. However, this was not the case in Tanganyika during this time.

In the late 1930s, Lord Hailey, a historian and theoretician of British colonial policy, expressed the attitude towards Africans at that time; "It is clear that by treating the native reserves as reservoirs of manpower, there is, in effect, saving in that outlay on social services which in other circumstances might have to be incurred on behalf of industrialised labour" (Hailey, 1938:710). It is no wonder that, until the Second World War, most measures in the realm of social policy benefited Europeans almost exclusively (Kaufmann, 1982; Fuchs, 1985, both cited in Eckert, 2004:473).

In November 1942, a social security scheme, the Provident Fund (Government Employees) Ordinances, was set up by the British regime in Tanganyika. This policy was intended to provide funds for lower-rank workers (including native Africans), and offered, at least, small payments in the case of a premature inability to work and subsequent retirement (Tanganyika Labour Department, 1950, cited in Eckert, 2004). African workers expressed some reservations and resistance regarding how they were being dealt with by the British administration, which controlled all social and economic aspects of life. Reflecting on the situation, Eckert wrote: "The manifestation of capacity for industrial action by African workers was instrumental in raising voices to be fairly and equally treated as workers. The Africans workers demanded to be treated as workers as opposed to Africans" (Eckert, 2004:8). Black Africans' request to be merely known as workers rather than Africans could be interpreted as a demand to be treated on the same basis as other workers regardless of race, ethnicity or skin colour. These frustrations that native black Africans in Tanganyika expressed are an indication of the impacts of social inequality in the workforce. They were racially profiled by their British employers when it came to individual rights in the workplace. Eckert (2004) explained that the marginalisation of African workers was symptomatic of how, in general, Europeans viewed black African people at that time. European colonisers likened Africans essentially to "primitive tribesmen." The extraction of casual labour or unskilled work and the conservation of tribal African structures was a common practice.

While social welfare provision was perceived to be a complicated matter at the British colonial governmental level, other organisations within the voluntary sector took up the responsibility of social welfare provision in Tanganyika during that time. Jennings (2014) stated that the voluntary sector comprised almost entirely Christian missionary organisations. History reveals that British missionary work in Tanganyika increased steadily from 1924 onwards (Leubuscher, 1944). History indicates a formal voluntary sector and an alliance between the colonial state and Christian missionary organisations in Tanganyika from the 1930s (Jennings, 2015). The voluntary sector's work was acknowledged and made an integral part of the British colonial government in Tanganyika.

Retrospectively, voluntary and charitable work have historically played a central role in social problem-solving. Manji and O'Coill (2002:568) pointed out that:

"Market and voluntarism have a long association; the first and most celebrated period of "free trade," from the 1840s to the 1930s, was also a high point of charitable activity throughout the British Empire. In Britain, the Industrial Revolution opened up a great gulf between the bourgeoisie and the swelling ranks of the urban proletariat. In the 1890s, when industrialists were amassing fortunes to rival those of the aristocracy, as much as one-third of the population of London was living below the level of bare subsistence, and death from starvation was not unknown. At this time, private philanthropy was the preferred solution to social need and private expenditure far outweighed public provision."

Indeed, as the above quote indicates, charitable groups composed mainly of Christians, for example, the Salvation Army, the Church Missionary Society, and other church groups/philanthropists played a part in helping those affected by social problems in the United Kingdom during the 18th and 19th centuries.

Christian mission institutions played a most significant role in meeting the social welfare needs of the indigenous populations, including addressing Tanganyikans' health-related needs across the country. Jennings' research indicates that from the 1930s, the colonial state gradually incorporated mission-run services into its health system. By the 1950s, we can see Tanzania's health system operating as a public–private partnership model (Jennings, 2015:2). Large- and small-scale hospitals were established, addressing various aspects of health-related matters that affected natives. Missionaries seemed to be closer to the local people than the overall British colonial establishment. The British colonial state in Tanganyika acknowledged positively the contributions and social services provided by mission organisations. Jennings (2013) explained that under British rule, cooperation between the medical services operated by the colonial state and those of the voluntary sector increased steadily from the 1930s until the late 1940s. During this time, the British colonial state provided limited funding for voluntary sector services. In return, those voluntary providers agreed to subject themselves to greater regulation and direction from the state. The funding did not cover all costs, did not include capital costs, and official grants were only made for mission hospitals with resident doctors, not for dispensaries and clinics (Jennings, 2015:2). The state support level was predicated upon the assumption that voluntary services would also receive funding from external sources. So, the mission organisation was expected to match half of the total state grant from external sources (Tanganyika, 1952).

A formal public–private model for healthcare service delivery in Tanganyika was established as a partnership between the state (with overall responsibility for regulating health service provision) and Christian mission providers. Mission work was contracted through grant-in-aid provision to provide services where the state could or would not do so (Jennings, 2013).

Some authors have questioned the extent to which British missionaries in Tanganyika and Africa were committed to promoting and protecting the social well-being of native black Africans in colonial times. The argument is that British missionaries exhibited a contradictory and ambivalent attitude towards injustice and inhumane treatment endured by native black Africans under the colonial regime. Some literature indicated that the attitude and work of missionaries in Africa helped the colonial power fulfil its plan in the country. The mission stations strengthened the colonial regime's hold over the country, missionaries inducted native black African people into the best kind of civilisation, and mission structures were an essay in colonisation (Temu 1972, Okon 2014). Also, missionaries' social welfare programmes that served black native people were associated with purposes other than redressing the social circumstances that caused impoverishment. One apparent view is that British missionaries used the British Empire's resources, and then, in turn, the Empire coerced them into using their teachings to subdue the native Africans. In this way, missionary organisations actively helped to suppress anti-colonial struggles (Manji and O'Coill, 2002). These authors see that voluntary welfare provision by mission organisations was easily adapted for social control (Manji and O'Coill, 2002). Other authors see a similarity between Britain and Africa regarding how welfare provision was used. Woodroofe (1974:13) wrote: "in Britain and the colonies alike, politicians frequently alluded to the threat of revolution and actively encouraged greater interest in works of benevolence as a solution to social unrest." Of course, colonialism and its injustice and brutality impacted many lives, and missionaries were in a position of power compared to native Africans. They could have championed justice and the fair treatment of native Africans. However, for reasons unknown to us of which we can only speculate, they chose not to interfere and instead turned a blind eye to the colonial regime and its activities. It is difficult to establish whether this indifference and lack of interference by mission organisations was caused by a lack of courage to confront their fellow compatriots of the British Empire or whether, indeed, the colonial agenda, upon which economic and material gains depended on the exploitation and utilisation of native Africans as a labour force was a plan known to missionaries, and they, therefore, restrained from interfering.

While there may be some truth in the criticisms levelled against missionary organisations operating during the colonial era, it is essential to note that the voluntary sector did address the social circumstances which affected native people to some extent. For example, hospitals and clinics in Tanzania were built and helped native people whose well-being was threatened by diseases. Schools set up by missionaries linked to different Christian denominations a long time ago continue to provide primary and secondary education, making education available to a large population in Tanzania (Mushi, 2009:187).

Both Christianity and Islam characterise the religious identity of the country of Tanzania, so is the contribution in addressing social problems and enhancing social welfare services in the country. Islamic involvement in social welfare issues has a history in Tanzania. It emerged in pre-colonial, colonial, and post-colonial Tanzania and continues today. Historically, traditional Islamic Education was introduced by the Arabs in the coastal area of Tanzania, where Islam first arrived. It thus preceded Western-style schooling by centuries. Generations of walimu (teachers), some more trained than others, provided religious education to the young. This education was offered in what is known as the Quran schools at the primary level (Chande, 1993:1). The establishment of Muslim schools and the spread of education carried out in Tanzania and elsewhere in Africa has always been done to consolidate Islamic religion and its cultural identity in a society (Pouwells, 1987; Chande, 1993).

Furthermore, Muslims of Arabic descent who lived in Kilwa, Tanga, and other coastal cities had a good level of literacy in Kiswahili written in the Arabic script. They took the Islamisation agenda by offering education in coastal and mainland Tanganyika. History indicates that Muslims of Arabic and Indian descent were used by the German colonial administration as interpreters and assistants consolidating the colonial regime and operation in Tanganyika because of their good level of literacy in Kiswahili and local awareness. From the time Islam arrived and its development in Tanzania, education has been a tool to the public.

Though initially education was concentrated more on traditional Islamic religious teachings (Lienhardt, 1959), today's education led by Muslims tries to embrace other dimensions of academic fields, modern subjects that reflect broader life experiences, and charity work. Literature indicates efforts by Islamic religious groups to address social problems and provide social welfare services before and after independence. Islamic social contribution is evident in the country's health care and education (Lange et al., 2000). Islamic social efforts in providing education to local Muslim Africans did not receive warm approval from the British colonial administration when Tanganyika was under colonial occupation. Reflecting on this situation, Chande (1993:6) wrote: "As far as the matter of awarding subsidies to mission schools was concerned, the British administration had quite early made it possible for many of their schools run by the voluntary agencies to receive financial assistance. By providing them such assistance the British were seen by the Muslims to be subsidising Christianity, particularly in view of the fact that they refused to grant aid to Quran schools on the ground that these were exclusively religious institutions."

Consequently, due to missing financial support from colonial masters, they took measures into their own hands. Muslims, through their then leader, the Aga Khan (Sultan Muhammad Sha), leader of the Ismailis, collaborated with like-minded Asian and African Muslims established, and initiated the East African Muslim Welfare Society (EAMWS). The expressed aims of this association were as follows: "a) to promote Islam in East Africa; and b) to render assistance in the advancement and the betterment of such Muslims and in particular African Muslims who in the opinion of the society, stand in need of such assistance in the fields of education, both secular and religious, and in the spheres of health and social services." (Kiwanuka 1973:49, cited in Chande, 1993:7). This organisation began to function fully in 1945, the year marking the end of World War II (Chande, 1993).

Islamic organisations are among the organisations that are active in social service delivery today in Tanzania. Their impact is not only limited to the private sphere of the believers but also extends to the public sphere (Weiss, 2020:1). A study by Lange et al. (2000) found out that Muslim organisations run a number of hospitals and 15 secondary schools around the country. Two of them provide training for future religious leaders; the rest are open to all, including Christians. Other studies have explored the beginning and impact of Islamic education and social activities in Tanzania (Mushi, 2009).

The voluntary sector in the colonial era may have served as a foundation and catalyst for the development of the current local non-governmental welfare organisations in Tanzania. Today, the voluntary sector plays a significant role in eliminating poverty and fighting against other social ills affecting the general population's wellbeing, especially those from socially disadvantaged backgrounds, and challenging injustice in social structures. History reveals more efforts to address social welfare concerns. The British administration set up a formalised social welfare structure arranged for native Africans, as discussed in the following section.

6.3 More Formalised Welfare Arrangements During the Colonial Period

The Second World War was a significant turning point in the thinking of the British colonial administration regarding their involvement with the social welfare needs of the indigenous Tanganyikan people. The British administration in Tanganyika could see the social impacts of the Second World War on the local population, especially local Tanzanians who had participated in war abroad. Hence, during and after the Second World War, the British colonial regime in Tanganyika deliberated on activities focused on social welfare, and some reasonable attempts to address the issues did surface. History indicates that the British colonial Government tried to set up social welfare programs that targeted specific social groups. These social programmes were social welfare centres in some cities, including Dar es Salaam. To realise the social welfare centres' vision, the British administration back in London allocated £50,000 from the Colonial Development and Welfare Fund to establish social welfare centres throughout Tanganyika. (Tanzania National Achieve 34257: Report on Social Welfare for the Year 1945. Cited in Eckert, 2004:477).

The welfare centres were an integral part of a vision that sought to promote social development and social security initiatives in urban areas (Cooper, 1996). One objective behind these initiatives was to bring the natives of Tanganyika into the 20th century, so the established social welfare centres focused on increasing literacy (Cooper, 1996). The opening of these social welfare centres was deemed crucial in the early 1940s, as many African soldiers returned from action overseas (Burton, 2008). Before and at the beginning of the Second World War, some established welfare initiatives did exist, for instance, literacy programmes for adults in the Eastern Province and specifically in Dar es Salaam (Eckert, 2004). Eckert provides us with this historical information to understand the deliberation and steps taken to this policy based on the archive's information. TNA 34257, cited by Eckert (2004:477), reported:

"Already in the spring of 1944, the chief secretary did mention in a circular to all provincial commissioners (TNA 61/782/1) plans "for the establishment after the war of associations of ex-servicemen, clubs, general welfare centres having particular regard to the need of the returned soldier." The establishment of various social or welfare centres would act as a gathering place for the most progressive Africans, both ex-soldiers and others, would have particular regard for the needs of the ex-soldier and would be in some measure recognition of the services he had rendered to the territory in the war. Such a centre would also fulfil some of the functions of a club – for which there is an ever-growing need amongst Africans and an educational centre for adults. And might, if properly organised, be a useful agency through which District Commissioners could keep in touch with the more advanced elements in their districts."

The British Information Officer in Dar es Salaam 1944 declared a territory-wide mass education programme targeting the African soldiers returning from overseas service. The British colonial establishment believed that due to their exposure to different places and lifestyles, returning soldiers would be hungry for education. Therefore, they were described as the sole object of this programme (Low and Lonsdale, 1976). This quote by an Information Officer on 11 July 1944 (Tanzanian National Archives (TNA 61/67/5) best describes the background behind establishing these social welfare centres. The Information Officer's words in Eckert (2004:477) read:

"the soldiers themselves have seen many strange things, have visited, in many cases, distant lands and have acquired a taste for knowledge…When they come back from the war, they will want to have at home the same opportunities they had in the army; they will wish to continue their studies and will want their friends and relatives to study with them and to keep pace with them."

Eckert's information officer's account indicates the underlying principle of thinking by the British colonial administration. The idea of setting up social welfare centres as a response to the potential needs of returning soldiers seemed an appropriate social programme.

To implement the social welfare centre programmes, a social welfare organiser, Mr Baker, was appointed, and he acted as a chairman to oversee the entire project (Eckert, 2004). The British Government set out to establish 40 centres, mainly in urban areas, within a short period of time. Initially, the objectives of these centres were unclear (Tanzania National Archives –TNA Paper, 1954). Each provincial administration created a separate unit that played a role in taking care of the reintegration of returning soldiers, and in 1944, welfare centres were a focal point of this endeavour. Historians provide more explanation for the establishment of these social welfare centres: besides becoming outlets for ex-soldiers ambition, these centres had other tasks associated with them. Citing information from the TNA (540/3: Circular Social Welfare Office, Oct. 1945), Eckert (2004:478) maintained that these centres served a bridge-building purpose. "The function of the centres is to endeavour to bridge the gap between the proletariat and the intelligentsia and to inspire the latter with the ideal of service which it so badly lacks. Many policy documents followed, listing numerous potential functions and tasks of the centres, such as providing leisure and adult learning for local populations and creating a community spirit of self-help." These social programmes were bridging the gap between the intelligentsia and the proletariat and inspiring the intelligentsia with the country's ideals of service, which were seemingly lacking. However, it seems unclear how the welfare centres were to serve as the bridge between intellectuals and the working class. It is not clear who belonged to the intelligentsia and who was part of the proletariat. Was it returning soldiers bridging the gap with ordinary native Africans, or were British colonial officials and experts interacting with returned soldiers? Other functions attributed to these centres were the provision of adult learning and leisure for local populations and the creation of a community spirit of self-help. Activities which took place in these centres included debates, lectures, theatre performances, sports, dance, and reading and writing courses (Eckert, 2004).

Other activities in these centres focused on women. It was believed that women promoted better conditions in the home, contributing to higher overall standards of living. Hence, much effort was spent on educating women in the ways of improving living conditions, as women prepared the food, clothing the family, were responsible for bringing up the children, and were generally accountable for cleanliness, domestic health, and behaviour patterns (Eckert, 2004). In Dar es Salaam, female welfare officers, who were mostly the wives of European officials, organised courses for women, as did voluntary workers from the Women's Service League of Tanganyika, offering activities such as knitting, sewing, healthcare, ironing, domestic hygiene, and English. They were met with enthusiastic responses, although little is known about the experiences and the motives of the women frequenting these welfare centres (Eckert, 2004). These centres received small government subsidies; however the British colonialists refrained from entirely financing these centres, using membership payments as a way of encouraging the 'self-supporting' nature of the centres. British officials believed that this form of financing would improve the Africans' sense of responsibility in social and financial matters, and they defined welfare centres as analogous to local government institutions, a kind of training ground linked to future democracy (Eckert, 2004).

History indicates that the programmes which were run at the social welfare centres received criticism and were not fully embraced by Africans. For example, the Tanganyika African National Union (TANU) representatives regularly attacked the British education policy in the Legislative Council (Nyerere, 1966). The Government of Tanganyika patently neglected the educational aspects promoted in the British social welfare education system extension and development policies. Most nationalists and Africans, in general, were not comfortable with the kind of civilisation instruction and training offered in the social welfare centres (Nyerere, 1966). Additionally, questions about the effectiveness of these centres emerged, with varying opinions surfacing regarding the success of the social welfare centres.

British officials attempted to explain this situation with a mixture of self-criticism and paternalism. For example, Richards, the then Social Development Commissioner, assessed that the lack of success was caused by the two most crucial user groups of the centre, who failed to fulfil their role adequately as designed for them. The Commissioner highlighted that the 'educated class', mainly government clerks, were 'social snobs', unwilling to mingle with manual workers and the latter's interest 'was limited to fun and games and in particular dances' (Richards quoted in Eckert, 2004:480). Equally, another perspective on the matter was that "as far as the less educated sections of the community are concerned, the centres appear to be unattractive in comparison with the customary and traditional relaxations. At the same time, they lack the full support of those the more educated by whom welfare is regarded as something which should be provided and paid for by the State. The result is a degree of apathy towards the centres and a continuing reluctance to contribute even nominal subscriptions towards their upkeep and maintenance" (Annual Report to UN for 1957, 121., quoted in Eckert, 2004:479).

Furthermore, Mnyampala (1954) made a point that a strong community of interest was deemed to be a feeling that was alien to tribal exclusiveness; that, in their sense, "Africa is not club-minded." A further explanation for the lack of success of the social welfare centre programmes was that very few ex-soldiers stayed in Dar es Salaam or other cities. In his annual report for 1947, the British Social Welfare Officer noted that no soldier felt the need to commit actively to social progress contribution because "tribal life" had absorbed them again. Only a few former soldiers seriously engaged in political, social, or cultural activities. Their military experience impacted more on village beer party conversations than on political organisations (Iliffe, 1979). A survey conducted on the impact of the social welfare centres in the Tanganyika provinces and districts resulted in frustrating conclusions. The summary report reads:

"No District Commissioner claims more than moderate success for the centre in his area. Two centres have failed, and twelve are regarded as being more or less failures ... The basic difficulty is that illiterate and semi-literate African peasants are unable quickly to assimilate twentieth-century ideas of community life and development. Particularly, is this so when the ideas are associated with the word "welfare," which has a war-time association with the ex-servicemen for whom the centres were primarily designed in the first place? This word, for many, has the connotation of "getting something for nothing." Other difficulties have been insufficient staff (European and African); the gulf between the 'educated' African and the artisan-peasant; ...and, finally, the fact that dancing, often the most popular community activity, has incurred the hostility of missionaries." (Tanganyika re. Community Centres, Summary Report, [Apr. 1952] in Eckert 2004:480). However, others have argued that it was a big mistake to have imposed these centres on African communities without first cultivating the African understanding of these institutions' main aims and objectives (Burton, 2003). While the other above explanations are valid, the lack of consultation, partnership, and working relationships between the British colonial administration and the indigenous communities contributed significantly to the failure of the social welfare centres. How could a group of people be expected to embrace and carry on a project if they had no participation in its construction? Could such a project bear any value or meaning in people's lives through coercion alone? The social welfare centre programmes sounded as though they were a positive vision. However, the implementation process appeared to overlook essential steps, namely, collaboration in the formation and implementation of the project between stakeholders, including British colonial officials, ex-soldiers, and local communities.

The colonial occupation of Tanganyika ended in 1961 when the territory gained its independence from Great Britain. In 1964, the mainland region of Tanganyika joined with Zanzibar and Pemba Island and formed what is known today as the United Republic of Tanzania. Following independence, the country entered another era, and the elected Government had to grapple with how to address the social problems that affected its population. Therefore, in the following section, we discuss the path, steps, and actions that the Government took to address social issues in the country.

6.4 Formal Approach to Welfare Arrangements Following Independence

The colonial invasion of Africa and Tanzania marked a point of no return, both in terms of indigenous populations' understanding of life at the time and their experiencing of life in the subsequent post-colonial era. For example, Settles (1996:1) remarked: "the imposition of colonialism on Africa altered its history forever. African modes of thought, patterns of cultural development, and ways of life were forever impacted by the change in political structure brought about by colonialism. The African economy was significantly changed through the process of imperialism and the economic policies that accompanied colonisation." The colonial activities impacted people significantly and left them trying to navigate a new path as an independent nation, which required political leadership that could bring about social and economic development in the country. Soanes and Stevenson (2003) defined politics as the ideas and strategies of a government or the public affairs of a nation. Political leadership can have various meanings. One meaning which seems relevant to this discussion is the understanding of political leadership's role in giving vision and strategy to a nation and creating a conducive environment for implementing formulated policies. These policies aim at, among other things, bringing about economic development and social change (Ngowi, 2009:261). After gaining independence from the British colonial Government in 1961, Tanzania faced the daunting task of creating its own Government and addressing its people's welfare. Mwenzwa and Waweru (2016) asserted that, after obtaining freedom, African states needed to revisit their social and economic development strategies through self-directed formulation and the implementation of policy processes. Hence, to be useful to its people, the Tanzanian Government adopted a political philosophy that has influenced the formation of the economy, the society, and the social welfare arrangements. Under Nyerere's leadership, the new Government's administration had the sole responsibility to bring about economic system change that would benefit every citizen and not just a privileged few. One responsibility that the Government and policymakers sought to fulfil was the extension of all necessary public social services (health, education, and water) and other social services to the entire population (Manyama, 2017).

Historians have explained that the analysis of the socio-economic reality and the vision of necessary services was motivated by some observable factors: firstly, the realisation that even after independence, the economy continued to be mainly within the hands of the British colonial masters and Asian businessmen, primarily Arabs and Indians, who controlled industries, plantations, banks, mines, and a relatively large number of commercial activities. The economy continued to be market-oriented, with private sector capitalism dominating (Ngowi, 2009; Wangwe and Rweyemamu, 2001). Secondly, Tanzania inherited a colonial economic and public sector structure that benefited few people. For example, the education system in colonial times was stratified by racial categories (White, Asian, and African). The quality and accessibility of African schools were relatively poor and under-resourced, and most of the black population did not receive any education (Ngowi, 2009; Wangwe and Rweyemamu, 2001).

Furthermore, at that time, the healthcare system consisted of a few hospitals and private doctors in urban areas and religious mission services and traditional healers in rural areas. In the water sector, most households, mainly rural, obtain water from natural sources. Therefore, considering all of these deficiencies in the social and economic sectors, the country, through its Government, declared war on what they named the nation's three archenemies: poverty, ignorance/illiteracy, and diseases (Wangwe and Rweyemamu, 2001:3). A single party characterised the political structure, the Tanganyika African National Union (TANU), until 1964. Tanganyika and Zanzibar united under the leadership of Julius Kambarage Nyerere, who became the first president of Tanzania (Ngowi, 2009).

After gaining independence, changes did not occur straight away. The new Government made a political decision to continue with the capitalist mode of production inherited from colonial masters. With regard to this decision, it can, therefore, be argued that at this time the relationship between political actors and economic policy was one in which the leaders followed the procedures inherited from colonial masters (Ngowi, 2009). Operating within the inherited old economic framework, the Government implemented a five-year plan (1961–1967) to change the economy and the social condition of the country. This strategy was the first effort, as Kaiser (1996:229) explained: "Immediately following independence... efforts were made to implement a programme which depended on foreign investment to support massive, capital-intensive industrialisation and agricultural development projects. By the middle of the 1960s, it became apparent that this ambitious five-year plan was not yielding anticipated results, and that Tanzania was on a path towards increased dependence on the North."

Factors that indicate that the five-year economic plan seemed to be unsuccessful in producing its intended results are documented. Wagao (1992) explained that during the five-year plan urban–rural income differentials increased dramatically, rural-based development was ignored, local expertise remained inadequate, and finance became synonymous with capital projects at the expense of mobilising underutilised labour and land resources. It was within this social and economic context that the Government decided to introduce drastic measures. President Julius Nyerere presented an alternative vision in 1967 as outlined in the Arusha Declaration. The governing Tanzanian African National Union (TANU), later named the Chama Cha Mapinduzi (CCM), called into question the benefits of modernisation policies by challenging the basic tenets of capitalism (Kaiser, 1996). The political leadership seemed to be facing the dilemma of deciding which economic model would bring about the social and economic changes they wished to see on the ground. Their final decision to embrace a socialist economic philosophy model, as opposed to a capitalist economic model characterised by capital markets and private enterprise, seems to have primarily been influenced by the historical experiences of colonialism and associations between the capitalist economic model and the country's colonial history. Capitalism had already failed to bring the desired economic and social changes to the large, scattered Tanzanian population. However, the Government was entering uncharted territory, with little known about how a socialist economic model emphasising self-reliance would work. This was also the first time Tanzania had become a nation with one political structure. Still, they pressed ahead because they believed that the new economic policy model was relevant and could bring about social and economic change to all.

The political and economic landscape of Tanzania changed dramatically in 1967 as a result of the political decisions that gave birth to the Arusha Declaration proclaimed this year. The Arusha

Declaration served as an ideological foundation, a blueprint declaring that Tanzania would follow 'Ujamaa', a kind of African socialism policy, in its social and economic pursuit. The Ujama (familyhood) political ideology was deemed essential to the attainment of a self-reliant socialist nation and as a solution for marginalised communities in Tanzania. Julius Nyerere, the then first president of Tanzania, wrote: "The developed ujamaa ideology would cater and care for the sick, care for the orphans, widows, the aged; the unmarried, other people marginalised people in villages as a whole, just as the traditional society was up to the task" (Nyerere, 1968:352).

The impact of implementing this new policy became quickly evident on the ground. Kaiser (1996:229) explained that Nyerere's Government decided to retreat from the capital-intensive industrialisation that it had planned in its first five-year plan, as it was deemed an expensive project requiring vast amounts of foreign money and technology. The Government's focus and priority were now given to the development of the agricultural sector through Ujamaa Vijiji (Ujamaa Villages). The Government's actions seemed to be in line with TANU's Policy on Socialism and Self-Reliance (1967). The policy of the ruling party, TANU, stipulated that foreign grants, loans, and investments were to be discouraged in order to eliminate the complete dependence on outside help, as this endangered Tanzania's political independence and autonomous policymaking ability. To this end, the Government tried to channel monitored external assistance to increase domestic productivity carefully to limit imports to only those goods that could not be produced domestically (TANU's policy 1967:11).

The Government took more drastic actions to implement the socialist-oriented economic and political policies. The capitalist private sector and market-led economy that was inherited from the colonial powers at independence was replaced by a state-owned, centrally planned and controlled economy. All the essential means of production in the country (industries, agriculture plantations, commerce, mines) were nationalised, as were private-led institutions and social institutions under the voluntary sector, including schools and hospitals. The state became the principal owner, controller, and manager of these state-owned enterprises (SOEs) (Ngowi, 2009:262).

While during the colonial era, the voluntary sector and non-governmental organisations (NGOs) were at the frontline of welfare service provision, all of this changed after Tanzania gained independence, starting with the so-called Nyerere era. The status and functioning of the voluntary sector and NGOs were quashed, and their influence was reduced and pushed to the background during the first two decades of Nyerere's premiership. Additionally, in order to reach as many people as possible with public social services and other social interventional mechanisms, the Government decided to create villages and relocate people into these newly constructed villages. In his account of the history of Tanzania after independence, Kaiser (1996:229) remarked: "Since the population was widely dispersed on small plots of land, peasants were moved to newly constructed village settlements to promote efficient agricultural production and to facilitate the equitable delivery of essential services that had not occurred during the early years of independence. The process of villagisation was intended to integrate the logic of economic efficiency with the goal of social equity."

President Nyerere hoped that socialism would promote a classless society and serve all of the people of Tanzania, instead of creating wealth only for some (Jivani, 2010). The Tanzanian central Government tasked itself with providing the social services essential to the well-being of its population. Services, such as free health services, water, and education, were provided until the late 1980s, when the Structural Adjustment Programme was introduced by international donor communities, mainly from Western countries.

However, the Government encountered obstacles in meeting the costs of public services. It ran out of steam in terms of finances, resources, and personnel. The period between 1979 and 1985 witnessed economic stagnation in Tanzania as investors pulled out of the country. Poverty was high across society, and the productivity levels in agriculture and industry were very low. By the late 1980s, it had become clear that the central Government alone would not be able to fulfil its desire to meet the needs of everyone in the country without involving citizens and other stakeholders, including the voluntary sector and NGOs (Wangwe and Rweyemamu, 2001). According to Wangwe and Rweyemamu (2001), the failure of social service provision happened because:

"The cost burden following significant capital investments in health, education, and water services, and training of large numbers of personnel was enormous. While donors had been willing and able to finance much of the capital costs of developing the infrastructure, financing of the recurrent costs was primarily left to the Tanzanian Government, which in turn depended on too small a tax base. Overextension of the health, education, and water systems was compounded with rapid increases in the costs of imported materials and financial demands of other sectors, and overall decline in growth of the economy." (Wangwe and Rweyemamu, 2001:6).

Other reasons were that the Government could not manage the vast networks of water systems, health facilities, schools, and associated staff. Additionally, the poor transportation and communication network in rural areas made effectively managing social welfare service supply more difficult. At the top of the communication chain, there was a lack of coordination and accountability between central and local governments (Wangwe and Rweyemamu, 2001).

The economic struggles the country experienced and the inability of the state to meet the social needs of its people triggered reactions from the international community, especially donor countries. In the 1980s, Western countries, through international non-governmental organisations (INGOs), such as the World Bank, the IMF, and UNICEF, gave the Tanzanian Government an ultimatum. If it was to continue receiving financial aid, it must change its way of operation. Among the requirements demanded by the INGOs was that the Tanzanian Government must abandon its socialist model and the government-centralised social welfare provision model. Additionally, the INGOs required that NGOs in the county be involved in providing public welfare services to the people. Tanzania had no choice but to bow down to these stipulated conditions and reinstate the voluntary sector NGOs (Shivji, 2004; Ngowi, 2009).

Other perspectives see the demand for economic and social policy change in Tanzania, as well as in other parts of Africa, not as an isolated incident linked to the failure of the state to provide for its people but instead as a deliberate push by the powerful and rich northern countries of the world to reorder the world's economic structure by forcing the developing world to be part of a globalised market economy. Concerning this point, Ravenhill (1988:181) remarked:

"With the end of the Cold War and the progressive globalisation of trade and capital markets, developing countries are encouraged to look to private enterprise as the motor of development and the means for meeting their economic and social needs. It is believed that by the adoption of open market economies, the world stands on the threshold of redirecting resources, sharing technological advances, and attaining levels of human prosperity never before imagined."

While other external factors may have contributed to the state's economic failure and its efforts to provide social services, the main reasons for this could lie within the country and especially the Government itself. Poverty was high, and productivity levels in agriculture and industry were deficient. The idea that the state could alone manage to meet the social service needs of every individual in every corner of the vast country without partnering with private and voluntary sectors itself was a bold, over-ambitious, and unrealistic plan. For a country that at the time had a meagre economic engine, high unemployment, no functioning manufacturing industries, and a low number of locally educated and qualified experts in various fields, cooperation with other stakeholders would have been a sensible decision. The country could have benefited from a collaboration between the Government, the private sector, and the voluntary sector, which could have minimised the extent of the economic crisis. Following the international community's demand, Tanzania signed an agreement with the International Monetary Fund to adopt structural adjustment programmes in 1986 (Kiondo, 1993). The conditions of this agreement included the control of the money supply, devaluation of the currency, and a reduction in government expenditure for social services, among other sweeping changes (Kiondo, 1993). These decisions created space for civil society and NGOs to address human social welfare in the country. Henceforth, development and service delivery expanded dramatically, and the number of registered NGOs in Tanzania increased from only 17 organisations in 1978 to 813 organisations by 1994 (Kiondo, 1993). The active participation of international NGOs and other forms of voluntary organisations in welfare provision has, since the late 1980s, become significant service providers, working alongside, in some cases supplanting, state providers (Jennings, 2014).

One argument for using international and locally based NGOs was that they were more efficient, less corrupt, and able to operate in a closer manner with people experiencing poverty than government bureaucracies. Therefore, NGOs actively filled in the gaps created as the Government retreated from its front-line service role due to severe budgetary restrictions (Jennings, 2014). These developments created a situation whereby NGOs, especially international NGOs in the country, freely tackled vast social issues. However, due to the vastness of social problems in the 1980s through the 1990s, such as the HIV/AIDS epidemic, challenges arising from a high level of urbanisation, swelling of towns' populations often without proper social structure, high level of unemployment, poverty, and lack of appropriate sanitation, services such as water, education, health-related services, and social protection, remained a challenge. The responsibility of tackling these issues could not solely be left to INGOs/NGOs, no matter how capable they might be. The Government's involvement in putting in place structures, infrastructure, and policies was needed to spearhead long-term social and economic goals while working together with the voluntary sector (INGOs/NGOs) to address social issues affecting people's social well-being. The state relegation in providing welfare services in the 1980s and 1990s retarded the national development efforts of the economy and social progress (Manyama, 2017).

As people realised the willingness of donors to give direct support to NGOs and community-based organisations (CBOs), the number of organisations exploded (Lange et al., 2000). Additionally, the rise and demand for certain social groups, such as women, people with disabilities, and older people, to organise and articulate their interests in the country contributed to the rise. They strengthened local NGOs' role (Manara, 2009). Another factor was the move by international aid agencies to bypass the state and also the retrenchment programmes that increased the number of unemployed people who found voluntary organisations as an employment alternative in the country (Patel et al., 2007). In 1985, Nyerere stepped down from the presidency. The new Government under Ali Hassan Mwinyi developed new policies to bring about socio-economic development. This era is known as the country's 'neo-liberal' era. The presidency under Ali Hassan Mwinyi introduced new ideas, and the World Bank and the IMF supported liberalisation. Mwinyi was nicknamed 'ruksa' (all is permitted) (Lawi et al., 2013) and led the country from 1985 to 1995. He opened up the economy and allowed individual and privately led enterprises to operate in the country. For instance, in the health sector, the National Health Policy was endorsed in 1990, and private investors in the health sector were officially allowed in 1991 (Private Hospitals Act, 1991). The most significant change that occurred in the healthcare provision was the growth in non-governmental healthcare facilities, particularly at the initiative of healthcare entrepreneurs during the 1990s. The total number of healthcare facilities in the country increased from 3577 in 1995 to 4961 in 1999 (Ministry of Health, MoH 1998). Of these 4961 healthcare facilities, only 3035 were government-owned (URT – MoH, 1999, Health Statistics, cited in Wangwe and Rweyemamu, 2001:11). More workers in the public sector were made redundant and became self-employed in response to this. One aspect of information that could have added knowledge to our understanding of the voluntary sector development was to know how many healthcare facilities were Government-owned at the start of the period. Also, how many were transferred from the Government and how many new institutions were financed privately or voluntarily? Unfortunately, this information could not be obtained.

In contrast with Nyerere's period, during Mwinyi's leadership and the subsequent Government that followed, other forms of welfare organisations whose common interests were based on religious, regional, ethnic, or professional affiliation increased (Lange et al., 2000). The private sector became particularly important in the provision of social welfare services. For example, Manyama (2017) maintained that, by 1986, the Government was calling upon the voluntary sector—largely made up of churches and other non-governmental organisations—to play an even more significant role in providing education and healthcare services. From 1984 to 1992, the number of NGO-run schools tripled from 85 to 258 (Lange et al., 2000). The information about the total number of primary and secondary schools in Tanzania between 1984 and 1992 is not available for comparison. The Tanzanian Department of Social Welfare (2012) pointed out that the current social and economic contingencies could be attributed to the changes that had happened in Tanzania between the 1970s and 1980s. These contingency plans have helped, to some degree, to eradicate poverty, family problems, poor health, the rising rate of crime, alcohol and drug abuse, and issues related to HIV/AIDS (Ministry of Health, Social Welfare Department, 2012). Introduced by neo-liberal supporters, this structural adjustment did not produce the expected economic growth in Africa, and the World Bank introduced another condition described as "good governance." It emphasised the need for the private sector and civil society to cooperate with the state to achieve "sustainable growth" (World development report by World Bank 1989). The World Bank report of 1989 gave a broader picture of the economic and financial crisis of countries in sub-Saharan Africa and clearly expressed what actions they wished to see happening: "The financial systems of many developing countries require restructuring, however. Their present condition reflects the approach to development taken by many countries in the 1960s and 1970s, an approach that emphasised government intervention to promote economic growth. Today, many countries are revising their approach to rely more heavily on the private sector and market forces. For the financial sector, this implies a more minor role for the Government in the allocation of credit, the determination of interest rates, and the daily decision-making of financial intermediaries. Relaxation of these economic and operational controls calls for an effective system of prudent regulation and supervision." (World Bank Report, 1989).

In Tanzania, corruption, fraud, and forgery among government officials affected the Government's performance. Welfare services for the people who most needed them, and the Tanzanian relationship with donor partners, deteriorated again (Lawi et al., 2013). The appearance of corruption and fraud at the leadership level, and a drop in investment in health, education, and other essential welfare services became apparent. Perhaps this resulted from the Government's loss of complete control as it moved quickly from one extreme economic model to another within a short period, without the substantial maturity required to run a neo-liberal, free market-based economic system. The World Bank and IMF's demand for structural adjustment was a bitter pill for the Tanzanian Government and most Tanzanians. The section below expounds more on the further developments and improvements made to social service provision in the country.

6.5 The Role of Voluntary Organisations–NGOs in addressing welfare needs in Africa–Tanzania

The term 'non-governmental organisations' (NGOs) is recognised worldwide to describe organisations operating to address various social issues alongside governments (Lewis, 2009), and is often associated with organisations that focus on relieving various social or political issues through different long-term or short-term approaches (Cleary, 1997; Kusmanto, 2013). Hence, it would be fitting to consider the voluntary sector as the realm of social activity undertaken by non-governmental organisations, non-profit organisations.

While elsewhere other organisations may be called 'non-profit organisations' (NPOs), in Tanzania local NGOs consider themselves as non-profit organisations, with not much difference to be distinguished between the two terms. Both terms refer to almost the same thing; organisations that belong to the voluntary sector realm that work not to make a profit but for the social good. These organisations work outside the government body. The government may raise funds for an NGO or NPO, but they maintain a non-governmental position, with no need for government representation. Because of the variety of literature contributed to the discussion here, readers will see the two terms surfacing throughout.

The social services provided by voluntary organisations/NGOs are hugely significant in most people's lives, especially those in a vulnerable situation, whose social well-being and function are affected by problems in Tanzanian society. Where governmental social interventional programmes do not exist or are poor and unreachable, voluntary organisations/NGOs are significant. However, there is an acknowledgement that even though non-governmental and non-profit organisations appear to be filling the gaps in providing services and public goods, these organisations are limited in the extent to which they can effectively fulfil their roles. Looking at this subject matter in the African context and Tanzania in particular, the following observations are apparent.

In Tanzania, voluntary organisations/NGOs face limitations and challenges too. The literature indicates evidence about the operational reality and situation non-governmental welfare organisations face as they fulfil their social work mission of intervening and supporting those who face issues to address problems in Tanzania. For example, Noboye (2013), who investigated the effectiveness of NGOs in rehabilitating street children in Dar es Salaam, identified some problems that impede and limit local NGOs' efforts to accomplish their mission. Some of these problems include a lack of enough funds and community support, poor working environments, the poor educational backgrounds of the rehabilitated, and a lack of trust between children and their minders. Another literature has observed that although the civil society in Tanzania has been fast-growing, particularly the NGO sector, it is still considered weak by international organisations working in the country (Lange et al., 2014:3). Similarly,

Ottka (2010) observed that a common problem local NGOs face is finding financial means to implement activities. The most significant support comes from international governments and donor agencies, especially Western countries. However, Ottka recommended that funding from local and national government sources is urgently needed with a long-term view. Additionally, local people in business and corporations, and those benefiting from economic growth, should take on more social responsibility within society (Ottka, 2010).

Another issue facing NGOs is a lack of professionalism in their operation and long-term sustainability. According to Okorley and Nkrumah (2012), a sense of professionalism involves proper leadership, accountability (good governance), and good management and is necessary to help NGOs stand out from their environment and become more competitive. NGOs that stand out from the rest tend to have more success in receiving donations. Kusmanto (2013:37) clarified further this matter of professionalism, stating that this also means adopting best practices to address dysfunctionality within organisations (Kusmanto, 2013). Likewise, Šešić (2011) suggested that improving NGO's professionalism and management as a practice and science needs to be introduced through management consultancy and training, which is known as organisational capacity building in the context of NGOs. Additionally, organisational capacity building can benefit NGOs by equipping them with adequate strategies, techniques, and logic for long-term goals to improve management performance and address immediate challenges such as funding reductions and operational dysfunction (Šešić 2011). Indeed, insights emerging from this discourse help us understand particular problems and areas that NGOs in Tanzania must consider, including those appearing in this research. One crucial issue that needs to be worked on is the relationship between local NGOs in Tanzania and the Government (Lange et al., 2000). Local NGOs must take the necessary measures to improve their

internal professionalism, including organisational capacity building, and create an accountable culture and creativity in addressing finance-related issues. They must maintain close working
relationships with the communities they serve for their organisation's sustainability.

Another observation is that NGOs face a lack of good governance. This challenge is perceived as an internal threat to NGOs'
sustainability. Interestingly, although this challenge comes from
within the NGO, it strongly correlates with the first challenge: reductions in funding (Jepson, 2005). Research sees a lack of good
governance as one reason for reducing donor funds. Consequently,
donors reduce their contributions to prevent the NGOs from
abusing funds. The failure of NGOs to handle the lack of good
governance can negatively affect their accountability in the long
run (Edwards and Hulme, 1995; Edwards, 2000; Kusmanto, 2013).
Helpful insights shed light on limitations NGOs experience in
fulfilling their role from past scholarship. It helps us understand
the importance of the government's help towards what NGOs
seek to fulfil. For example, Salamon (1987) explained some basis for governmental involvement in social service provision; he
justified government intervention on what he saw as limitations
that mark the voluntary sector. Salamon, who articulated the
'voluntary failure' theory, described four reasons behind its occurrence as follows:

Philanthropic insufficiency refers to the situations in which the
resources available for NGOs and non-profit organisations are
insufficient (Salamon 1987).

Philanthropic particularism refers to situations in which non-
profit organisations focus on specific demands for ethnic, religious, geographic, and ideological groups, duplicating efforts
in some cases and neglecting other needs (Salamon, 1987).

Philanthropic paternalism: this limitation refers to situations
where non-government organisations and non-profits rely on
philanthropic contributions and volunteers. The contributors'

interests govern them among donors and volunteers who decide on priorities rather than having the beneficiaries set these priorities (Salamon, 1987).

Philanthropic amateurism refers to situations where non-governmental organisations rely on volunteers who lack professional credentials and specialised knowledge in certain action areas (Salamon, 1987). In cases of voluntary failure, the market and government sectors take roles in providing services and responding to public needs (Powell and Steinberg, 2006).

6.5.1 *Why must government and local NGOs collaborate to solve issues and provide social welfare services in Tanzania?*

One aspect that has drawn attention in the literature is how the Government and Local NGOs can collaborate to address social issues. Establishing a good, effective working relationship between the government and Local NGOs in the country is necessary for meeting people's welfare needs. This aspect of knowledge is relevant to the discussion concerning the situations of NGOs in Tanzania. Studies about the involvement of NGOs in social service provision in other cultures have indicated partnership and collaboration between governments and the voluntary sector in the daily endeavours to address people's social welfare needs (Salamon, 1984; Salamon, 1987; Lewis and Kanji, 2009). For example, Salamon (1987:29) revealed that the voluntary sector in America had been an integral part of the Government's strategic plan to address its citizens' social welfare needs. The Government relied on non-profit organisations to deliver government-funded human services. Salamon observed that non-profit organisations receive more of their income from the Government than from any other single source (Salamon, 1987:29) in America.

Another aspect Salamon discussed is recognising the need for government involvement and the legitimate government accountability requirements to NGOs. The participation of the Government in social welfare provision and working with NGOs in service delivery has certain advantages. Salamon (1987) perceived that government involvement could strengthen the relationship with the voluntary sector. He mentioned some benefits of this relationship, firstly, those that benefit an organisation from a "financial perspective". Salamon argued that one could not rely solely on private giving and voluntary activity to address human services; hence, financial government involvement is crucial. Second, in functioning as a body that oversees funding distribution, the Government can ensure equity in distributing voluntary services. Third, the Government can ensure diversity in the service delivery system as the non-profit sector may, e.g., monopolise the flow of funds, limiting their access to newer or smaller groups. Fourth, a central tenet of a democratic society is that the public should set priorities through a democratic political process and then muster the resources to address these priorities (Salamon, 1987:45).

Another vital point to emphasise here is that there is always a need for improvement in the partnership management between the Government and the local voluntary sector. In order to strengthen this relationship, according to Salamon, "it may be appropriate to consider ways to achieve a greater degree of dialogue on questions of resource allocation, division of responsibilities for meeting community needs, and joint public–private ventures." (Salamon, 1987:46). It is also worth noting a further insight from Salamon that the Government is advised to respect specific structural elements and the needs of non-profit organisations to strengthen the relationship.

Voluntary organisations/NGOs can play a role in addressing social problems and social service provision, making a difference in the lives of people whose wellbeing and functioning are impacted by issues in Tanzanian society. Salamon advocates that the Government should support the voluntary sector. In the first ten years of Tanzanian independence, the voluntary sector struggled to contribute to the social wellbeing of people in Tanzania. Part of this seems to have been the new Government's choice of socialist philosophy, which influenced its approach to economic and social welfare provision and its drastic action of the mass nationalisation of structures (Tibaijuka, 1998). This decision weakened the private sector and the voluntary sector. Since the voluntary sector was represented mainly by Western mission organisations and NGOs, anti-colonial sentiments, which were high in the post-colonial-independence era, affected the voluntary sector's place and status in the country. Today in Tanzania, the voluntary sector is actively tackling various social issues affecting the wellbeing of individuals and society (Manyama, 2017).

In Tanzania, one issue of concern is the partnership and working relationship between the Government and voluntary organisations/NGOs. The Government has a responsibility to recognise and endorse voluntary sector services as necessary and legitimate to the population, become responsible for NGOs in terms of verification, and oversee the voluntary sector for the public's sake. The Government should show support towards the work of the voluntary sector, and in this way, the voluntary sector and the government-led sector can work together. However, a study conducted in 2007 indicated a mixed picture of the relationship between the Government and NGOs.

The Research on Poverty Alleviation (REPOA) in Tanzania asked the question: How are tripartite relationships among non-governmental organisations (NGOs), donors, and the State perceived in poverty reduction efforts? The paper reported issues perceived as obstacles to collaboration between NGOs and the Government in poverty reduction and addressing general social problems. It stated that 'viewing the Government as an adversary is counterproductive. Knowing the Government's position and forming relationships with key officials can help effectively influence policy debate' (REPOA, 2007). NGOs should continue monitoring and scrutinising the Government to strengthen their impact to protect their 'public investment.' The critical issue here is that voluntary organisations/NGOs can hold governments to account.

Furthermore, the report suggested that individual NGOs must build skills and capacity to overcome their organisational weaknesses to improve their impact. Advocacy efforts need to be well-informed and organised (REPOA 2007). Moreover, NGOs can channel and interpret information between government and grassroots communities and help fill gaps where the Government does not or lacks the capacity to provide services (REPOA 2007). The report also emphasised that NGOs should analyse government policy and enhance outcomes wherever possible by providing information and offering creative solutions. Indeed, how the Government relates to the voluntary sector or vice versa is vital, as it has a bearing on the functioning of said organisations. This relationship is essential in understanding the role MAPERECE, Dogodogo Street Children Trust, and SMGEO are playing. These organisations try to care for marginalised groups of society that the Government does not directly support.

The discussion in this section clarifies two points: first, it acknowledges the importance of voluntary organisations/NGOs as social service providers, meeting people's societal needs. Additionally, it highlights that the relationship and partnership between NGOs and the Government in this respect are crucial. Indeed, a working relationship where the Government supports local NGOs might be beneficial for consideration in Tanzanian society.

6.5.2 The current Tanzania government's focus and the prospect of people's Realisation of Social Welfare Needs

Currently, the Tanzanian government seems to focus more on strengthening the country's economic status, hoping that economic improvement can help to realise public welfare services among the citizens. Indeed, public service offerings such as free primary and secondary education and the extension of water provision and health services to the population have shown some improvement in the last ten years (HakiElimu 2017; Goda, 2018; The United Republic of Tanzania- Ministry of Education, Science and Technology, 2018). Unlike the previous governmental regimes, the current president has made significant strides in addressing corruption since taking office in 2015, making it no longer a significant issue.

Despite the strides that the country has made in recent years surrounding the economy, the increase in employment, and the reduction of poverty, Tanzania still struggles to provide social services to its people. For example, government social efforts are still not sufficiently addressing the welfare concerns of the children living and working on the streets. Yet, this social group is an integral part of society. Gender-based inequality and discrimination against women at domestic/family and social/public levels are still problems that do not seem to feature much in the current government's economic and social improvement strategy (United Nations, 2016). Issues that negatively impact women's experience of life still exist, such as discrimination and abuse at a domestic and societal level (Rugira, 2015). Stigmatisation, discrimination, and the denial of fundamental rights were a problem for street children (Fredrick, 2010; Luena, 2011). Furthermore, the disabled experience discrimination at a domestic and societal level (Uromi and Mazagwa, 2014).

This project focuses on providing social services and especially the voluntary sector's involvement in addressing social issues in the country. It is a contextually based examination, explicitly looking at Tanzania. Hence, it is crucial to view what is happening and what has happened historically. The discussions surrounding the social welfare provision in the country indicate some key events that have shaped society and how it addresses social issues. As a country, Tanzania has gone through challenging times to reach where it is today. It has made significant progress in the economy and its efforts to address social problems. However, the citizens of that nation still face many challenges concerning their social well-being. This discussion also highlighted the importance of the voluntary sector in social problem-solving. However, despite progress, problems and their effects on the ageing population, street children, gender inequality, and disability persist; hence, the following chapter explores the role of three different voluntary organisations in tackling these problems.

6.5.3 Indigenisation of social work practice in Africa

Current literature on the debate concerning social work practice in Africa has called for indigenising or decolonising social work education and practice in the African context and emphasised the importance of social work by individuals or groups to consider local African traditional ways to address social problems among communities in Africa. For example, reflecting on indigenous social innovations in rural West Africa, Matthews (2017) cautioned against the common practice of externally induced innovations targeting poor rural communities. He argued that since humanitarian and development agencies are usually outsiders to their target groups, rural communities face the danger of being overpowered by exogenous ideas and processes

(Matthews 2017). The inclusion of local indigenous knowledge systems is a prerequisite for what has been called the 'indigenisation' (Rankopo and Osei-Hwedie, 2011) and 'decolonisation' of the social work profession in Africa (Ibrahima and Mattaini, 2019). Therefore, the debate on social work practice in Africa suggested the inclusion of local epistemologies and methodologies into social work theory and practice. Rankopo and Osei-Hwedie (2011) pointed out that the starting point of this process must be the community. They see that rural communities, with their resourceful coping mechanisms of helping and healing, are under-researched and underestimated and must, therefore, be at the forefront of this discourse (Rankopo and Osei-Hwedie, 2011). Many of these arguments have been echoed by Spitzer and Twikirize. For example, Spitzer (2019) observed that social work in many African countries is still mainly based on imported, Western-oriented theories, concepts, and methods. In this way, it disregards culture-specific indigenous knowledge systems. However, Twikirize and Spitzer (2019b) showed that rural communities show resilience and exhibit innovative ways of handling their problems at a grassroots level, thus improving their lives by themselves. Therefore, Spitzer and Twikirize (2021) advised that policymakers, academics, international development actors, and social workers in rural communities must seek to discover and utilise the potential rural grassroots innovative approaches to social problem-solving.

Spitzer and Twikirize (2021) highlighted two examples of indigenous rural innovative problem-solving models in African countries. One example of the rural social innovative model comes from Uganda (akabondo, a household cluster model to fight poverty). It is a community-based concept model to promote rural development in Uganda. The other example of the rural social innovative model comes from Rwanda, known as "umugoroba w'ababyeyi', which refers to a community-based family strengthening model. This model is mainstreamed into government policies. Rwanda's model developed in the challenging context of a post-genocide society (Spitzer and Twikirize, 2021). Indeed, the two highlighted examples of rural indigenous innovative models from rural Uganda and Rwanda rural communities indicate the potential of rural communities and the possibility that they can play an active role when engaged in the strategic process of social problem-solving.

Literature indicated that the terms "decolonisation' and "indigenisation" represent the academic effort to formulate and promote Africa's social work methods. Consequently, the deliberation effort has developed a new approach known as the 'developmental social work model'. The developmental social work model stresses the importance of linking the so-called "micro" and "macro" to address social problems by social workers. The "micro- focus" orientates social work practitioners toward such questions as "How do I improve your life?" In comparison, the 'macro' focus is concerned with addressing the social structural circumstances that make the lives of individuals difficult. Whether local or international NGOs work with rural communities in Africa, addressing social problems necessitates understanding and considering how a society operates. Social work practice must evaluate local people's capacity and resources and work with a community. Such consideration is beneficial in the long term as it could bring service providers, community, and service users into a more symbiotic working relationship. However, I would like to comment on how the debate concerning social work practice in Africa has been framed: whether to adopt "Western" or "indigenous" approaches. Concerning this issue, I argue that the discussion should not be about choosing between Western methods over indigenous-African approaches or indigenous approaches over Western methods in addressing problems. Thinking in this way perpetuates the superiority of one method over the other. Instead, the academic discussion should objectively acknowledge the strengths and weaknesses of Western and indigenous methods in social problem-solving. Those involved in social problem-solving must consider the socio-cultural and economic context in which they operate what seems to work in that context, and not consciously think which method is African or European. However, any welfare organisation addressing social problems must see that it works with communities rather than upon the community it seeks to help.

6.5.4 Social-cultural Changes and How They Impact the Care for Vulnerable Populations in Africa

Another critical reality a contemporary debate on social work practice in Africa must consider is the realisation of social change in African societies. In particular, the destruction of the traditional extended family support networks system as a reliable mechanism of social protection for older people results from (a) their more limited relevance to urban settings and (b) the impact of depopulation on their application to rural settings.

Destruction of the traditional extended family support networks system illustrates that society and its cultural ways of life and practice do not remain static but constantly evolve as they interact with external social forces that often produce internal changes. In this regard, it is incorrect to talk about indigenous or traditional ways of addressing social issues that social workers in Africa or East Africa-Tanzania must adhere to as if the methods of dealing with social problems that characterise traditional African society are readily there. This view assumes that the community remains the same, unchanged at all times. Therefore, when one advocates the need to use traditional African ways to solve social problems, one must also consider thoroughly the social-cultural and economic changes that characterise contemporary communities in Africa today, including

Tanzania. Literature shows that the traditional extended family network that characterised traditional African societies is diminishing as a reliable mechanism for problem-solving in Tanzania (Manyama, 2017; Evans, 2005; Aboderin, 2006). Other studies have observed the same social phenomenon in other parts of Africa (Akuma, 2015; Apt, 2000; Theron, 2013; Eboiyehi and Onwuzuruigbo, 2014). This social reality change requires that those involved in social work practice and the academic debate in Africa be in tune with the new social reality. They may acknowledge that social work practice in some circumstances might not just seek to preserve local cultural identity in their way of finding the solution for social problems. Instead, their approach must be objective, employing whatever methods may be effective on the ground.

Another crucial point of reality we must bear in mind is the realisation of the extent to which contemporary Tanzanians' problems are rooted in "traditional" cultural norms and practices. While we talk about the benefit of knowing and using existing "traditional" cultural practices and ways in communities to address social problems, we must also know that not all aspects of social-cultural values and traditions are conducive to the dignity and well-being of persons (Linda, 2014; Essien and Ukpong, 2012; World Bank, 2003; Klasen and Lamana, 2008).

These observations align with and mirror the viewpoints and social experiences of Tanzanians who participated in the initial research. The study noted that many of the issues addressed by local organisations originate from cultural attitudes and practices adopted by these communities. Some of the issues that specific individuals experience are caused by and relate to traditional prejudice against certain groups—for example, gender inequality, discrimination, and the abuse women experience in domestic settings. The patriarchal culture yields a misogynist attitude and discrimination towards female members of society. In some Tanzanian communities, many women experience domestic abuse, suppression, and discrimination when accessing certain rights, such as self-expression, social and economic opportunities, and inheritance. Women endure these challenges in their daily social living experience. A further example is that the traditional attitudes towards the roles of women and girls in domestic and societal settings underpin the negative life experiences of many girls and women in these communities. Also, the existence of witchcraft beliefs in these communities influences the harmful mistreatment of older women. This reality is an essential side of the story/social truth that one must consider. Indeed, MAPERECE, in the initial stage of addressing issues, understood that the victimisation and killing of older women were influenced by the superstitious beliefs embedded in the community. Therefore, the organisation sought to confront the root cause of the problems it identified by directing its response strategically at the community itself. Also, the disabled people experience isolation, stigma, and discrimination within the same culture due to held cultural beliefs, mindsets, and misunderstandings of disability. The wrong ideas about disability underpin society's hostile attitude and engagement with the disabled. Therefore, this awareness of where the source of problems lies necessitated SMGEO to focus its response on the community and its structures, challenging the underlying roots within the cultural mindset and traditional practices at the heart of the community itself.

This does not mean we should ignore the importance of a bottom-up approach or the need to draw on local communities' resources to address social issues where possible (see also Spitzer and Twikirize 2021). The key characteristics and strengths of the bottom-up approach are that it considers seriously the views of service users, community involvement, and methods that rural communities might use in dealing with social issues. The current thesis has raised this point as one of the critical issues affecting the working relationship between service providers and service users in Tanzania. Take the following example from the MAPERECE organisation. MAPERECE, as indicated on page 60 of this thesis, believes that for changes to happen in older people's lives, they must involve the entire local community. Hence, they help older people within their local communities to help themselves and challenge families and communities to support them. MAPERECE delivers its clients' services through the community's older people council. However, the degree to which the organisation considers the opinions of the clients it serves is not profound, as the empirical report provides a different picture. There is a sense that the older people whom MAPERECE help see the organisation coming in from the outside, with its view on how things ought to be changed on the ground. According to female respondents' reflections on their service experience, MAPERECE does not necessarily consider what the older people (service users) think about their situations and solutions to their problems. This lack of the organisation closely working with its clients indicates that in its working manner, MAPERECE may not be able to draw on or harness the local resources (including local people and communities) to promote empowerment and resilience.

By way of emphasising, the above discussion has highlighted some critical points to note. It emphasised the need for any welfare organisation to address social issues to work with communities and utilise the capacity and resources available within the community rather than belittling and imposing ways or solutions to solve problems upon the communities it seeks to help. However, it is necessary to understand that some of the difficulties people face may lie in or be an integral part of the communities themselves. Therefore, it would also be required for a social work organisation to be prepared to take account of the new perspectives provided by 'non-indigenous' approaches in challenging the problems embedded in those communities.

They must seek to know whether the overall operating culture underpins issues experienced by individuals in that community. Chapters Seven, Eight, and Nine show the outcome of this investigation. These chapters provide an accurate picture of the local non-governmental welfare organisations' social issues and the interventional approaches to solving and providing services to their clients.

7 Case study 1: MAPERECE

The historical background provided in chapter six outlines the emergence and involvement of the voluntary sector, with a focus on the role of missionaries and NGOs in social welfare provision for Indigenous people during Tanzania's colonial periods under German and British rule. Chapters Seven, Eight, and Nine present a current and evidence-based overview of NGOs' efforts in addressing social issues in present-day Tanzania, drawing from empirical data collected for original research. The discussion in this chapter is founded on empirical data and showcases the unique approach of MAPERECE in addressing social work with older clients in rural Mwanza areas. This local non-governmental organisation is dedicated to addressing the social welfare concerns of older people, highlighting the diverse involvement of NGOs in social welfare initiatives.

Older people face various challenges concerning their livelihoods, social welfare needs, and fundamental rights in Tanzania's rural areas. Until the start of the 21st century, older people in Tanzania could often rely on their children and grandchildren to care for their livelihood and wellbeing. Adhering to family traditions was important. Within this culture, it was a well-acknowledged view and the proper expectation for a young person to look after an older person, but in recent times, this long tradition has been affected by forces of change (Aboderin, 2010; Spitzer and Mabeyo, 2011). Amongst these visible changes is a high flow of young people migrating from rural communities into cities and different regions (Tacoli and Agergaard, 2017), leaving older people struggling in unsafe living environments. Local non-governmental social welfare organisations are involved in addressing the social welfare needs and fundamental rights of older people in Tanzanian society. However, their contribution and impact on older people's lives are not widely known and researched. Hence, this knowledge gap prompted the inception of a study that involved collaborating with a local non-governmental organisation focused on social welfare, namely the Magu Poverty Focus on Older People Rehabilitation Centre (MAPERECE) in the Mwanza region. Let me first clarify one aspect regarding the name that identifies this organisation— specifically the use of the term 'rehabilitation centre' to which the organisation refers. Despite this name giving the impression that the organisation runs a rehabilitation centre or a rehabilitation programme for older people, the truth is that MAPERECE takes its social services to clients who live in rural communities, offering support at their homes.

This chapter presents and discusses the data findings related to this case study in the following order:

- The first section offers contextual information about older people's social situations in Tanzania and, more specifically, the Mwanza region.
- The second section discusses the origins and formation of the selected organisation, MAPERECE.
- Part three justifies the choice of this organisation for this research.
- The fourth section discusses the main issues that the organisation addresses.
- Part five discusses the organisation's services and how they reach clients.
- The sixth section discusses the organisation's service and impact on social situations from the perspective of older people who are service users.

7.1 Contextual Information about Older People in Rural Tanzania

This empirical research occurred in rural communities around the Magu district in the Mwanza region of northern Tanzania, which lies on Lake Victoria's southern shores. It is one of six districts in the Mwanza region, and the Magu district has a population of approximately 400,000, most of whom belong to the Sukuma tribe. About 19,500 members of the regional population (4.9%) are aged 60 or over, and 55% of older people are women over the age of 60 (Wamara, 1997; Forrester, 1998). As per the census of 2012, the population of Magu was 299,759 (National Bureau of Statistics, 2012). This amount is less than previously mentioned because the district was split up in 2012 (Wikipedia' Magu District,' retrieved on 11 July 2021). At the time of the research, no current data were available. Sukumaland (mainly Mwanza and Shinyanga regions) is notorious for being the area of Tanzania with the most severe problem of witchcraft-related killings. Statistics collected by the Tanzanian Women's Media Association (Sheikh, 1998) on such killings in the region showed that in 1997, 93% of women's killings had occurred in Sukumaland. Of 194 women killed in 1997, 86 were killed in the Mwanza region and 85 in neighbouring Shinyanga (Forrester, 1998). As references indicate, researchers studied these issues almost twenty years ago; however, the problem in question never disappeared. The Magu district is an area where many older people have lost their lives, especially older women, due to victimisation and witchcraft-related beliefs by various communities (Kibuga and Dianga, 2000). Studies indicate that in 2012, 630 older people were reported to have been murdered following witchcraft accusations. In 2013, this rose to 765, two-thirds of whom were women (the United Republic of Tanzania, Human Rights Report 2005; HelpAge Tanzania, 2014 Sauti Ya Wazee, Issue 05). The numbers show the widespread nature of these problems across society.

Older women have faced stigmatisation, physical and psychological abuse, and marginalisation because of witchcraft allegations in rural communities. The majority of those targeted have perished, and those who have survived physical attacks still experience physical and mental trauma (Spitzer and Mabeyo, 2011). Additionally, older people in rural Tanzania suffer and experience a general shortage of social welfare provision because of neglect and lack of support (HelpAge International, *Sauti ya Wazee,* Issue 06, 2016). Twenty years ago, research by Kibuga and Dianga described the social changes affecting the living situations of older people in Tanzanian rural areas; Kibuga and Dianga (2000:30) wrote:

"In the past, older persons lived within an extended family system. This system ensured that they were supported as their strength decreased and that there would be numerous family members to take over the more arduous household tasks. Nowadays, many older people report that their adult children have left the villages because of economic pressures, and the land is becoming scarcer. In the new economic climate of cost-sharing in Tanzania, it is more challenging to earn enough income through agriculture to pay for school fees and medical treatment than work in the cities."

The scarcity of the land stipulated in the aforementioned quote demands additional contemplation. In previous eras, where family members lived close together, lands or farms belonged to the family and not to individuals, as it is apparent today. Young family members would not demand land because the traditional practice was that the older generation would pass the land/farms onto their children. In the past, multiple generations tended to live under the same roof, in the same place and pursue the same activities for their livelihood; thus, rivalry over land-related matters within a family was not common. However, the reality of life today presents various challenges to young adults because of poverty, aspirations, desperation, and lack of resources. Urbanisation and modern lifestyles have made people realise how valuable an asset land is. Frictions emerge when those who leave rural areas for urban life return and demand individual ownership and usage of land at the same time as their parents or grandparents are still alive. Today, people use the land for many purposes, such as building houses and business infrastructures to enhance individual livelihood. The population is increasing; thus, the demand for land by the younger generation is high.

On a governmental level, the efforts to help older people have focused on implementing a social policy to facilitate the proper treatment of older people, creating a more favourable living experience for them. In 2003, the government formulated the National Ageing Policy. It expressed its responsibility and commitment as follows:

"The Government realises that older people are a resource in the development of our nation. The existence of Tanzania as a nation is evidence of older people's contribution in [the] political, economic, cultural, and social arena" (United Republic of Tanzania, 2003a:2).

In elaborating further, the following rights are part of the National Ageing Policy:

"Older people have the right to live like any other human. Older people have the right to free health treatment. Older people have the right to their dignity as human beings, like any human being. They deserve respect, acknowledgement, and honour. Older people have the right to have a good life, income and access to credit" (United Republic of Tanzania: National Ageing Policy, 2003).

The government established this policy eighteen years ago. However, the National Aging policy has not yet yielded a positive change in the practical living reality of older people in their communities. During the study, participants in rural communities explicitly remembered 2012, 2013, and 2014 as terrible years.

Many older people lost their lives, suffering horrific deaths due to victimisation that resulted in killing. These problems occurred when the government had already formulated their social policy. The policy has not impacted the mindset and attitudes of people in rural areas, especially in their way of thinking and treating older members of their communities. Others believe that most of the people in the villages are ignorant of the National Ageing Policy and its contents, with most not knowing about the existence of this policy (Spitzer and Mabeyo 2011). In their study of older people's social welfare needs and the importance of social protection systems, Spitzer and Mabeyo (2011:115) observed that:

"Older people acknowledged that it is not only them who lack sufficient knowledge about regulations, entitlements, and policy documents. They blamed the very government authorities responsible for implementing existing policies and laws for being inadequately informed and aware… Most people, even leaders at the ward and village levels, do not know the existing policies in our country. This lack of knowledge makes it difficult for them to fulfil their responsibilities."

Two issues can be said to underpin the problematic situation affecting older people's well-being, as indicated in the above discussion. The first issue is the effective destruction of traditional extended family support networks reflected in younger people's migration into urban settings and other regions. The consistent presence of young adults around older people in rural communities ensures social stability, safety, and provision. When this balance is disturbed, older people in rural areas find themselves vulnerable as they are alone and lack the necessary support.

The second situation that endangers older people is direct threats for either economic or cultural reasons perpetrated against them by young adults and close relatives. As various literature observes, victimisation and threats towards older people emanate from an embedded superstitious cultural belief that serves as a cover-up for true motives, which is often an economic reason. Individuals, because of a covetous desire for assets, such as lands, allege that an individual older person is a witch or involved in harming others in the community using witchcraft. The result is that the individual receives hate and threats and is eventually killed. Consequently, when the older person is out of the picture, those who concocted the witchcraft story can take the deceased's assets.

7.2 Origins and Formation of MAPERECE

Magu Poverty Focus on Older People Rehabilitation Centre (MAPERECE) is a local non-profit organisation (NGO) based in Magu town, working with older people around rural communities in the district. The organisation was formed in 1993 by Mr Shitobelo. Its main objective has been to promote community awareness of and care for older people. In 1993, MAPERECE carried out an informal survey in thirteen villages to understand older people's situation in the area. Their investigation found that older people were affected by various problems in various communities around the district. One of the most complex and disturbing of these problems was the allegations of witchcraft, which had a devastating impact on older people's lives, especially older women. Remarking on the beginning of the organisation, a male respondent at the managerial level said:
"The reason for establishing an institution dealing with older persons came to Mr Shitobelo after hearing about and witnessing many deaths of older people in the Mwanza region, especially Magu District. The massacre of older people was taking place in the village, county, the districts, which are also home to Mr Shitobelo. He had lost many of his elderly relatives to attacks, killed by swords. Victimisation and violence against older people

were happening so often. Older women were being accused of being witches and therefore attacked. They were stabbed with swords, and strangled while sleeping at night. Therefore, this organisation was established to eradicate violence, and brutal murder against older people." (Msuya)

Allegations of witchcraft leave older women exposed to various risks and vulnerabilities. The physical, social, and emotional trauma caused by this victimisation and the killing of older people prompted the formation and work of this organisation. The organisation's vision reads: "striving to create a conducive environment where older people over sixty live in peace, harmony, and are valued by their community" (Magu-guide, 2002:4). Furthermore, MAPERECE expressed its mission in the following statement:

"MAPERECE is a non-profit organisation based in Magu whose mission is to mobilise and sensitise the public to discard harmful beliefs and values that contribute to the killing of older people in the society. We do this through creating awareness and education among the community, the establishment of older people forums, lobbying and advocacy of leaders and policy-makers on a variety of issues that affect older people" (Magu-guide, 2002:4).

Administratively, MAPERECE has in place the following bureaucracy:
- General meeting
- Board of Directors
- Office Bearers
- Secretariat
- Committee/Branches

The general meeting is the decision-making body within the organisation. This meeting is held once a year, and every active member of MAPERECE attends, as do representatives of the elders' councils appointed by the MAPERECE organisation for the year. One of the responsibilities associated with the General meeting is approving the Board of Directors' recommendations.

MAPERECE works with communities through its established rural branches and relevant project committees. There are committees elected at various branches in villages where the organisation operates. These committees are comprised of elders' councils (respondent Paul, the project coordinator-MAPERECE). Currently, the organisation has both employed and volunteer members of staff. There are eleven workers: five paid staff and six staff working on a volunteer basis. Well-wishers, including religious groups and individuals across Tanzania, fund the organisation's work. Besides this, it receives financial support from different donors from abroad, including HelpAge Germany. Members of staff also make small contributions.

Since the organisation is legally allowed to operate across mainland Tanzania, it has, since its inception, spread its work beyond the Mwanza region, including Shinyanga, Simiyu, Geita, Mara, and Kagera. It seems that this expansion has been driven by the organisation's mission to create education and awareness of the welfare and rights of older people and the need to support them. The fieldwork undertaken with this organisation involved a total of twenty-two participants who all took part in one-to-one interviews.

7.3 Justification for the Choice of MAPERECE

The discussion of the social problems that emerged in the reviewed literature in Chapter Two influenced the selection of the organisations involved in this study. Since the research sought to learn how local organisations are involved in service provision and their impacts on service users, the researcher chose MAPERECE and its clients to learn from their lived experiences.

At the empirical stage, the research involved individuals representing three levels: managers, employees/social workers, and service users, enabling me to acquire the necessary and appropriate information for this study. Through interviews, the study learned about the social problems and service provision from the service provider and the service users, i.e., older people. Twenty-two participants took part in interviews. The identities of respondents who participated in this research investigation linked to the organisation are pseudo-anonymised to protect their identity. I translated the respondents' responses into English from the audio recordings made during the interviews in the Kiswahili language.

7.4 Main Issues Addressed by MAPERECE

The empirical evidence demonstrates the issues and concerns affecting the well-being and functioning of service users—older people—in the rural community. This section discusses the primary issues and needs that the organisation aims to tackle. Understanding and engaging with those problems that emerged in this study has been influenced by the researcher's worldview on the social world and knowledge creation, so-called social constructionism. Based on this, the researcher used a distinction of problems: People face immediate issues in their daily lives. But those issues are often problems that reflect broader circumstances. The study has found immediate problems and the underlying causes of those immediate problems. For example, a social problem like unemployment can lead to significant personal, immediate issues on the individual's well-being, such as depression or financial troubles (O'Donnell, 2002).

Understanding problems in this manner enabled me to acquire an accurate picture of the root causes of the issues affecting people's well-being and, to some degree, helped in deciding upon an appropriate interventional approach. Thus, for example, issues embedded within society and widely impacting everyone cannot sufficiently be addressed by solely focusing on the individual (a person-centred approach) while ignoring the underlying factors that emanate from broader social-cultural circumstances.

The discussion starts with problems that reflect immediate needs based on personal circumstances, often originating from social structural failure. In response to the question: "What kind of difficulties do you face in your life?" one woman (80 years old) replied:

"I am asking for cooking flour, cassava flour, and maise meal because there is no food in my house. If you help us older people, our lives will be prolonged, go forward, even become less burdened." (Esther)

This respondent's account describes the issue that has an immediate impact on her living situation; the main problem is a lack of food. Esther's narrative listed actual items or food-related materials that she desperately needs to meet her immediate needs. She sees these items as the solution to her situation in this context. Food is necessary for our human existence. A lack of food can create malnutrition, making an older person physically weak and potentially bringing about other issues that may affect their daily functioning. Her immediate hunger problem could have its root cause in older people's general food accessibility, e.g., as they are physically unable to farm. Also, it could be that the young adults whom older people relied on for acquiring basic needs and survival are no longer there or have never been there. Underlying issues include a lack of formal social security schemes and pensions, as those are hardly available for people living in rural areas and favour those in formal employment, mainly in urban settings. There are no local government structures available to support older people to access food, housing and security. Hence, this makes older people even more reliant on family support structures. However, those traditional support structures are in decline, which leaves older people in rural areas vulnerable and unprotected (refer to Chapter 2.2.1).

In line with the above, another female respondent named Mageni (78 years old) explained the challenge that she faces daily:

"I live alone. I have never had a child or a grandson who can say they can help me. Living alone, being old, the physical power that enables you to work or run here and there is not there and has made my life very difficult" (Mageni, who lives alone and is in poor health).

Mageni's account reveals her awareness of her diminishing physical strength due to ageing and the struggle to maintain her life and take care of herself. She explains that she struggles daily because no one can assist her with essential daily needs because of her weakening physical strength. This situation indicates the reality many older people in rural Tanzania communities experience. The diminishing of the social network of protection and lack of community support are the underlying causes of immediate problems that are apparent in the life of Mageni. Therefore, the issues expressed here find their root cause in broader social circumstances-structural problems.

On a similar question about the problems affecting study participant's well-being, a female respondent named Joyce (70 years old) describes the situation she faces, saying:

"I am old and in poor health. Taking care of my surroundings by myself is a major challenge for me. Getting food is a struggle for me. I am poor." (Joyce, who has no children).

The account indicates that poverty and poor health have an immediate negative impact on Joyce's experience in life, affecting her ability to take care of her living surroundings. Maintaining better living surroundings is vital for our human well-being.

Failing to keep one's living environment healthy can lead to other risky situations, such as health-related difficulties and illness arising from a lack of hygiene.

Mageni and Joyce indicate a cognitive awareness that something in their being and functioning has fundamentally changed, the ageing process and the direct impact. They seem to struggle when undertaking a simple chore, such as maintaining their surroundings.

A severe physical problem, such as a lack of physical strength, can severely affect other aspects of life. For example, it can lead to an older person's inability to cope with a simple task or failure to handle day-to-day challenges. Most respondents in this study indicated that as older people, they feel that the extent to which they can manage life independently is impeded.

The respondents revealed more issues. From a first reading, they immediately impact the respective individual, but looking closer at them reveals problems that reflect broader social circumstances. Therefore, they can be described as structurally caused. In responding to the question: "What kind of difficulties do you face in your life during an interview, a female participant (68 years old) expressed this answer:

"Water wells are too far away. It is difficult for me to walk a long distance while carrying a bucket of water on my head. I am an old person, and my body is weak. Whenever I try to carry a bucket full of water on my head, I fall." (Margaret)

This account indicates a social-structural problem because the well is too far away, and there is no easy access to water. The respondent feels powerless and vulnerable. Water, something she needs daily, seems inaccessible because of the distance involved. During the interviews, Maria, a social worker, explained the challenging situations that older people face in rural areas.

"The economic problem is a problem in rural areas. Because of age and diminished physical strength, our older people who used to work in agriculture now have no work to do which can bring them income. The lack of involvement in agriculture makes it difficult to meet daily needs such as food, clothes, and health treatment. Changing clothing is a problem; an older person wears the same clothes for a long time without washing. Also, maintaining their own house without help is a challenge" (Maria).

Indeed, farming is an essential source of income and livelihood for most rural communities, and the older generation has considered farming to be the sole source of income. Food production is used both for consumption and income generation. The inability to participate in agricultural activities means that older people have no means to survive. Thomas (72 years old), a service user, described the problems that he and other older people face in the area that he lives in:

"Our farming is in trouble. There is the unavailability of food; this is a significant trouble. And as you know, when a famine exists, without adequately yielding enough food, the person is restless. This situation impacts the life of an older person much more than any other person. The challenge is climate change, lack of rain, and the worst climate change for this time we have, different from the past. Climate change has harmed food acquisition. There is drought and hunger" (Thomas).

According to Thomas, climate change, in terms of shortages of rain and the rain coming late, seems to underpin the absence or deficiency of food production, affecting the community's source of livelihood. This situation appears to be more severely felt among older people. There can be no doubt that older people are more likely to be affected than, for example, young adults. Older people are more immobile, while young people may attempt to move around searching for new opportunities. The impact of climate change on food production is felt by many, a situation evident at the community level. The social structure supposed to represent and protect the community's social well-being must have effective strategies to intervene in this situation regarding a lack of food. This could relieve the pressures and remove the uncertainty that older people feel, enhancing their social well-being.

Health-related problems also affect the well-being of older people in rural areas. This aspect of the problem was echoed by Henry (67 years old), a village council representative, who described older people's situation:

"Health problems rank first in the order of problems here in our village. Older people struggle with many illnesses, including Malaria, physical pain, and stomach-ache. What makes this health issue even more difficult is the fact that health centres where people go for treatment are located far away. To reach the health centre, one needs transport, but the available means of transport here in our village are bicycles, and only young adults can ride bicycles for long distances, and not older people" (Henry).

Having good health is essential for our well-being and functioning as human beings. Henry's narrative reveals that older people struggle with various health issues affecting them directly in this community. The inability to access medical treatment because of the distance and the lack of appropriate transport complicate older people's health situations and their possibility of escaping from these health problems. Although health-related issues are felt directly by the individual, they find their root causes essentially at a social-structural level due to a lack of available medical support and transport. Society's awareness of this issue, especially local governmental awareness, indicates a structural failure, particularly considering that local government is a body that is supposed to represent society's interest and take care of its citizens' well-being.

Living with an untreated health condition may cause it to spiral into long-term severe health problems, especially if there are no available interventions or support to minimise this risk. Suppose many older people suffer from health-related issues because they cannot get to the medical centre for appropriate treatment. In this instance, a lack of proper transport means is the primary need in a community like this.

This study found that older people often lose their assets and resources by force to their adult children and grandchildren. This problem was reflected by a respondent, Masanja (60 years old), a male leader at the community level:

"One thing that has been the outcry for many older people is the denial of their basic rights. Young adults or relatives would demand the ownership of land and properties belonging to an older person. When an older person says no to their demand, she gets threatened. If the older person stands their ground, then they are attacked. Most attacks happen in the night-time. You would find an older person dead, mostly horrific death by being strangled. The unfortunate thing is that those who commit these terrible things are relatives. Even when the deceased's neighbours knew about the threat, they tended to remain quiet, not reporting the perpetrators to the local authority or police" (Masanja).

This account reveals a tragic situation where children and grandchildren turn against their older relatives by demanding their property. Masanja's report on older people's concerns indicates emotional and material abuse. Relinquishing resources and assets could significantly affect an older person's practical living experience in the village community, potentially increasing poverty and destabilising their lives, making them destitute. There is another further observational point in the narrative above worth pointing out. There seems to be a lack of collective responsibility, a neighbourhood failure and a general community failure to protect older people, especially those faced by these threats from allegations. The community must be the ear and protector of vulnerable people. Still, according to Masanja's narrative, they fail; therefore, their silence and failure to intervene contribute to the problems affecting older people's social well-being. Essentially, this is a social-structural issue.

A female social worker named Maria, explains what she sees as the problem facing older people in rural areas, saying:

"Older people, especially older women in rural communities, face threats and killings. The origins of these brutal acts are in perverted superstitious beliefs. These older women would often have been cooking for a long time using a "minyaa", a firewood that produces heavy and sharp smoke, leading to red eyes. Still, many people in this rural community do not see this as a factor; when they see an older woman whose eyes are red, they say this is a witch" (Maria).

Maria's narrative indicates how culturally entrenched superstitious beliefs blur people's understanding of the real reason that some older women have red eyes. Red eyes do not indicate someone being a witch; instead, they result from long-term exposure to burning firewood. The implication is that education must expel these erroneous ideas in rural communities. Furthermore, she described social situations and the causes of abuse of older people in rural communities:

"Inheritance claims are also the origin of the murder of older people in village communities. Children or grandchildren lacking wealth return home and begin to disrupt the life of the older person by demanding an inheritance, and if they are denied of property or estate of land, they so often resort to murder, killing their older relatives" (Maria).

As in Masanja's narrative, Maria's account raises two concerns: one is a human right, namely the individual right to access and ownership of resources; the other is intergenerational tension based on the availability of assets.

There is no doubt that this act of taking resources or assets belonging to an older person by force amounts to elder abuse (also known as the mistreatment of older people). It is generally agreed that the abuse of older people is either an act of commission or omission, in which case it is usually described as "neglect". It may be either intentional or unintentional (Ferreira, 2005:19).

The abuse may be physical, it may be psychological (involving emotional or verbal aggression), or it may include financial or other material maltreatment. Regardless of the type of abuse, it can undoubtedly result in unnecessary suffering, injury or pain, the loss or violation of human rights, and a decreased quality of life for an older person (Hudson, 1991). The abuse of older people is reflected in Maria's narrative, involving abuses related to material resources and emotional and physical harm.

Another category of problems facing older people is those associated with allegations of witchcraft. Such allegations often result in devastating social outcomes in the lives of the accused. Many respondents in this study have indicated the negative impact of, and problems caused by, accusations of witchcraft on an older person's life. A respondent named Peter, who is a manager, pointed to the issues affecting older people's well-being and explained the negative impact of witchcraft beliefs on the lives of older people in the community:

"When someone (becomes) ill or dies, especially in Sukumaland, people must go to the traditional doctors-healers to seek reason and solution. Since the so-called traditional healers want money, and material wealth, they feed people who go to see them with wrong information, saying, for example, the death is caused by your older aunt, grandma, or your mother, so go and get rid of them. Many young adults, ignorant of other factors and desperate for an answer, resort to consulting traditional healers and implement the recommended steps, only to find themselves in a more distressing situation and more difficulties befall them" (Peter).

The reasons behind the killing of older people in rural communities are complex. Peter, who was representing the organisation, disclosed that superstitious beliefs and the labelling of older people as witches had been used as a scapegoat to cover up something more sinister. 'Scapegoating' carries the idea of blaming or incriminating someone for something they did not do (Crossman, 2020). These superstitious beliefs are deeply socially embedded in the cultural mindset.

Another response came from Nelson (58 years old), a leader of an older people's forum and a village monitoring committee who looked after older people's welfare concerns in the community. Nelson describes the problems faced by older people in rural communities by saying:

"It is now about a year since the MAPERECE social project started operating in our village community. But the years back, before MAPERECE came to this village, it was very bad. Older people faced challenging problems, including security threats to their safety, freedom of movement, victimisation, and abuse of older people (especially older women) instigated by jealousy, prevalent beliefs, and witchcraft practices. Many older people are victims of vicious attacks, killed at night times when no one is awake or watching. Houses occupied by an older person would be attacked. Some older women have sustained injuries, scarred for life"(Nelson)

It is worth noting something important in the description that this respondent provides of the situation. Nelson's account describes two contrasting periods: The first period is before MAPERECE arrived in the village. This time is portrayed as dark and is characterised by horrible events and the victimisation and killing of older women. The second period is marked by MAPERECE working in the village when virtually all of the terrible events and difficulties older people endured, especially older women, stopped. Highlighting the positive impact, the presence of MAPERECE had made.

Responding to the follow-up question, "Which years did these terrible events take place?", Nelson answered:

"I would say the years of the 2000s were the worst period. From 2000 to 2010, each year in that period, you would hear six older people (older women) losing their lives to vicious attacks, hatred, victimisation and killing. These events created a sense of fear and terror among the older population in our community. Older people could not attend their farms or socialise openly. Some chose to sleep outside due to the fear that being inside something terrible might happen to them." (Nelson)

The respondent was retelling these horrifying stories regarding the abuse and killing of older people in this interview, indicating how older people in communities were physically, mentally, and socially troubled and were at risk and lived in a vulnerable social environment. It also suggests that families who lost their loved ones to these terrible events still live with the trauma and psychological scars even today.

The same respondent explained how young relatives contribute to their older relatives' difficult living conditions in rural communities. Nelson explained:

"Older people in our village have been experiencing many problems. Some have received a threat from their adult children and relatives, pressurised to relinquish their land, property, farms, and any valuable assets. Witchcraft allegations have been used as a ground for killing an older person, while the truth of the matter is that it is the older person's disagreement to give up their ownership of property, land, or farm." (Nelson)

There is a distinction between the idea that someone is a witch and that somebody else believes specific individuals are a witch and using this allegation to sabotage somebody's life and livelihood. So, in Nelson's account, it appears that people in these settings use their belief in witchcraft as a pretext for attacking older people to rob them of their assets and, hence, livelihood. A male respondent, Peter, the manager, elucidated further in his response about the situation:

"MAPERECE researched to find out what caused older people to face social isolation, lack of living space, discrimination, harassment, and torture… we found land issues and inheritance to be behind this problem. Today, the number of people is growing. Still, the land is decreasing. When there is land belonging to parents and grandparents, it is happening now that everyone is looking at that land as a resource for livelihood, and this is causing tension among relations. You find grandchildren wanting the land, and the quarrel arises. Young adults force grandparents or grandmothers to give up the landownership …and if parent, grandparents don't hand over that piece of land, you see the intimidations and killings happening." (Peter)

One may ask a question: If people leave the countryside for the towns, one might expect the ratio of land to people to increase, but as indicated in the above quote, scarcity of land is an issue. Having highlighted these points, I would like to incorporate other perspectives as I consider the effects of witchcraft allegations on a person's life. Being labelled as a witch carries with it profound adverse effects. Such allegations can profoundly affect a person's inner sense of being and social external reality. Since an older person is powerless, living alone may be an easy target. Stigma, as a process, is based on the social construction of identity. Thus, people who become associated with a stigmatised condition pass from being 'normal' to having a 'discredited' or 'discreditable' social status (Parker & Angleton, 2003). Equally, Goffman argued that stigma is a relationship of devaluation in which one individual is disqualified from full social acceptance (Goffman, 1963). Stigmatisation, at its essence, is a challenge to one's humanity. Crocker et al. (1998:504) explained that "a person who is stigmatised is a person whose social identity, or membership in some social category, calls into question their full humanity—the person is devalued, spoiled, or flawed in the eyes of others." Stigmatisation involves dehumanisation, threats, aversion, and sometimes the depersonalisation of others into a stereotypical caricature. Thus, stigmatisation is personally, interpersonally, and socially costly (Crocker et al., 1998). Eliminating oppression and creating better human living conditions, especially for older people, is critical for social change to improve the life experience of older people in rural communities.

This emancipatory framework recognises that some issues affecting individuals are profoundly rooted and prevalent in society and characterise the functions of social structures. From a social point of view, this implies that human emancipation depends upon transforming the social world and not just the inner self (Wright, 2007).

Another respondent described the issues affecting older people's well-being. Paul, the organisation's program coordinator, told of the challenges facing older women in the communities: "They face rights and law-related challenges. Some of the held traditions and customs in some communities tend to undermine and endanger older people's lives. Some of these traditions and customs hinder older women's life experiences and social development in some communities in Tanzania. A woman is still not seen as a person with certain rights, not allowed to own land or inherit property." (Paul)

It is suggested in this account that women often face unfair treatment when trying to access personal and social development opportunities as well as inheritance. Older widows, in particular, may experience the negative effects of gender discrimination due to various restrictions and denied inheritance. The vulnerability of women, especially older women without assets, is a cause for concern. To achieve gender and social equality in society, changes in legislation and legal systems are needed to reform social attitudes, behaviours, and misguided actions (Ndulo, 2011).

The findings of the research reveal that numerous social issues significantly impact the elderly, such as poverty, leading to financial insecurity, health challenges, social stigma, discrimination, and increased vulnerability. These issues are deeply rooted in societal structures.

7.5 Addressing of Problems by MAPERECE

I used Dominelli's social work model to understand how the organisation responds to the identified problems. I have clarified this social work model in the earlier sections. The model provides a way of understanding and categorising social workers' approaches towards problem-solving. Dominelli's model is made of three processes, namely the maintenance, therapeutic, and emancipatory practice.

In considering Dominelli's model, one can see that there may be a link between the way one understands or conceptualises a problem and the kind of solution to which one thinks a problem then lends itself.

A point about MAPERECE's mode of operation: this organisation distributes support to its clients through intermediaries rather than directly. Describing how the organisation identifies the needs of those who require its services and reaches them with help, Peter, the manager of the organisation, said:

"We have conducted meetings at village levels with the council of older people, and then the older people in that council could identify those most in need in their community. We work closely with councils of older people at the village level in providing services."

Equally, a female respondent, Margret (68), who is critical of the organisation's mode of operation, said: "If MAPERECE wants to give anything to the elderly, e.g., soap, food, or money, my advice is that they should not give it to the village councils or older people council…"

This account indicates that delivering needed immediate support to clients through intermediaries (such as the village councils) has some challenges and may require extra observation from the service provider.

(i) Problems that have an immediate impact:

The gathered information indicates how MAPERECE responds to the immediate and immediate needs of its clients.

In an interview, a respondent, Paul, representing the managerial level, explained that:

"MAPERECE is involved practically in providing tangible social support according to a client's needs, for example, building a house, counselling, building a friendship with older people (clients)." (Paul)

Commenting on the support he has received, Jonathan said: "Every time MAPERECE comes here, they bring soda, they give a piece of soap. We receive one Coca Cola, one soap." (Jonathan)

Immakulata, a social worker in the organisation, described the activities she does to support clients: "I provide cleaning services to keep his/her environment clean and safe. Make sure that his/her health is not affected by the surroundings." (Immakulata)

This response indicates that older people who cannot take care of and maintain their own living surroundings receive assistance from social workers employed by the organisation, like Immakulata, as demonstrated here.

There appears to be a difference between the client's perception—soap and Coca-Cola—and the organisation's—building a house, counselling, and building a friendship, as Section 6.6 will elucidate further.

The above response resonates with and reflects Dominelli's approach to problem-solving, the "maintenance" approach. This approach focuses on tackling an individual's immediate needs rather than addressing the broader social situation or more significant social problems beyond an individual (Dominelli, 2009). Furthermore, Immakulata's response indicates action, offering help directly to clients in their homes by cleaning their home environment. This sort of support aims to help older people maintain a good level of hygiene. This practical support activity directly offered to an older person's home setting demonstrates Dominelli's model's maintenance response, in this case, working with the client to maintain their independence at home.

In describing the process through which employees or social workers of the organisation fulfil their duty, Joanna, a female social worker, explained:

"A social worker of the organisation assesses the actual situation of the clients—older people—and decides the right support or course of action in accordance with the condition of our clients."(Joanna)

Likewise, Immakulata, a social worker, explained that:

"MAPERECE undertakes the assessment and provides advice based on the client's situation. For example, a client may have a personal concern, such as religious or spiritual concerns, or in need of legal advice. Then we can give appropriate direction and suggest a solution to this person." (Immakulata)

Joanna and Immakulata's accounts indicate some essential steps vital in determining a situation facing individuals and how best to help the individual recover normality. This process is called an assessment of need, and it is one of the essential steps a social worker must take. It involves examining and establishing an accurate picture of a client's situation, or people might be facing (Wilkins and Boahen, 2013).

During an interview, Joanna, a female social worker, described the tasks she fulfils with the clients:

"When I am with clients, other work is to teach them about older people's laws and rights and human rights. I also emphasise that older people are still needed in society because they have responsibilities for the community. So, there is a capacity building element, increasing awareness. My tasks include counselling, as the majority of our older people experience emotional and mental stress. Sometimes, due to high pressure, an older client will not feel comfortable and ready to see me and cooperate with you." (Joanna)

Joanna's narrative of her task, providing counselling and impart-ing relevant information as a response to older people experi-encing emotional and mental stress, demonstrates the 'thera-peutic' approach part of Dominelli's model.

In therapeutic interventions, the prime focal point is improve-ment through interpersonal relationships. This approach focuses primarily on what individuals can do to improve their position through targeted professional interventions. A principal aim is to enhance a person's psychological and emotional function-ing to handle their affairs (Dominelli, 2002a:12). In working with individuals therapeutically, the social worker's task is to open discursive spaces in which clients can develop their own inter-pretive story, which gives meaning to their experiences and en-ables them to understand how dominant discourses operate to suppress this story (Dominelli, 2002a).

It's worth noting that not all respondents affiliated with the or-ganisation and service users mentioned receiving this type of service to address their immediate needs. The majority of re-spondents indicated a lack of support and assistance for their pressing needs. While some acknowledged receiving support in the form of sugar and soap, the organisation claims to have constructed houses and staff members provide various forms of advice. These efforts align with Dominelli's maintenance and therapeutic approaches. However, the provision of frequent and ongoing tangible support and assistance to aid clients with their everyday needs is not consistently observed in the overall ser-vice delivery of the organisation.

(ii) The Social structure's defects are the underlying causes of immediate problems

According to the data, many older people find it difficult to ac-cess hospital treatment due to inappropriate transport and have difficulty accessing water on a daily basis. Upon close examination of these issues, it is evident that the problems' sources are structurally embedded within society. Institutions have created the perfect grounds for the emergence of these issues, affecting the functioning of individuals and their wellbeing.

The organisation goes beyond individual concerns and challenges the whole community and the social structures and institutions representing the people to respond to these problems. In an interview, a male respondent (Paul), who is the program coordinator in the organisation, explained the activities that are undertaken in response to these issues. Paul explained that: "MAPERECE is involved in educating the community about the welfare and challenges facing older people. We believe that giving education to the broader community can help bring a positive perspective and attitude towards older people." (Paul) Paul's narrative of the organisation's responsive actions to problems indicates that the organisation believes that the whole community and its social structures are responsible for the issues affecting older people's well-being. Thus, this realisation of the collective failure of responsibility leads the organisation to address the community in its approach to managing individuals' well-being.

The activity described above as a response by the organisation to the situation, which involves imparting knowledge about older people's welfare at the community level in a bid to affect change, reflects the emancipatory way of responding to a problem. The emancipatory approach changes society and seeks structural changes to ensure social justice. In this sense, the community addressed its issues for the sake of older people's wellbeing.

Paul, furthermore, explained in detail the involvement of MAPERECE in addressing the problems:

"We are involved in advocacy work, making the concerns of older people known to various stakeholders, including critical institutions in government, police, local, and regional social welfare offices. Also, MAPERECE is involved in educating multiple communities in rural areas about ageing, older people and the need to take care of older people." (Paul)

Paul's account indicates the organisation's effort at the structural level, targeting essential institutions representing the wider community's social interest. The idea behind reaching a wider society is to transform the community from being negative and hostile to being positive and caring towards its older people, who are valuable members.

MAPERECE's response and actions towards solving these issues, particularly their decision to address older people's welfare concerns at a community and structural level, resonate and reflect one suggested approach in Dominelli's social work practice model, the "emancipatory" approach to social problem-solving. The emancipatory approach to responding to social problems identifies the oppressive nature of social relations and argues that social workers are responsible for doing something about these whilst also helping people as individuals (Dominelli, 2002).

In clarifying the usage of emancipatory approaches from a practical point of view, Dominelli (2002b:85) wrote: "Practitioners who follow emancipatory approaches seek to achieve anti-oppressive practices by focusing on the specifics of a situation in a holistic manner and mediating between its individual and structural components."

MAPERECE understands that older people's issues span from the immediate needs of individuals to the community's social structure and are often culturally entrenched. In its effort, MAPERECE brings old and young people together to discuss the importance of their roles in the community. They also challenge long-held negative and cultural views, the negative impact of superstitious thinking, and misconceptions about ageing and older people. Their education package promotes awareness of older people's rights as enshrined in the Tanzanian national policy across the community.

Other observations are worth noting regarding the organisation's response to the highlighted issues and clients' social concerns. Reading and considering what the organisation does in response to social problems, older people face some specific problems that appear not to have been given any focus by the organisation, as revealed in the data findings. Because of the distance, older people cannot afford medical treatment and cannot reach where medical services are available. Therefore, they tend to live with health issues. There is no evidence of the organisation's activity to offer support to individual older people facing health issues who are struggling to reach medical services. Another issue flagged by the service users is living without water in the house. Older people struggle to get water from the water source, a well, because of the distance, and as a result, they sometimes go days without washing or drinking. Older people, especially older women, explained this problem with an anguished tone in their voices, indicating this considerable need and burden. Yet, there is no indication that the organisation supports this critical need in the data gathered.

Furthermore, most respondents mentioned a lack of reliable means of livelihood as the underlying cause of their challenging life experiences. For various reasons, older people who took part in this study in the community have no steady means to acquire a daily living, possibly because of their inability to cultivate. Considering that a person's existence is dependent on food, water, shelter, and good health, lacking these essentials makes the life of an older person very difficult, if not impossible, in rural areas.

If the organisation were to provide support in all aspects of older people's needs, this would be a massive undertaking for an organisation lacking resources and financial capacity. It would mean giving financial capital for starting a business as an alternative way for older people to earn a living instead of farming. It could mean MAPERECE becoming committed to supporting clients with daily needs—for sustenance—whatever that may mean for each older person involved. Such an undertaking would require a significant reservoir of finances and other resources. The lack of complete coverage and response to all the highlighted issues implies limitations to what MAPERECE can do in responding to its client's problems and needs. Hence, it makes sense for MAPERECE to devote at least some of its time to campaigning and to advocate to achieve the more significant changes necessary at the structural level.

The section below examines the impacts of the organisation's work on the situations mentioned above.

7.6 Impact of MAPERECE's Activities: From a Perspective of Service Users

This section deals with the impact of the organisation's services on their clients, and it considers MAPERECE's effect on the broader population in the communities they serve. In considering the organisation's impact on clients who experience their services, the study has revealed a contradictory set of perspectives from service users concerning how they see MAPERECE's impact.

A male respondent, Nelson, commented on the impact of the organisation's work in his community, saying:

"It is now about a year since the MAPERECE social project started operating in our village community. But the years back before MAPERECE came, it was very bad." (Nelson)

Although Nelson did not elaborate on the specific activities by MAPERECE that contributed to this change of affairs, there is an acknowledgement of the organisation's vital role in supporting older people. However, some respondents expressed dissatisfaction with the organisation's impact on a personal level.

Phrases used by respondents in describing their experiences that surfaced in interviews included "I have not been helped," or "I have not received any support." In an interview, a female respondent, Margret (68), explained:

"I have not been helped by MAPERECE. They only encourage us older people to come into groups, being part of the older forum, older people group at village-level councils. But privately in my trouble, I have not received direct support from the organisation or seen anyone coming to want to know the realities of my life. Older people meet and talk about the problems and challenges they have. You see the benefits of being part of a big group. Meeting other older people in the area reduces loneliness, sadness, and depression. When you are with others, you feel a little happy, peaceful, and laughing, but problems continue." (Margret)

Margret's account seems to acknowledge the impact of MAPERECE's work at the community level. She seems to value the coming together/peer support among older people in the community but does not feel that it is helping in solving her problems. She says that she has not been helped directly by the organisation. She uses the term "privately," and this could mean on a personal level. Her dissatisfaction with the organisation's handling of the social problems facing older people appears to emanate from her awareness of her circumstances. She believes that her requirements cannot be resolved by mere peer support or meeting with other older people in the community. She sees that the only way to solve her problem is by receiving direct, tangible support or one-to-one contact with the organisation. She claimed that she has never received any support directly from the organisation, although she may be associating 'help' with being 'given' something. It may be the case that, in this context, the idea of help is taken literally to mean "give."

In further discussion with her in an interview, it became apparent that Margret's dissatisfaction could arise from the lack of trust in the system set-up, which is supposed to serve as an intermediate structure for MAPERECE's work.

For example, answering the question, "What do you think MAPERECE should do to help older women?" Margret, who lives alone, replied:

"The best way to help us older women is for MAPERECE to come to visit the older women and listen carefully to the ideas, know our needs. If MAPERECE wants to give anything to the elderly, e.g., soap, food, or money, my advice is that they should not give it to the village councils or older people council. Still, they should meet one older person after another, in person, and listen to her and give that relief and support. Through this way, I believe MAPERECE will see the reality of older people, older women, and elderly female widows. Because so often the assistance that is being passed onto the council of older persons, does not reach the targeted audience, especially older women, and it is not clear what is happening with that support." (Margret)

Margret's remarks suggest that the organisation provides services and resources through intermediaries, such as the councils, but there is uncertainty about whether these materials reach the intended recipients. It seems that older women, in particular, face challenges in accessing these services. Based on her feedback, it appears that there is a lack of trust and integrity in the operation of these councils. This could possibly explain why the participants express a preference for direct, one-on-one services from the organisation.

The older people's councils and village councils were formed on the initiative of MAPERECE in collaboration with the local government. These councils are supposed to be the bridge and channel that can process older people's concerns and support. The issues she raises here are severe, and they can potentially jeopardise the organisation's good work. If the systems that are in place function in a way characterised by dishonesty and a lack of transparency, honesty and gender discrimination, then criticism arises.

Another reflection on the organisation's service delivery came from Joyce, a female respondent. In an interview, she said:
"MAPERECE does not help me with anything directly. But we, older people have been encouraged to come together, forming an older council group. We meet and talk. We meet on Friday. At our meetings, we share ideas and encourage each other in this life. So, I can say that I have never received help from MAPERECE: food, soap, clothes, or otherwise. Many times, when people from the organisation come, they speak only words, and then you are left in the same situation in your trouble." (Joyce)

Joyce's account shows that she, too, feels that she has never received any help from MAPERECE that could enable her to address her immediate needs. However, she does acknowledge that MAPERECE has helped older people in her community to come together and meet regularly. Bringing older people together helps against isolation and loneliness and provides some sense of solidarity and belonging. However, this mixed reaction to the service might be driven by the clear differentiation between what a service user regards as their immediate essential needs and the organisation's perception of clients' needs. The immediate needs of these service users often take precedence over waiting for societal-level changes, underscoring the complexity of the situation. There appears to be a disconnect between the organisation's activities and the service users' expectations, further highlighting the intricate nature of service provision. Balancing the hopes and aspirations of service users with the agency's approach to solving issues presents a significant challenge, adding to the complexity.

Another female respondent named Mageni expressed the following perspective on her experience of the organisation's service provision. Mageni (78 years old), who lives alone, gave this view of the organisation:
"Sometimes ago, they gave me soap, and another time, they gave me a little bit of money. But I do not see the representative

of the organisation visiting me. It would be beneficial if they were aware of my life situation, and how I am. If there will be someone around to help me, the burden of my life will be a little easier." (Mageni)

This response indicated the existence of some direct tangible support. Mageni acknowledged receiving soap and money, but she used the word "sometimes"; this may suggest that receiving physical material support is not a daily occurrence. She said that she had never seen a representative of MAPERECE visiting her at her home, highlighting the lack of personal connection in the support system.

Another reflection on the organisation's service provision came from a male respondent named Jonathan (70 years old). He had this to say:

"I thank you, MAPERECE, for being willing to help us older people. However, the thing that bothers me is that when MAPERECE comes here, they bring soda and give a piece of soap. We are given soda, Fanta, one Coca-Cola or one soap. Older people are happy. But if you look or overthink this kind of help from a far-reaching perspective…mhmm. Does drinking soda, or being given a single soap help us? Where will one soda lead us? Helping an older person by giving one soda!… I don't know." (Jonathan)

His perspective reflects a contrasting response to the physical or material assistance offered by the organisation. While Jonathan acknowledges the organisation's willingness to assist elderly individuals, he raises doubts about the effectiveness of the aid provided to clients. Specifically, he questions the extent to which providing a Coca-Cola or a bar of soap can truly improve the situation of an elderly person living in a rural area. The respondent's inquiry may stem from an understanding of the complex challenges that older individuals face in such environments. The study highlights the immediate and future needs that contribute to the difficulties faced by elderly individuals in rural areas.

Even though the organisation recruited service users for this study, they were not afraid to criticise the organisation's type and manner of involvement with them. This attitude may indicate an independent mind, awareness of circumstances, and what individuals might wish to see happening.

As shown in this chapter, MAPERECE plays a significant role in addressing issues that impact older people's well-being in rural areas. This social group faces immense challenges but does not receive sufficient solid support from the government. Data findings indicate the active involvement of the organisation and its impact on the ground. However, the data revealed criticism expressed by the service users for not having received tangible help to address their immediate needs. This observation suggests an expectation mismatch between service users and what the organisation thinks it is doing or has set out to be doing. Clarifying expectations is vital to ensure a smooth and meaningful relationship between the clients and the organisation. Though support delivery through intermediaries, i.e., the village council of older people, may indicate a close working relationship between the organisation and the community, it appears that operating in this mode complicates the service provision process. Coming together in these forums helps older people be part of and engage with their peers who have similar experiences and concerns. This social gathering creates positivity and, hence, is more beneficial than they are willing to recognise. Situations within society and its social structure seem to underpin many issues affecting older people's well-being. This explains why the organisation is directing its efforts at the societal level by challenging society to create a socially conducive living environment for older people. This effort has been particularly successful regarding witchcraft allegations against older people. However, as revealed in the data, primarily through the clients' reflections on the service, the organisation seems not to meet all the perceived needs, especially the immediate ones, due to its limited capacity.

8 Case study 2: Dogodogo Street Children Trust

The original investigation of this study aims to understand how social services provided by local non-government social welfare organisations in Tanzania address social problems and their impact on service users such as street children. One of the local organisations recruited to participate in this research was the Dogodogo Street Children Trust. This organisation addresses the social welfare needs of street children in Dar es Salaam, Tanzania. The phenomenon of street children is among the most challenging social issues in urban Tanzanian society. According to observations in social studies, Dar es Salaam is one of the many cities with a high influx of street children exposed to unsafe living conditions (Luena, 2011).

Social researchers and the international community have offered various perspectives in understanding the distinctiveness of this social group. Accordingly, a street child is: "any girl or boy who has not reached adulthood for whom the street (in the broadest sense of the word, including unoccupied dwellings and wasteland) has become his or her habitual abode and source of livelihood." (Thomas de Benitez, 2011:7). Another perspective construes street children as those for whom the street, more than their family, has become their home, a situation in which there is no protection, supervision, or direction from responsible adults (Parveen, 2014; Bhukuth and Ballet, 2015). These interpretations are adopted in this study and resonate well with the social reality of street children in the context of urban Tanzania.

During the research, I carried out a series of semi-structured one-to-one interviews to understand the social problems and social service provision from both the service providers and users of the services linked to the Dogodogo Street Children Trust. Hence, this chapter presents and discusses the data findings related to this case study in the following order:

- The first part discusses contextual information about street children in Tanzania. This part also includes information about Dar es Salaam and the social situation facing street children.
- The second part explains the origins and formation of the Dogodogo Street Children Trust.
- Part three discusses how the organisation identifies its clients.
- Part four discusses the central issues and needs the organisation seeks to address and how they undertake this responsibility.
- Part five explains the organisation's response to each problem through the lens of Dominelli's social work practice model, as discussed previously.
- Part six looks at the impact of the organisation's work on clients' situations and the broader society.

8.1 Contextual Information About Street Children in Tanzania

In Tanzanian culture, having children is considered a significant blessing and a sign of wealth. Society sees children as a symbol of high social status and insurance for the future older generation's social well-being (Mbilinyi and Omari, 1996). However, in the light of such a dominant pronatalist culture, it seems surprising and contradictory to learn that, in the same society, there are cases of child neglect, child abandonment, and homeless children living on the streets of cities across Tanzania today (Rwezaura, 2000; Rwegoshora, 2002; McAlpine et al., 2010). It is recognised globally, including in Tanzania, that all persons under the age of 18 years old are children. All children in Tanzania are protected by the Law of the Child Act 2009 (UNICEF, June 2012-Tanzania). The parliament of the United Republic of Tanzania enacted the Child Act's Law, No.21, 2009. This law applies to the whole country concerning promoting, protecting, and maintaining children's welfare and rights.

The Law of the Child Act 2009 combines child-specific provisions from a range of national laws into one document. The law enshrines the fundamental rights of children drawn from international and regional agreements. It establishes a framework for protecting children from abuse, violence, and neglect at local and national levels. Existing provisions for children who need care outside their own homes and restrictions on child employment are strengthened in this law (UNICEF, June 2012-Tanzania).

In order to understand how important this research project on street children's social well-being is, we must place this matter in the context of the local social reality. Additionally, it is vital to understand how the inactiveness of the social structure and legal provisions potentially contribute to the miserable social conditions that affect children in general.

The Law of the Child Act 2009, Article 8(1) expresses whose duty it is to maintain a child:
"It shall be the duty of a parent, guardian, or any other person having custody of a child to maintain that child. In particular, that duty gives the child the right to—food, shelter, clothing, medical care, education and guidance, liberty, right to play and leisure." (United Republic of Tanzania: The Law of the Child Act 2009, Article 8(1), p. 14).
The Law of the Child Act 2009 further states that: "If a child's parents die, and there are no other relatives to care for the child, or if a child is neglected, abandoned, or abused by their parents, the state should ensure they have a safe place to stay." United Republic of Tanzania: The Law of the Child Act 2009.
The Law of the Child Act 2009, part iii, titled "Support Services for a Child by Local Government Authorities," Article 94 (4) and (5) states that:
"The local government authority shall have the duty to keep a register of most vulnerable children within its area of jurisdiction

and give assistance to them whenever possible in order to enable those children to grow up with dignity among other children and to develop their potential and self-reliance." (United Republic of Tanzania, Law of the Child Act 2009, Article 94 (4)). "'Each local government authority shall, within its area of jurisdiction, be required to provide assistance and accommodation for any child who appears to the authority to require such assistance as a result of having been lost or abandoned or is seeking refuge." (United Republic of Tanzania: Law of the Child Act 2009, Article 94 (5))

These few quotes above indicate the Tanzanian government's efforts to address children's social welfare needs at the policy level. It also appears to set out the duties of the local government to intervene and provide support and protection. Notably, the Law of the Child Act of 2009 lays out some dangerous social circumstances that could potentially affect children's well-being and, therefore, necessitate the government to intervene and practically support children in unsafe social living environments. Despite having these rights and legal provisions in place, children have continued to experience social difficulties. Tanzania has witnessed a tremendous increase in unsupervised children living alone or working on urban streets in the past three decades. Tanzania is home to over 54 million people, most below thirty years of age. Half of the adult population lack employment. Children under 15 constitute approximately 46% of Tanzania's people, whereas the urban population is estimated to account for about 26% (Luena, 2011). Studies indicated in 2012 that one in four children lived in an urban centre, which "is projected to be one in three in the short time span of one generation" (Riggio, 2012:6).

The emergence and growth of the street children phenomenon in Tanzania are caused by many interrelated factors (McAlpine et al., 2010). The diverse factors exacerbating the problem mainly originate in the rural villages. The rise in the number of street children is usually in response to the deterioration of the living conditions in these rural villages and the hardship faced by poor communities on the outskirts of cities. For many, the perception that larger towns offer more significant economic opportunities makes the streets more attractive than a weaker rural economy (Kopaka, 2000). However, life waiting in the city is often difficult. These children often do not have the education and basic skills necessary to deal with the risk factors and to cope with adversity in cities (Ayuku et al., 2004; McAlpine et al., 2010), finding themselves in more risky situations, with their personal and social well-being and development deeply affected.

A further observation is that the family institution in Tanzania has gone through a significant period of upheaval. Fewer and fewer children have stable and loving family environments. Absent parents, alcoholism, and domestic violence increasingly have characterised many families (Kopaka, 2000, Consortium for Street Children—2009 Survey Tanzania). Juma (2008) observed that most extended families lack adequate resources to provide for orphans and other children in their households.

The street children phenomenon is an acute social problem in big cities such as Dar es Salaam, Arusha, Tanga, Mbeya, and Mwanza, where urban population growth rates have exploded (UNICEF- the United Republic of Tanzania, 2009). Rapid urban population growth has been associated with an increased number of children living alone on municipal streets or spending most of their day on the roads in their quest for survival. Street children, or 'Watoto Wa Mitaani' as they are known in the Kiswahili language, are among the most vulnerable groups of the urban poor (Nyoni, 2007). In 2012, an estimated 849,054 street children lived in Tanzania (Government of Estimate–International Labour Organisation Survey; 2012). However, other sources in 2016 stated that the number of street children aged fourteen and below had increased by forty per cent between 2012 and 2015 (Tanzania Daily News, 2016). When one calculates the forty per cent increase of street children from 849,054, the result is 339,622, indicating the total number of street children reached an estimated 1,188,676 in 2015. When I was conducting this research in 2018/2019, there existed no reliable statistical data to show the current number of street children in Tanzania. Others consider the number of street children to be higher.

The following section provides information on street children's situation in Dar es Salaam.

8.2 Street Children in Dar es Salaam

Dar es Salaam is the largest industrial city in Tanzania and is located on the coast of the Indian Ocean. The city's land area is 538 square miles, equivalent to 1,393.41 square km, with a population density of 12,457 people per square mile. The city's current population is estimated at 6,701,650 (World Population Review—https://worldpopulationreview.com/world-cities/dar-es-salaam-population,July,2020). This big city is made up of five municipalities or districts. The present study was conducted in the Ubungo district, located on the southern central side of Dar es Salaam. This area is one of the places where the Dogodogo Street Children Trust operates.

Since colonial times, Dar es Salaam has led urban population growth and accommodated over a third of all urban dwellers in the country (Lugalla, 1995). According to the census conducted in Tanzania in 2012, Dar es Salaam had 4,364,541 inhabitants (The United Republic of Tanzania, 2013:14). Since the 1960s, Dar es Salaam has grown and is Tanzania's biggest, most developed city and has experienced significant economic growth. Dar es Salaam city has been represented as the principal concentration of wealth, population, and modernity. Therefore, the city has acted as a magnet to many Tanzanians, especially young people, from the surrounding areas and other parts of the country.

Nevertheless, large slum areas have been growing along with the city, and many families struggle to provide for their children. Like most urbanised cities in Sub-Saharan Africa, urbanisation in Dar es Salaam is characterised by the fragmentation of a formal economy, unplanned and planned inhabitant areas, poverty, weak institutions, a lack of employment, and non-existent public service provision for people's welfare (Mkalawa et al., 2014). The city receives children from different parts of the country, including from the outskirts and slum areas to the city centre (Consortium—survey on Street Children, 2009). Other studies indicate that poverty drives children into the streets, where they hope to make ends meet, only to find themselves being embraced by a harsh living environment characterised by severe poverty (UNICEF, 2012).

Other investigations indicate that street children in Dar es Salaam experience severe difficulties, hardships, and violence daily. They are often harassed, physically, and verbally abused by adults and law enforcement institutions (Kibassa and Lugalla, 2003; Sanga, 2014). Indeed, Luena (2011) explained that street children's day-to-day life is a continuous struggle for survival. Street children who live in the city experience loneliness, homelessness, loss of parental contacts, parental protection, a lack of love and care, and frequently extremely squalid living conditions. Likewise, Shrestha (2009) described that street children in Dar es Salaam are among the most vulnerable and marginalised members of society, often lacking access to food, shelter, healthcare, security, and education. Equally, another reality is that street children share the streets with hundreds of thousands of adults, many of whom regard them as nuisances if not as dangerous "mini-criminals" (Mbunda, 2011; Niboye, 2013). During the day, children work informally as car-parking boys, vehicle security guards, car washers, or baggage loaders. They use the money they receive from these jobs to buy cheap food in shanty hotels, commonly known in Dar es Salaam as "Magenge" or "Mama Nitilie." Others get their daily food by begging. Bathing or washing is not considered especially important (UNICEF, 2012).

Another perspective insists that street children in Dar es Salaam are among the most invisible populations, overlooked by government, law, policymakers, and the public. The lack of responsible actions by the establishment contributes to the plight of street children who are living and working on urban streets (Consortium for Street Children, 2019). This observation corresponds with an assessment study by the Tanzanian Ministry of Health and Social Welfare (2012:1), which reported that:

"In Dar Es Salaam, street children are seen as a problem by many, which further compounds the nature of an urban crisis. Politicians, policymakers, and urban planners seem to be helpless in their efforts to either solve the problem or to assist street children and other vulnerable children and have failed to prescribe plausible concrete solutions. Street children are considered to be hooligans, vagabonds, and prone to commit crimes. As a result of this, they have routinely been the target of harassment by law enforcers. There are many cases of street children being beaten by police, rounded up, detained, and sometimes repatriated to their rural homes against their will. Nevertheless, these measures have not provided long-term solutions to this social problem. The number of urban street children and children trafficked for different purposes has continued to escalate every year in Dar Es Salaam."

Other studies stress the importance of understanding the social concerns that affect the welfare of both street children and children in general. Such knowledge could identify social problems, the elements that lead to the negligent conditions of orphans, and the factors that expose street children to situations detrimental to their overall well-being (Spitzer et al., 2014).

Although the exact total figure of street children dwelling and working in the city is unknown, Dogodogo's perspective is that the numbers have increased. The government has not done enough to understand who these children are, where they come from, their reasons for leaving home, how they survive, and the issues they face (Nyakwesi, 2012). However, let there be no doubt that living on the streets can potentially have severe long-term effects on a child's mental and physical well-being. In Tanzania, the efforts and support towards street children's welfare needs seem to come from non-profit, non-governmental social welfare organisations operating in the cities. In Dar es Salaam, the Dogodogo Street Children Trust has stepped in to address street children's welfare needs and rights.

8.3 Origins and Formation of the Dogodogo Street Children Trust

The Dogodogo Street Children Trust is a Tanzanian local non-profit, non-governmental social welfare organisation (NGO). It was established in 1992 by Maryknoll Sister Jean Pruitt (Maryknoll Sisters are a group of Roman Catholic religious women, initially based in New York, but also involved in mission) in collaboration with local people in Dar es Salaam.

The arrival of the Dogodogo Street Children Trust was a story of hope for street children experiencing various problems in the city. These children appeared to be forgotten by the central and local governmental authorities. The organisation's representatives said that the Dogodogo Street Children Trust was created in response to the growing number of vulnerable children who had moved from various parts of rural Tanzania to Dar es Salaam. The term 'Dogodogo' means 'little ones' in Kiswahili. The organisation learned of various reasons for children living on the streets, including child abuse and the desire for a better future. The organisation adopted a holistic approach to addressing the children's needs in its consideration and response. Thus, the organisation sought to provide shelter, education, promote justice and children's rights, and overcome the poverty and exclusion of this vulnerable group. At its inception, Dogodogo's vision was to see a Tanzania where all children were empowered to enjoy their fundamental rights to survival, development, protection, and participation in society (Dogodogo Street Children Trust—27 November 2019).

To realise its vision, Dogodogo took the following actions. In 1992, the Dogodogo Street Children Trust opened a drop-in shelter, the Dogodogo Centre, in Dar es Salaam. The history of the organisation's work reveals that in the first sixteen years of its existence, more than 1,500 street children passed through the centre's services and programmes, including education and vocational training. Aside from this, the organisation helps many children and young people return to their families or move into the wider community (Maryknoll Office for Global Concerns, 2011).

In 1996, the Dogodogo Trust took another significant action when it opened the Kigogo Home in Dar es Salaam's suburbs. Here, trained staff members provide vital services for up to 60 street children at any time. The Kigogo Home provides shelter, nourishment (body and soul), education, healthcare, arts and culture, sports, counselling, and family reunification. They also run other programmes, including a vibrant programme on HIV and AIDS, using theatre and the arts to reach street children in more than twenty villages, as well as a successful anti-drug programme.

The Dogodogo Street Children Trust, through its work, is also involved at a governmental level. The organisation has served on a government-led steering committee to promote policy development on the issues affecting vulnerable children, pioneering the National Network for Children and the Global Network of Religions for Children.

Furthermore, the organisation works with other public bodies nationally and internationally. The Dogodogo Street Children

Trust has also served on another government-led steering committee to promote policy development on issues affecting vulnerable children, pioneering the Tanzanian Child Rights Forum (TCRF), of which it is the current Chair. Dogodogo works closely with other like-minded organisations to promote children's best interests, both nationally and internationally, such as UNICEF, Save the Children, the Global Network of Religions for Children (GNRC-Africa), and Plan International. Dogodogo is also a member of the Implementers Partners Group (IPG), meeting monthly to share ideas and new developments, progress, and challenges regarding children. Additionally, Dogodogo is also a member of the Children Agenda (CA) and is part of the CA Advocacy Task Force.

The tasks and responsibilities carried out by the organisation can be described as follows:

- First, Dogodogo is involved in advocacy and lobbying for children's human rights, especially those living and working on the streets in Dar es Salaam.
- Secondly, they facilitate and subsidise street children attending secondary schools, and they do the same for marginalised street children in vocational skills training.
- Thirdly, they offer guidance, counselling, and psychological support to street children attending secondary education and those at Bunju Vocational Skills Training School.
- Fourth, they provide medical treatment, assisting street children in need of medical treatment by taking them to the hospital.
- Fifth, they monitor and evaluate their work regularly.
- Sixth, the organisation provides daily sports activities, including jump rope and football.
- Finally, they carry out mobile education, offering primary school lessons on Dar es Salaam's streets.

The organisation revealed that more than 4,500 children have benefited from their services in the last 28 years, including medical, educational, and vocational training. They have also helped 500 children to return to their families (Dogodogo Centre, 2020).

However, it is a challenge to obtain information on how many people have lived as street children in Dar es Salaam over these twenty years, as no data records exist. It would also be interesting to know the overall proportion of the street-child population that the organisation has helped in the twenty years of its existence; however, records of this information seem unavailable. Dogodogo has an organisational structure in place that guides its decisions and actions in its social care practice. Organisationally, Dogodogo is governed as follows:

- Board of Trustees
- Director
- Executive Committee
- Programme Co-ordinators
- Employees

This structure determines how the roles, power, and daily responsibilities are assigned, controlled, and coordinated and how information flows between the different levels of management. The organisation recruits its employees and volunteers following its needs, which are very much based on its overall purpose. To be part of the organisation, staff must know or have received education on social work, community development, and management. For a person to work in the organisation, they must have received education and qualification in one of these areas. Financially, regarding resources, the Dogodogo Street Children Trust is not self-reliant. It relies on donors and well-wishers from inside and outside Tanzania. It is this dependence on donors that has both enabled, as well as limited the organisation in adequately addressing the needs of street children in Dar es Salaam.

A male respondent named Shija, who represented the managerial level, reflected on this fact during an interview. He explained: "During the period between 2008 and 2010, there was a global economic crisis. During this period, the organisation's performance struggled due to financial difficulties. The global economic crisis led some of our donors to withdraw and stop funding our programmes and others to move away from Tanzania, and aid in our programme declined. Due to a lack of funding and money in 2010, we were forced to close the centre at Kigogo A. We had to ask the kids to go back to their homes. So, we decided to take them back to their homes for the young people who were ready to go back home. For those who did not want to return home, we requested a place for them in other centres run by other organisations in Dar es Salaam. So, from December 2010, the centre of Kigogo A was closed. In December 2017, we sold the Kigogo A building to the Government in the Kinondoni municipality in Dar es Salaam. Since then, this centre has been used as a clinic facility." (Shija)

This quote shows that the organisation has seen highs and lows in its work. In the first seventeen years of its operation, Dogodogo's work attracted attention from donors outside the country who were financially and materially supportive. As a result, various aspects of its work thrived. However, the global economic crisis had a significant impact, as donors could not sponsor Dogodogo's work to the same level. This forced the organisation to scale back and stop some of the programmes that required more funding, a difficult decision made in the face of unprecedented challenges.

One of the programmes the organisation had to stop offering due to financing limitations was the material services provided to street children from low-income families from the surrounding communities on the outskirts of Dar es Salaam. Previously, these families received school materials, such as pens, pencils, school notebooks, school uniforms, and daily counselling.

Consequently, after the financial crisis, the organisation decided to reduce the services given to this group. Instead, it concentrated its full assistance to the children and young people in the street permanently. These children do not have relatives or a family to be part of in Dar es Salaam.

The organisation put these children in what they refer to as the 'twenty-four hours' category, denoting children who consider the streets to be their permanent dwelling. They are in the streets twenty-four hours a day, seven days a week.

In their daily operation, the organisation has categorised their clients—the street children—into two groups, 'twelve-hours' and 'twenty-four hours'. These categories reflect and help identify an individual's street child, determined by the duration of time spent on the streets. The following Section 7.3 will clarify this matter further.

The research enquiry used one-to-one semi-structured interviews to acquire relevant information. Interviews were conducted with staff members and the organisation's service users (street children). Interviews were audio-recorded in the Kiswahili language, audio-recorded, and then the transcribed transcripts were then transcribed into English.

I interviewed a total number of fifteen participants. The interviews involved individuals representing three levels: managers, employee/social workers, and service users. The respondents' identities who participated in this investigation are pseudo-anonymised to protect their identity.

8.4 Identification of Clients by Dogodogo Street Children Trust

The organisation has guiding factors by which it can identify and ascertain an accurate picture of its client's circumstances and, therefore, fashion services relevant to the client, presented in this section. Two critical questions led to information generation: What kind of street children does the organisation support? How does it identify the client's needs? Respondents at the managerial level revealed factors or criteria that guide them in identifying and determining their clients' needs.

A male respondent (Shija) at the managerial level pointed out age as a criterion for including a person in the organisation's service provision:

"Street children aged 7 to 17 years old are welcomed to be part of the Dogodogo program as clients. Children within this age range are influenceable and could be guided. The individual is expected to finish and leave our programme at the age of 19 years. This street youth would end his time with the organisation and get on with life independently." (Shija)

The age at which children are enrolled is an intriguing topic, especially in Tanzania where the law mandates that children must start primary school at seven years old. I didn't inquire whether the organisation chose this age due to the existence of this law. Furthermore, the organisation's service program accepts street children up to the age of seventeen, and they can participate until they turn nineteen, at which point they must leave the program. During my time with the organisation, I had the opportunity to interview three individuals who had previously lived on the streets, gone through the Dogodogo program, and now have successful careers in the city. This led me to think about what would happen if a worker encounters a child below the age of seven wandering helplessly in the streets.

A male respondent named (Mayunga), a staff member, explained. "We would send a child below seven years of age to other non-governmental organisations that are involved with abandoned children of that age here in Dar es Salaam." (Mayunga)

Apart from the age factor, the organisation uses other factors to determine the needs of a street child and decide who should be part of its programme.

In responding to this question, described in another way, Mayunga explained:

"A "twelve hours category" is another group of street children that we have identified. This category comprises children, and young people who spend twelve hours working in the streets each day. They have family, relatives, and a home to go to at the end of the day. So, they do not sleep in the street, and relatives or parents may know their whereabouts and activities." (Mayunga)

Mayunga elaborated on the second category that the organisation uses to understand street children and their needs. He said:

"There is a "twenty-four hours" category of street children. This category comprises young street people who are without family connections in Dar es Salaam city. These are young people who work and live on the streets. For them, the street is a permanent home. The organisation pays much more attention and focuses on those in the streets for twenty-four hours." (Mayunga)

Mayunga's accounts indicate the organisation uses a "duration factor" as a basis for deciding which street child is in need of which type of service.

This way of identifying the street children, based on the "duration factor", agrees with other social science research conceptualisations of street children, which tend to categorise children into two groups: "children on the street" and "children of the street'. This distinction is based on two criteria: the amount of time the child spends or has spent on the street and their relationship with parents or other responsible adults (Apteker and Stoecklin, 2014).

The phrase 'children on the street' represents children or young people who work on the streets in the daytime but return home at night where they sleep, although some occasionally sleep on the streets (UNCHS, 2000; Ibrahim, 2012). On the other hand, "children of the street' refers to homeless children for whom the streets in urban areas are both their source of livelihood and where they sleep and live (Ibrahim, 2012:1). Dogodogo Street Children organisation refers to the 'children of the street' as 'twenty-four hours' children. The children in the 'twelve-hour' category may have different problems and needs. There may not be concerns regarding them sleeping rough on the streets because they may have a family to go to at night. However, it might be the case that spending twelve hours on the streets may be instigated by the level of poverty or an impoverished life in a family. No food to eat and other basic needs characterise their families.

The problems and needs of the children in the 'twenty-four hours' category may be more complex. Children in this category may lack a safe place to sleep, food, and clothing, be vulnerable to harassment or sexual abuse at night, and be susceptible to exploitation.

Another strategy that the organisation uses to identify and determine its clients and their needs is face-to-face interviews with street children. In response to the question, 'How do you determine that a person is a street boy or girl, who deserves your services?' A respondent (Shija) at the managerial level explained:

"A method we use to determine whether or not this boy or girl deserves our service is one-to-one interviews and face-to-face conversations. We also conducted some observations, trying to map the whereabouts of the person. The activities they are involved in while in the streets. Otherwise, the interview does reveal a lot about a person." (Shija)

Ascertaining an individual's eligibility to be part of the organisation's program takes time, as respondent Mayunga, a social worker, explained:

"It takes time and more than one encounter to establish an accurate picture of a person's identity. For a street boy to trust you in the first encounter is difficult. Perhaps that is to be expected. Therefore, what we do is to go to talk with this person more than once, getting to know him, befriending him, and letting him ask us questions. It is a two-way traffic conversation. After a second time, you leave him alone and work on the information gathered at the office level to discern the type of service suitable for him. For the street children belonging to the 'twelve hours' category, we talk with them and acquire permission to speak with their parents. We try to have a conversation with both parents and children involved in the same room." (Mayunga)

This section's discussion, particularly the respondents' accounts, indicates how important and seriously the organisation considers its role as a service provider to street children. As elucidated above, it has devised strategies and an approach to know its clients and address their needs. In general, it seems that they consider every street child as important and deserving of support. The organisation's strategy for identifying who is a street child and their individual needs is through face-to-face interviews. This way of determining its clients also ensures a genuine picture and the right client who deserves to be part of its service programme. Section 8.5 considers the issues and needs that the organisation currently addresses, as revealed by the data findings from the interviews.

8.5 Main Issues Addressed by Dogodogo Street Children Trust

The empirical evidence displays the issues and concerns affecting the service users' (street children) well-being and functioning in Dar es Salaam. This chapter discusses the main problems and needs the organisation seeks to address. Data revealed issues that represent immediate needs that affect respondents' well-being. And the existence of those issues often finds their root cause from within the broader social structure.

The discussion starts with those immediate problems. However, considering these issues, we must know that their underlying root causes are embedded in society- broad social circumstances. Responding to the question: 'What problems do street children face?', Kulwa, a staff member, explained the circumstances that present danger to street children, saying:

"Working and collecting empty bottles in slums, areas hygienically not safe; most of our children and youths have contracted infections because they touch anything; they walk over anything with bare feet." (Kulwa)

Kulwa's account indicates physical and health-related challenges and circumstances in which children are likely to contract health problems. Street children are vulnerable health-wise because they live and work in a hygienically poor environment. These issues form part of the environmental concern in which street children live and work. So, the nature of the problems does not simply reflect immediate health issues, but it is structural, too. Nicolas, a street boy, demonstrated how harmful the streets can be as he focused on his physical injury:

"My leg is injured, and it is hurting, troubling me. I was running, and I fell at the bridge of Ubungo station. I fell on a sharp metal, and it cut me so deep, as you can see. It is now a week since I got this injury." (Nicolas)

Another street boy (Kevin) described the physical health problem affecting his person's well-being and attributed this health issue to his lifestyle and poor living conditions:

"I have been feeling weak physically for three months now. Young people here are sleeping in the same place, use one toilet—even the food we share. We also eat from one container, plate. So infectious diseases in this environment are very easily getting transmitted from one person to another person." (Kevin)

Kevin's account shows that street children are susceptible to various health situations and incidents that potentially harm their physical well-being because of poor living conditions and living arrangements.

In an interview, Mayunga, a male social worker, highlighted that finding a safe place to sleep is a problem that street children face. He explained:

"Street children sleep in unsafe environments in a rough place. When you walk around Dar es Salaam during night-time, you see many children sleeping on floors without clothing, some sleep in the heap of boxes of rubbish. When the weather is unfavourable, for example, raining, cold, or scorching, street children have no choice but to endure the harsh living conditions." (Mayunga)

Indeed, the challenge of finding a safe place to sleep during the night featured as a significant concern for street children in Dar es Salaam.

"The challenge in street life is to get a safe place, to feel safe, sleeping safely. Living in the streets without fearing being attacked, beaten, without being harassed, ridiculed or chased by police around." (Kevin)

These accounts indicate how vulnerable, powerless, and unprotected children are on Dar es Salaam's streets; they operate in a hazardous environment.

Sleeping is one of our human needs, and it plays a significant role in our development as human beings (Connolly et al., 1996). Indeed, going through days or nights without sleep because there is no safe place to sleep can negatively impact a person mentally, emotionally, and physically, yet this is the experience that a child living in the street is likely to face.

In Kevin's account of street children's problems, he mentions being chased around by the police, an aspect worth attention. Indeed, the police institution plays a significant role in society, with a mandate to protect and ensure all citizens' safety, particularly vulnerable people, including children and street children

(Millar et al., 2019). Hence, how police officers respond and interact with street children is hugely important, as they could increase or decrease street children's feelings of safety and well-being. Various studies have explored and contributed to understanding the role of policing in children experiencing abuse and the realisation of children's social well-being (Richardson-Foster et al., 2012; Millar et al., 2019). Other investigations into street children's reality exposed instances where police officers abuse street children in Dar es Salaam (Fikowski, 2013).

The accounts above by the respondents demonstrate aspects of the vital immediate needs of street children, namely health and safety. Hazardous environments threaten those they find themselves in. Basically, there is a broader underlying issue here: society's, including government and police, responsibility to create a good and healthy living environment to ensure the safety, health, and well-being of children.

Economic problems due to the lack of stable means of livelihood are other pressing issues that immediately impact street children in Dar es Salaam. Timothy, a social worker in the organisation, explained that:

"You know, many children from rural areas, are being misled by others, believing that life in Dar es Salaam city is good, there is no problem, there is food, there is work. However, the reality is always different. The truth of life in the streets is not the same as it was promised or conceived. Many children, youths come here to the city and find that no one is interested in them, there is no reception, not accepted and no one to help them. So, a child or youth finds himself in a worse situation never expected." (Timothy)

As indicated by the above account, the problem is that a child accessing their basic needs faces incredible challenges without a source of income.

Similar concerns were expressed by Lydia (20), who had previously lived in the streets but was enrolled on the Dogodogo programme and received vocational education. She explained what it was like for her to be homeless and the challenges she faced:

"Poverty in our family, my mother was struggling to meet our basic needs, and education made me leave home. I desired to have a better life, so I decided to run to Dar es Salaam city life, hoping that my life in the city would be better than in the Singida village. However, life in the city proved the opposite. Without proper education and work, it was tough for me to earn a living. Besides, being a girl in an unknown place, wandering around in a city was a threatening experience for me." (Lydia)

This narrative reveals why street children lack basic needs: street children lack financial capital, job-related skills, education, and other resources vital for their existence.

The immediate issue for those children is making a livelihood in Dar Es Salaam. But behind that are various underlying issues like poverty and lack of education. Lydia came to the city without any means and education, hoping for a better life; however, she encountered a contrary environment.

In an interview, Nicolas, a street boy, expressed how having a physical injury can disrupt any engagement in earning-related activities: "No, this collection of empty bottles are not mine; it belongs to my friend. I have not managed to go collecting bottles because of the wound on my leg. When you have a health issue, life is tough, currently, I do not have any money to buy a drink or food." (Nicolas)

Nicolas's account reveals how vital being in good health is for a street child because engaging in any survival activity depends on how healthy and physically strong an individual is.

Kevin echoed this: 'A challenge I do face, and every street boy faces, is how to get the basic needs, as it is not guaranteed that one can get money through selling items in the street.' (Kevin)

Our existence as human beings depends on our ability to make a living and acquire food, water, and other necessities. In this context, the failure to obtain basic needs puts street children at high risk and more vulnerable.

Even though a street boy or girl may be involved in selling items, there is still uncertainty surrounding acquiring money. It may be that the items themselves are in poor condition, obtained illegally, or irrelevant to the needs of a buyer. The fact remains that the failure to sell items or earn income negatively affects an individual's life on the streets, including causing them not to afford to eat. In trying to understand the street children's reality of life and their involvement in activities to sustain their lives, two concepts feature in the debate: resilience and vulnerability. The aspect of resilience is demonstrated by street children's positive attitude and actions to survive. Commenting on the necessity of employing some coping and survival strategies, Kebede (2015:48) wrote: "To cope with their day-to-day challenges, street children resort to several coping strategies to avert their adversities. These survival strategies include ways they use to make money, acquire food, and other basic needs. The lifestyle inherent to living on the streets exposes children to a range of harmful situations. Hence, their survival is often dependent upon engaging in risks to their health and general well-being while on the streets; they have to battle fiercely to keep alive."

The concept of resilience is understood as "the capacity of individuals to face up to an adverse event, withstand considerable hardship, and not only overcome it but also be made stronger by it" (Sondhi-Garg, 2004:70). Other studies have indicated that resilience is attributed to social support networks on the streets that provide support, acceptance, and companionship (Evans, 2002). The perspective expressed by this research corresponds with the experience of street children in Tanzania. As the current study findings indicate, street children exhibit resilience, ingenuity, and determination to survive. Lugalla and Mbwambo (1999) found that Tanzanian children living in the street are organised into peers who share resources, strategies, assets, and care.

It is also crucial to accept the aspect of vulnerability that they encounter in their lives. Although street children have and must show resilience for their survival, they remain vulnerable. Constant talk of resistance and resilience strongly indicates a continuous struggle (Lalor, 1999). It is this struggle faced by a child when moving from one vulnerable situation (the home environment) to an unpredictable situation (street life) that needs to be acknowledged and explored in terms of vulnerability (Kilbride et al., 2000; Ali, 2011). We should not take the resilience shown by children living and working in the streets to mean that it is acceptable for an underage boy or girl to live and work in the streets. As various studies on this matter across the globe have shown, the street environment is not conducive to a child, as it is full of hazards to children's well-being (Connolly, 1990).

The vulnerability immediately impacts the unsafe environment street children find themselves in. This situation is accentuated by the lack of support from a structural level, i.e., local and central government, which could potentially eliminate the dangers and protect those children in unsafe and challenging environments. By living and working in a hazardous street environment, children are more exposed to risks potentially harming their well-being. Hence, street children are vulnerable individuals as they are unprotected, lack primary care, and experience physical injuries and mental and psychological trauma resulting from living in an unsafe environment and involving in high-risk behaviours.

The concept of vulnerability is used in several fields to refer to the potential for poor outcomes, risk, or danger (Arora et al., 2015). According to Arora et al. (2015:194), the term "vulnerability" relates to the state or condition of being weak or poorly defended. Hence, when the concept of vulnerability is related to young people/children living on the streets, it implies the ones who are more exposed to risks than their peers. They can be vulnerable in terms of deprivation (food, education, and parental care), exploitation, abuse, neglect, violence, and infection with HIV (Arora et al., 2015:194).

Illiteracy and a lack of education are among the issues that street children face. These issues featured in the response by Mayunga, a male social worker, who explained that:

"The inability to be able to read puts many street children at risk. For example, you find someone sleeping in a dangerous area, even if there is a label forbidding anyone to sit or sleep, but because this person does not know how to read, he ends up sitting or sleeping in that area. Some children sleep under the hanging electrical wires. So, mobile education does consider the environment or living condition children are in and educates them in those concerns." (Mayunga)

Mayunga's narrative reveals that ignorance, characterised by an inability to read due to a lack of education, can lead individuals to conduct their lives in an environment potentially dangerous to their well-being.

Another response from Timothy, a social worker who lived a street life before becoming part of the organisation, described street children's problems. Timothy explained:

"Lacking education is an issue. When a child arrives in the city, he finds himself not attending school, and he loses his goals. For example, I left home believing that I would find someone to help me here in town, but that was not the case." (Timothy)

As stated in Mayunga's account, Timothy's narrative highlights education issues. Lack of education contributes to many other problems and increases potential immediate dangers. But not only the immediacy of the matter is to be considered. Lack of education has a long-term effect and may prevent street children from obtaining work-related skills and excelling socially and economically in life. Issues, as expressed above, have an immediate impact on the life of a street child but are further exacerbated by the failure of the social structure. Hence, the paragraphs below elaborate on those issues and conditions embedded within society.

The community's careless attitude and negligence towards street children put children in vulnerable situations where they are unprotected and lack vital support. This fact is reflected in Shija's response to the question regarding which issues affect street children's well-being, where they explained:

"A lack of community support, support from the extended family relative to youth who is without parents. Society lacks a positive attitude and sympathy for children living in difficult circumstances. You find all parents dead, the child or the children are left alone without any help, and unfortunately, even the surrounding community around them does not care. The struggle and hardships facing street children are visible to society, but the level of care towards them is non-existent." (Shija)

Shija's account highlights the social and life challenges experienced by street children, which are exacerbated by the community's apparent indifference to their plight. This indifference has a profound impact on these children, prompting important questions. For instance, unaccompanied children undertake perilous journeys to urban areas like Dar es Salaam, where they end up living on the streets. They use public transportation without anyone showing concern for their safety or well-being. Moreover, community members often witness children working and living in difficult conditions on the streets, yet they choose to ignore the situation. It's clear that the community's indifference is a significant issue that needs to be addressed for the welfare of these vulnerable children, and it's our empathy and compassion that can drive this change. In answering the question: 'What problems street children face?' A male staff member, (Kulwa), responded:

"Some people see street children as those outside the usual circle or system of life and hence unreachable, but the reality is that street children are in the front face of society. They are everywhere; everyone sees them in their impoverished life. Therefore, one cannot say that they are hidden from public sight. Their loss and pain are visible to all of us." (Kulwa)

Kulwa's account indicates that the public ignores street children in their vulnerable situations because, for some, they are not in what one may call a normal environment, such as family. But he points out that those children are part of the community, and their problems are visible. This response highlights an issue of the community's attitude towards street children.

Kulwa also further explained:

"Most people in our society blame and judge harshly the young people who live in the street. But they seem to forget that these children are not in those situations voluntarily, but because of neglect of parents, relatives, and society." (Kulwa)

The above narrative indicates the judgemental attitude of the community towards street children, hence the stigmatisation they are faced with. The community disconnects with street children by blaming and devaluing them for their situation.

Although there may be a range of factors that lead a child into this situation, their family and the community play a significant role. Lenski et al. (1974) noted that when a community is involved in projects involving street children, it comes to realise that the problems of street children are problems for the whole community. It also comes to understand that the issues affecting street children have multiple causes and need various responses. Current studies on the street children phenomenon also share this same observation (Friberg and Martinsson, 2017). Although Lenski et al. made this comment over four decades ago, it still rings true that the protection of street children is a shared responsibility involving the family, community, and governmental bodies.

Kulwa further described the problems that street children face in Dar es Salaam. He explained that:

"Children and youths encounter beating and harassment from people and the police, too. A street youth is regarded as a troublemaker undesirable socially. Whenever a police officer sees a group of more than five street youths together, his/her reaction is to chase them, disperse the group, and children run, and some end up hurting themselves, even some end up with broken legs." (Kulwa) Kulwa's account of the street children's social situation indicates that the public's reactions often exacerbate the circumstances of already devastated children. Negative perceptions produce a repressive response by the public and police, reinforcing the social isolation of street children. Indeed, other studies on street children in different cultures have observed that street children's perception and public image influence people's responses. For example, a study conducted in Latin American countries by Connolly and Ennew (1996) found that:

"The public image of street children has acted as a barrier to success in both research into their lives and programmes intended for their welfare…the emphasis should shift away from attempts to define street children towards an analysis of their relationship with the street environment." (Connolly and Ennew, 1996:131). Another response by Andrea, a youth living on the street, echoes the physical abuse that he encounters. Andrea explained: "As you can see, problems everywhere, not a nice place. You frequently receive threats from the police, and you get beating from other people in the streets." (Andrea)

This short account shows that it is not just the general public but also the police, a law enforcement body supposed to protect citizens, including the vulnerable, who seem to be some of the perpetrators most frequently physically harassing these children. These attitudes can only be a sign of an embedded culture insensitive to and stigmatising street children.

As mentioned before, stigmatisation and discrimination run deeper in society. These issues are featured in Kevin's response in an interview. He, a street youth, expressed his sadness regarding how the public sees street children:

"Most people in our community have a horrible view and attitude towards street children. The public sees us as second-class citizens, not treated in a dignified way. We are laughed at and debased. We are called names such as thieves, hooligans, dirty people, and dangerous people. This type of language and views creates a big chasm between street children and the rest of society in terms of a good relationship. However, street children are human beings at heart, and they dream of a better life, regardless of how they may look on the outside, as shabby, dirty, rough, and confused. We deserve fair treatment, respect, and support. Each morning, we get up with our daily schedule, go to the cars, sell bottles, clean up, wash cars, and work hard to meet our basic needs." (Kevin)

Kevin's account emphasises the existence of stigmatisation against street children, which appears to manifest itself in the form of condescending language, labelling them as unusual and dangerous human beings. Stigmatisation can profoundly affect a street child's self-image and confidence to engage in life socially and make better decisions that can improve their lives.

Sadly, stereotypes, stigma, and discrimination are also apparent in the educational system, as the Dogodogo organisation discovered. Shija, a respondent at the managerial level, explained their campaigning efforts for street children to join public schools in Dar es Salaam encountered resistance:
"When we approached Dar es Salaam's government authority to enrol street children into public schools, they agreed. They allowed us to enlist the street children into their schools. However, the implementation of this decision and process was met with resistance. Teachers' reception and attitudes in some schools towards street children were very ambivalent and showed a discriminatory attitude. Some school authorities, teachers, and individuals in local government did not like the idea at all. But we pressed on with the idea, and the central government agreed." (Shija) Shija's account reveals how street children are disadvantaged because of the entrenched culture of stigmatisation in the

establishment or public institution. The stigmatisation culture creates interpersonal, internal, and external social repercussions on the children's living experience. Moncrieff (2006) observed that children often struggle with low self-esteem, a lack of self-confidence, and a sense of worthlessness and shame. Indeed, discrimination against street children and obstructing them from acquiring an education deny their fundamental rights. Education has the potential to change children's lives positively, offering skills that can lead to employment opportunities and social empowerment.

In summary, this section indicated problems that affect street children's well-being according to the data findings.

(i) Problems that have an immediate effect according to the data findings include:
- Health issues caused by poor hygiene and hazardous environment
- Safety
- Lack of livelihood
- Vulnerability
- Lack of access to education

(ii) Underlying causes for immediate problems according to the data findings include:
- Indifference and ignorance by the community
- Lack of acceptance and protection, including harassment by police
- Lack of creation of a safe and conducive environment
- Stigmatisation and discrimination

8.7 Addressing of Problems by Dogodogo Street Children Trust

Data findings reveal some of the actions by the organisation to address these issues. For example, the organisation provides services to alleviate the poor health of those with physical and medical problems. This fact is considered by Josephine, a social worker, who explained her responsibilities:

"In my position as an employee, Dogodogo has assigned me this responsibility because health-related problems concern almost every street child/youth we encounter in the street. I do make an assessment, and usually, it is me who takes the person for the medical evaluation and subsequent treatment. I must carry with me the First Aid Box whenever I go to the street, and if a person requires more medical treatment, then I talk with the team about his case, and then appropriate measure follows. Those with a severe health problem we help by taking them to the hospital for treatment." (Josephine)

This account shows that a first aid service is provided for physical wounds and minor health conditions. Additionally, there appears to be practical help in transporting those with severe health conditions to a good hospital, made available by the organisation.

In an interview, Kevin, a street boy, explained the support he receives from the organisation. He said: "They help us with advice, take us to receive medical treatment when we need it. The workers of the organisation helped me when I was not well." (Kevin)

In an interview, Nicolas, a street boy, described the medical help he received for his wounded leg. When asked: What treatment did you get and from where? Nicolas responded: "A social worker, the teacher, came from Dogodogo, cleaned me, bandaged my wound, and gave me some ointment to put on the wound." (Nicolas)

During my time with the organisation, individual workers told me that street children's health concerns dominate the organisation's daily work. Providing support to those with wounds and other serious health issues has been a priority for the organisation to ensure survival and maintain the well-being of these vulnerable people, as health-related problems represent an everyday occurrence for the children living in this environment. The absence of a safe place or shelter to sleep is another problem this vulnerable group encounters. The local social welfare organisation opened a drop-in centre for street children to address these issues.

Shija, a representative at the managerial level, reflected this fact in his description of what they do to address the issue:

"The street children and young people could come to this centre to have a shower, sleep and during the morning could go back to the streets. So, the street children were free to come and go at any time." (Shija)

The organisation's actions and response to these issues resonate and reflect the maintenance approach of Dominelli's model, which mainly focuses on individuals.

Economic problems which occur due to the lack of a stable means of livelihood are also issues that the street children in Dar es Salaam face. The organisation does not address the economic concerns directly or provide sustenance for the street children. However, its helping method is characterised by other services rather than fixing one such economic issue.

Andrea, a street youth, explained. "A large part of our daily life, we support ourselves by picking cans, collecting empty plastic bottles, and selling and washing cars at road junctions and roundabouts. Sometimes, we receive help, such as soaps. If you get an injury on your body, staff from Dogodogo do come to help. Dogodogo teaches us how to protect ourselves against disease, dangers." (Andrea)

In his account, Andrea says, "Dogodogo teaches us how to protect ourselves against disease, dangers." This activity is an example of the therapeutic approach within Dominelli's model, which involves providing knowledge that serves as a tool to help the individual improve their life.

Another identified issue that street children face is illiteracy, the lack of education and the accessibility of formal education. The organisation has put activities and programmes that promote literacy among street children in place. One of the programs carried out by the organisation is called 'mobile education. It is a type of educational programme carried out in the street, and it is tailored to the living environment and life of the street children through being set in the streets. Kulwa, a staff member responsible for this programme, described it as follows:

"This sort of education does not follow a ready-made curriculum or syllabus. Some of the elements in this type of education include listening, observation, and observing the environment and conditions in which these children live and operate. Other elements in this education package are reading and writing. As a social worker/educator for street children, I listen to the story, observe the condition, take notes on key issues, and then take a short class to discuss these observations with the children. For example, it deals with the questions, such as taking care of themselves, maintaining hygiene, and not eating randomly. Also, infom them about not sleeping in dangerous areas, for example, in places where there is loose electric wire, under heap of rubish, or under parked cars. This education is very much related to their living environment and experience." (Kulwa).

This account highlights the role of mobile education in empowering street children. It is designed to educate and train them to be aware of their surroundings and teach them how best to take care of themselves. Mobile education equips them with tips on identifying danger or anything that could potentially harm their well-being, thereby empowering them to navigate their environment more safely.

In addition to this, part of the organisation's efforts to ensure that street children receive their education involves speaking with the education authority in Dar es Salaam to allow street children to access education in public schools. In this way, the organisation assists street children and young people in obtaining public schooling in Dar es Salaam. Shija, from the organisation, explained:

"We explored ways in which street children can enter the formal education system to attend school. In partnership with the City Council's leadership, we were able to ask the Government education authority to allow the street children who desired education to be given places at some of the local public schools across the city. Therefore, some children and teenagers began to go to government schools. They go to school in the morning, and after school hours they return to us, sleep at the centre during the night-time." (Shija)

Formal schooling in public schools is essential. A proper education could enable a street child to see what pathway of higher education or career they might follow.

Another education service the organisation provides for street children is a vocational training school. Students choose a study tailored to their career interests and undergo training for two years. They can select subjects that focus on, for example, carpentry or joinery, house construction, tailoring or sewing clothes, or house painting and decoration. Lydia, a respondent who once lived on the street, gave her views on her own experiences of this type of educational service provision:

"The Dogodogo organisation financed my education at their vocational training centre. I decided to make tailoring my career because I loved it. Receiving education gave me a sense of purpose and an occupation for my life. At the end of my studies,

I did well and graduated. The organisation gave me a certificate. The organisation gave me a sewing machine as a gesture of kindness to help me to have an easy start in my tailoring career and helped me start my independent life." (Lydia).

The organisation's activities indicated in Lydia's account concerning career-oriented education mirror the emancipatory approach and transformative service of responding to the problem in Dominelli's model. Dogodogo provided an emancipatory solution to Lydia's situation. Lydia received vocational education service; this education has the possibility of emancipation as a purpose.

The emancipatory response gives power to a person by freeing the person from the shackles of social problems and discrimination and providing a person with mechanisms and skills for life that potentially give an individual power over her affairs. In this case, vocational education with an emancipation purpose engages Lydia mentally and psychologically, equipping her with relevant knowledge and skills that potentially enable her to make a fundamental difference in her life.

The organisation challenges the community's long-held negative views and actions that affect children and impede good interactions between street children and the community. Issues such as stigma, discrimination, and the deprivation of children's human rights receive attention. Shija of the managerial level described the action the organisation takes:

"The Dogodogo organisation felt the need to run an awareness programme in those schools, sensitising teachers and other people in those structures about the welfare of street children, child rights and a healthy way of embracing and dealing with street children in schools. We emphasised to them that just because a child or youth has been working and living in the streets, that does not make them less of a human being, or an unusual child or a bad human. It is the responsibility of all of us to ensure that each child in our society experiences love and good care and receives basic rights, including a good education. The need to protect street children and young people from the feelings of being unwanted, unworthy, discriminated, unwelcomed in other social groups is the key to street child progress." (Shija). The organisation's response reflects the emancipatory approach to solving social issues, an approach associated with radical social work that questions the balance of power in society and resource distribution. It identifies the oppressive nature of social relations (Dominelli 2002:13; Adams et al., 2009). Here, Dogodogo engages with the social structural bodies supposed to represent the community. Yet, these bodies are often the stumbling block to street children's well-being, development, and possible economic progress.

The organisation's support for its clients and its efforts to address the issue of street children may not fully address the underlying causes that lead children and young people to leave their homes and migrate to cities. These causes often stem from family and home environments and social structures. The organisation's services primarily focus on addressing the immediate situations that can harm and impact the well-being of children living on the streets.

The organisation prioritises providing immediate relief and long-term support to enhance the lives of children and teenagers on the streets. Their approach involves addressing the children's immediate needs and psychological well-being, while also integrating elements of the emancipatory process, such as advocating for the rights and importance of education for street children. Looking at Dominelli's model from a practical point of view, it is a valuable framework. However, the boundaries between the different types of activities are not always clear-cut. It all comes down to how the service provider conceptualises the social work task at hand. Practitioners can use this model by utilising one or more of these approaches, and in many cases, these three approaches overlap at times. Like in the Dogodogo Street Children Trust practice, where their social work tasks are more of maintenance and therapeutic form, one can see an emancipatory task as the organisation focuses on society and structure. Other structural issues appear not to be addressed by the organisation. For example, Dogodogo can work closely with law-and-order enforcement institutions, such as the police force. The police must be aware of the street children's vulnerability, rights, and social welfare and ensure that street children are not harassed or abused but protected. But as data indicates, police members are part of the problem; they relate and respond to street children in a repressive and forceful way.

8.7 Impact of Dogodogo's Activities: From a Perspective of Service Users

This part looks at the impact of the organisation's work on both clients' situations and the broader society on the ground. This reflection is based on the respondent's perception of their service experience.

Concerning this objective, the service users were asked what support was provided to them and their reflections on their service experience. Kevin, a service user, described the service he had received:

"They help us with advice, take us to receive medical treatment when we needed. They helped me when I was not well." (Kevin)

This account testifies to the organisation's actual work regarding health issues. The reports seem to give a positive impression as the individual received support relevant to his needs. The account also reveals another aspect: Dogodogo's service provision is carried out one-to-one.

Another respondent, a female service user, (Suzan), explained her experience:

"I received education for two years in tailoring, how to make clothes, mending clothes. Where I am in life at this moment is because of the organisation's effort to support me sacrificially." (Suzan)

Suzan uses the word 'sacrificially' to highlight the invaluable support she had received from Dogodogo and how much that had had a positive impact on her life.

Another respondent, a male service user who lived in the street, named Seba, described his experience of the organisation's service provision:

"I enrolled in the Dogodogo vocational training school in 2011. My studies lasted for two years. I specialised on carpentry career. In 2013 I graduated. Now I am standing on my own feet, I have my own career." (Seba)

This account and previous accounts give a positive reflection demonstrating how significant the work of Dogodogo has been in these individuals' lives. Through its vocational training school, the organisation has brought long-term positive impacts to the respondents' lives. They feel emancipated as they have gained professional skills valuable for the rest of their lives.

There are, however, some opposing opinions regarding how service users experienced the service provided. There are service users who are not so enthusiastic about the organisation's involvement with them. For example, Andrea explained.

"The organisation does not give us money directly, which can help. But, when you are sick, ill, or injured, they would take you to a hospital for treatment." (Kevin)

Andrea does acknowledge the practical support provided by the organisation but reveals that receipt of money directly from the organisation would be his preferred type of service and is of concern. This different picture might come from his individual way of understanding the concept of help. His life experience in the street may inform his perception of support.

Another respondent, Kishishi, gave this response when asked about how the organisation helps: "I have never received any support, except for advice on how to protect yourself and protect yourself from problems. They have taken me to the hospital for treatment." (Kishishi)

This response is first to deny being given anything. However, Kishishi then remembered receiving advice on looking after himself and being taken to the hospital by the organisation.

It is not easy to make sense of this mixture of feedback. On the one hand, the respondents say, "The organisation has not done anything," or "They have not given me anything, but on the other hand, they say, "They have done something".

It is worth reflecting on these varying responses. Service users seem to associate "help" with being 'given' something. This contradictory reflection may not necessarily mean that respondents do not see and appreciate other forms of services and the organisation's impact at the societal level. However, this position might be caused by the respondents' more profound awareness and focus on their pressing issues in a particular situation. Hence, when one is in crisis, "help" takes on a certain level of immediacy. The Dogodogo Street Children Trust provides vital medical services, including first aid and hospital visits, for street children. They also contribute to the education of these children, with the goal of enhancing their employability and improving their chances of finding sustainable livelihoods. Users of these services have reported positive outcomes. Additionally, the organisation actively raises awareness about the hardships faced by street children and advocates for their rights. However, there are prevalent misconceptions about street children that need to be addressed within the broader community. Efforts are required to dispel these misconceptions at the family, community, and societal levels. It is also crucial to help street children understand how their actions can lead to positive long-term outcomes in their lives.

In order to solve the street children phenomenon, governments and other vital social institutions that represent people in society must be concerned and genuinely dedicate their efforts toward intervening in the problems children face at the earliest stage possible. Collective efforts to understand what causes children to take up street life will provide a better starting point for bringing genuine solutions. The community and the established social structures and institutions must represent and defend all citizens' welfare, including the vulnerable children living on the streets.

9 Case Study 3: SMGEO

The existence of gender inequality and discrimination against certain social groups is an obstacle to human development in society, as the UNDP-Human Development Report (2019) highlighted:

"Inequalities in human development hurt societies and weaken social cohesion and people's trust in government, institutions, and each other. They hurt economies, wastefully preventing people from reaching their full potential at work and in life. They make it harder for political decisions to reflect the aspirations of the whole society, as the few pulling ahead flex their power to shape decisions primarily in their interests."(UNDP-Human Development Report, 2019:1).

However, inequality is the reality for certain social groups of people in Tanzania, as this research has found. In this society, women still experience discrimination at domestic and structural levels, and some suffer abuse in their domestic setting. The study examined the impact of gender inequality on women's life experiences.

This study also involved people with disabilities, another social group in society whose daily social life experience is marked by discrimination and mistreatment domestically and in the public sphere.

The original thesis has centred on three case studies. This chapter looks at the work of the Social Mainstreaming for Gender Equality Organisation (SMGEO). SMGEO, a local non-governmental welfare organisation, addresses gender-based inequality issues that impact women's social well-being and their experience of life in society. Additionally, this organisation is involved with disabled people.

The organisation's work is evident in the Morogoro region, where the office headquarters is located. I conducted this research in

Chamwino, a suburb area of the Morogoro District, where the organisation operates. The study was interested in learning how SMGEO, as a local non-governmental welfare organisation, addresses the problems associated with gender-based inequality that impact women's life experiences and social well-being. Additionally, the study wanted to find out how this organisation is helping people with disabilities affected by discriminatory social situations in their community.

Before going further with the discussion, let me clarify why the organisation addresses the social concerns of people with disabilities. Gender inequality and discrimination are social phenomena naturally associated with harmful actions and attitudes towards women at a domestic and social level. However, asserting that inequality and discrimination happen only to female members of society does not truly reflect the reality of life in all cultures globally. In some cultures, such as Tanzania, other social groups experience the negative impacts of the attitudes and actions that stem from social and cultural discriminatory attitudes.

The name "Social Mainstreaming Gender Equality Organisation (SMGEO)" gives the impression that this organisation focuses on women's social welfare needs, and for the most part, this understanding is correct. However, due to the realisation that other social groups aside from women also experience discrimination in Tanzanian society, this organisation began to direct their work towards these groups. Disabled people are another social group whose experience of life and meeting their social welfare needs are hampered by an unequal and discriminatory culture. This reality may explain why SMGEO embraced people with disabilities as a disadvantaged social group who need to be supported and defended in society.

This research aims to understand how the organisation helps its clients and its impact on the ground and the service users' concerns. Therefore, the case study involved those with experience providing service and receiving social assistance from this organisation.

During the research, I conducted a series of semi-structured, one-to-one interviews to understand the social problems and the social service provision present from both the service providers and service users linked to SMGEO. Hence, this chapter presents and discusses the data findings related to this case study in the following order:

- The first part discusses contextual information regarding gender inequality and the impact of discrimination against women and discrimination against people with disabilities in Tanzanian society. This part is divided into two segments: (i) gender inequality and its effects on women's lives, (ii) inequality and discrimination and the impact of this on the lives and well-being of people with disabilities.

- The second part explains the origins and formation of the Social Mainstreaming for Gender Equality Organisation (SMGEO), the organisation's structure, and the resources upon which it relies.

- The third part discusses the main problems and needs the organisation seeks to address. This part is divided into three segments: (i) problems affecting women's social well-being and development, (ii) how the organisation addresses these problems, and (iii) viewpoints of female service users regarding the organisation's impact on their situations.

- The fourth part discusses problems affecting the social well-being of the disabled. This part is divided into three sections: (i) what are the issues affecting the social well-being and functioning of the disabled, (ii) how the SMGEO addresses these problems, and (iii) what do people say about their experience of service?

9.1 Contextual Information about Gender Inequality and Discrimination

The end of the twentieth and the beginning of the twenty-first century witnessed a global effort to end inequalities and discrimination based on differences such as sex, ethnic origin, economic status, and political ideology. Human rights activists and oppressed groups have placed these issues on the front pages of the media. As a result, research on women's roles in social, economic, and political progress worldwide reveals their positive impact. It stresses the need to maintain gender equality and social and economic equity in society (Matotay, 2014). This research uses Therborn's description of inequality:
"Inequality is a violation of human dignity: it is a denial of the possibility for everybody's human capabilities to develop. It takes many forms, and it has many effects: premature death, ill health, humiliation, subjection, discrimination, exclusion from knowledge or of mainstream social life, poverty, powerlessness, stress, insecurity, anxiety, lack of self-confidence and pride in oneself, and exclusion from opportunities and life chances. Inequality, then, is not just about the size of wallets; it is a socio-cultural order, which reduces our capabilities to function as human being." (Therborn, 2013:15)
Studies show the impact of gender inequality on women's experience of life and their functioning in Tanzanian society. The following section expounds upon this aspect in more detail.

9.1.1 Gender Inequality and Discrimination of Women

Gender inequality is an issue of great concern in Tanzania. In Tanzanian culture, women and girls receive unequal or disadvantageous treatment compared to men. Literature indicates a range of efforts, including conferences on women's rights and gender equality at international and African regional levels, such as Beijing 1995, the New York summit in March 2005, and the Maputo Protocol on the Rights of Women in Africa 2003 and the Istanbul Convention 2014. Despite these mentioned conferences, many voices from Africa and Tanzania lament the prevalence of domestic violence, widespread poverty, and various forms of discrimination directed against women and girls (Mutume, 2011).

The prevalence of inequality in society goes against the first article of The Declaration of Human Rights. This article states that 'all human beings are born free and enjoy equal rights. They are embedded with logical consciousness to act towards each other in their unity of purpose,' United Nations: Universal Declaration of Human Rights (Article I).

Why do women and girls experience discrimination and subjection in Tanzanian culture? One major factor that underpins these discriminatory tendencies is that the root cause of women's oppression in African societies is found in long-held customs and traditions (Olatunji, 2013). Various studies observed that most of these customs and traditions are patriarchal in their orientation. In patriarchal societies such as Tanzania, women are viewed as inferior, and so they face discrimination in accessing various opportunities, regardless of their experience and qualifications (Mbepera, 2015; Bhalalusesa and Mboya, 2003).

Nevertheless, other studies say that the resilience of gender inequality may be in part due to stereotypes, which portray women and men as innately different and unequal. Such stereotypes may create interactional processes that help maintain inequality (Ridgeway et al., 2004; Shafer and Malhotra, 2011). However, I argue that stereotypes do not exist independently of the customs and traditions present in communities. Stereotypes are a manifestation profoundly embedded within cultural perspectives, the patriarchal system, and practices that generally impact women's social status and social well-being. These observations stress that internal attitudes can have significant external impacts on society-wide levels of inequality and public policies. Indeed, any effort to address gender inequality must consider the customs and traditions underpinning social living reality, as these are often the root cause of inequality and discrimination. Shafer and Malhotra (2011:209) suggested that "changing beliefs about the appropriate roles of women and men in social structures, such as marriage, family, and the workplace, may therefore be one of the keys to promoting gender equality."

The Gender-Related Development Index (GDI) and the Gender Empowerment Measure (GEM) are structured social measures that use specified gender indicators to understand women's social situation. Their goal is to reveal how a country is performing in the case of addressing gender inequality and its commitments to gender equality and sustainable development. The Gender Empowerment Measure considers various aspects relating to women's progress. It focuses on education and economic aspects of women's empowerment and gender equality (Klasen and Schüler, 2011). Other indices, such as the Women, Peace, and Security Index, ranks countries based on the additional dimensions of social inclusion, justice, and security (Klugman et al., 2017). However, other salient domains of women's empowerment must also be considered; some of these domains include women's self-reported human, social, and economic resources for empowerment (Miedema et al., 2018). Other aspects to be considered are the attitudinal and behavioural evidence of empowerment, such as women's attitudes about gender and violence against women, freedom of movement, and domestic, sexual, and reproductive decision-making (Mistry, Galal and Lu, 2009; Yount et al., 2016).

Gender equality indicators at the national level reflect structural equality and inequalities (such as policy commitment, legal frameworks, and national legislation). They may measure manifestations of gender inequalities (such as a lower retention rate of girls in education compared to boys or the prevalence of violence against women), or they could refer to the impact of a lack of government provision of essential services on both women and men (Grown et al., 2005).

As a country, Tanzania exhibits a lower Gender-Related Development Index (GDI). Both government and society have not yet addressed and demonstrated gender equality within the social, cultural, political, and economic spheres. Some of the issues facing women in Tanzania include access to education, resource ownership, freedom of expression, participation in decision-making at the domestic and social level, gender-based violence, participation in economic production, and personal development. (The United Republic of Tanzania-National Five Years Developmental Plan 2016; Human Development Trust 2011; Idris, 2018).

The government believes that gender equality has a significant role in shaping society and individuals' lives. However, its efforts to bring about gender equality have been slow. One area in which change can be observed is in the Tanzanian parliament, where there has been an increase in female representatives. Currently, the country has a female president; however, the general living reality for most women across the country, particularly in disadvantaged areas, is of enduring problems. Likewise, Idris (2018) examined factors that cause women to experience economic inequality and exclusion from economic progress in society, observing that women in this culture are often time-poor, spending more time on household chores than men. They have primary responsibility for the strenuous and time-consuming job of water collection and fuel (firewood) collection tasks, leaving limited time and opportunities to engage in productive (as in paid) work. Idris (2018:2), elaborated 'unpaid care work/household chores are seen as predominantly female activities. This perception and cultural norms and religious values, which can impose restrictions on women's interactions in wider society, hamper women's engagement in productive (paid) work' (2018:2).

Studies on gender inequality stress the importance of female empowerment. Indeed, the idea of women's empowerment holds relevancy and contributes insights that shed light upon the situations women face and potential solutions to inequality and the mistreatment of women. Empowering women in various areas is an indicator of social change and a priority for sustainable development goals (Miedema et al., 2018).

The concept of female empowerment is understood to be multi-dimensional (Agarwala and Lynch, 2006). Kabeer (1999:436) construes women's empowerment as "the process through which individuals attain the ability to make choices under conditions in which choice was previously denied." The dimensions of female empowerment include resources for empowerment, agency, or the ability to make choices, including concerning one's gendered attitudes and beliefs, achievements in the political, economic, social, and cultural realms, and the intergenerational transmission of resources and opportunities (Moghadam and Senftova, 2005; Kabeer, 2011; Cornwall, 2016; Eger, Miller and Scarles, 2018). Women's empowerment is contingent on social transformation across these interrelated domains (Kabeer, 2005). Female empowerment is an individual and a collective process (Eger et al., 2018; Kabeer, 2011) and involves claims on new resources and control over beliefs, values, and attitudes (Cornwall, 2016).

Studies on female empowerment have resulted in the theory-based validation of women's empowerment measures. In attempting to gain information about the implementation of the concept of female empowerment in a particular culture or country, researchers have tended to focus on three interrelated domains of female empowerment measured as in the DHS (Demographic and Health Surveys): (1) access to assets and enabling resources, (2) the ability to exercise choice in the household (instrumental agency, or power to), and (3) the expression of equitable gender beliefs and attitudes (intrinsic agency, or power within) (Cornwall, 2016; Kabeer, 1999; Kishor, 2000).

Indeed, these three domains represent areas where women have and are disadvantaged.

For example, on the point of 'enabling resources', Kabeer (1999) considers enabling resources the precondition of empowerment. Similarly, Kishor (2000) stresses that positive economic, social, and human resources and conditions can enhance women's potential to exercise instrumental agency. Other studies consider enabling resources from the perspective of women's schooling attainment. They stress that women's schooling attainment, the acquisition of economic resources, and a later age at pivotal life events (for marriage and childbirth) predict greater instrumental and intrinsic agency and wellbeing (Yount, Crandall and Cheong, 2018). Equally, others see schooling as enhancing women's cognitive abilities (Kabeer, 2005), which, in turn, is associated with greater wellbeing (Carlson et al., 2015; Pratley, 2016; Rieger and Trommlerová, 2016).

On the intrinsic and instrumental agency point, Kabeer (2005) explained that agency is a woman's ability to make choices about her life under conditions when an option exists. The agency can be instrumental or intrinsic. The instrumental agency is often measured as women's ability to make household and family-level decisions (Becker et al. 2006; Gammage et al. 2016). This aspect is also about women's political and community participation (Moghadam and Senftova, 2005) and freedom of movement (Ghuman et al., 2006; Yount et al., 2016). Measuring women's participation in family decision-making is a time-invariant indicator of women's agency (Cheong et al., 2017). Additionally, Gammage et al. (2016) also see the voice of women and their ability to express beliefs that may run counter to dominant norms as essential elements of women exercising their agency.

Realising female empowerment in East Africa and Tanzania encounter specific contextual challenges. The implementation of the empowerment of women is conceptualised and mainly operationalised in classic patriarchal settings (Kabeer, 2011; Kishor 2000; Santhya et al., 2010; Yount et al. 2016). Entrenched traditions, customs, and cultural practices emanating from a patriarchal framework within African settings create conditions for the limitation of female empowerment. Female empowerment is measured mainly in the family and household context (Kishor, 2000; Mason and Smith, 2003; Yount, 2005).

In patriarchal settings, where women occupy a lower social status than men, the distribution of power within a household systematically favours men (Kandiyoti, 1988). Compared to classically patriarchal settings, for example, in South Asia and the Middle East, women in East and sub-Saharan African countries may hold greater autonomy, particularly in the operation of economic decision-making, due to women's roles in community and household economic activities (Dolan, 2001; Larsen and Hollos, 2003). At the same time, women often control low-revenue commodities (Njuki et al., 2011). Asset differentials reflect gender power relations and the gendered nature of household cooperation among agricultural communities (Njuki et al., 2011). The processes of female empowerment in Africa must consider these cultural conditions. However, it is an under-researched area with much of the literature on the empowerment of women focusing on South and South-east Asia (Schuler et al., 1996; Kabeer, 2011), with some studies conducted in the Middle East (Kishor, 2000; Yount, 2005; Yount et al., 2016).

Women's control over household assets and income increases household nutrition among specific pastoral communities in Tanzania. In general, social life in Tanzania is characterised by patriarchy. Interregional variation of gender systems may moderate women's strategies to negotiate and attain power in Tanzania and East Africa (Mason and Smith, 2003). The Tanzanian society is a large one and comprises more than 125 ethnic tribes characterised by different cultural traditions, customs, and practices. The question of gender inequality and women may consider factors specific to the region in which a tribe is situated and, at the same time, consider how the situation may differ in the other areas and tribe groups. Likewise, the United States Agency for International Development (USAID) Health Policy Initiative Task Order 1 (2008) revealed how gender roles and norms disadvantage girls in their progression and independence compared to boys in Tanzania. They reported that focus group participants affirmed that boys' education tends to be valued more than girls, especially in low-income families. Girls may be taken out of school to assist with domestic responsibilities or marry. The quote below illustrates this observation:

"Girls in the family, we have been placed as workers. Therefore, a girl, even if she goes to school and gets more knowledge, the parents believe that if she continues, she will be a mother of a house, she will get pregnant… and there will be great loss. Therefore, the parents do not see the importance of continuing the education of girls to go farther to help their future lives. Each parent thinks their girls will go and get pregnant and have a baby, that is it." (Adolescent females focus group participant-USAID | Health Policy Initiative Task Order 1. 2008:8)

Measures at the policy level show that the United Republic of Tanzania (URT) constitution protects the equality and rights of every person (Ministry of Community Development, Women Affairs and Children, 1992). Tanzania has policies and acts geared towards promoting gender equality in leadership roles, including the Women's Gender Policy of 2002, the Public Service Commission (on all-sector gender equality), and the National Employment Promotion Service Act of 1999. Tanzania has also adopted the Convention on the Elimination of all Forms of Discrimination Against Women (Muro, 2003) and the Beijing Platform for Action 1995 (United Nations, 1995), whose objective is to increase women's participation in decision-making by 30% (Muro, 2003). However, as the above observations indicate, women in Tanzanian society face discrimination and mistreatment at domestic and social levels. They are often denied opportunities that would enable their personal and social progression.

Another social group experiencing social discrimination that impacts their welfare needs in Tanzanian society is people with disabilities. The following section explains this matter in more detail.

9.1.2 *Discrimination against the disabled People*

The United Nations Convention on the Rights of Persons with Disabilities (UNCRPD), as an international treaty, identifies the rights of people with disabilities and stipulates that governments must promote, protect, and ensure that these rights are realised. Studies on disabilities have highlighted the potential effects of a disability on a person, including the loss of their freedom and independence, practical problems—transport, choice of activities, accessing buildings—and frustration and anger at having to rely on other people (Tavares, 2011). The Tanzania Disability Survey Report 2008 acknowledges that disabled people are among the most vulnerable groups in society. It adds that the disabled in this culture are often uneducated, frequently unemployed or underemployed, and poor, especially women, young people, and those living in rural areas (National Bureau of Statistics, 2008; Sida, 2015). Other significant challenges facing people with disabilities in Tanzania are access to transport and information; negative attitudes at home, school, and work; inaccessibility of public services or premises; poverty; and inadequate representation (Tanzania Disability Survey Report, 2008). In Tanzania, there has been a long-term effort to ensure that everyone is valued equally, with and without disabilities. The Government has legally enacted different documents to recognise the rights of people with disabilities. In terms of international instruments, these steps include signing and ratifying (in 2009) the United Nations Convention on the Rights of Persons with Disabilities (CRPD) and the optional protocol, the first international, legally binding treaty aimed at protecting the human rights of disabled people (Aldersey, 2012).

The Tanzanian Government has also signed and ratified the UN Convention on the Child's Rights, the African Charter on Human and People's Rights, and the Convention on the Elimination of All Forms of Discrimination against Women. All these treaties reference protecting the rights of the disabled, fair treatment, appropriate care, inclusion, and full participation in society. Tanzania is also committed to the East African Policy on People with disabilities (2012), which outlines joint policy commitments in line with the CRPD and country-level recommendations (Sida, 2015). The 1977 Constitution and its amendments recognise the rights of persons with disabilities and prohibit all forms of discrimination against them. The new Constitution adopted in 2015 has some disability-specific provisions (URT Constitution 1977:44) which express explicitly that a person with disabilities has the right to:

- be respected, recognised, and treated in a way which does not lower a person's dignity;
- an education through specialised equipment and to participate in social affairs.
- have the infrastructure and an environment which allows an individual to go wherever they please, use transport facilities, and acquire information.
- use sign languages and written language with the aid of special machines or other appropriate methods.
- learn with persons without disabilities; and
- get a job and contest leadership posts in various sectors.
- The country's authority shall specify the procedure for enabling disabled people to participate in representative activities (United Republic of Tanzania, Constitution, 1977).

In addition to this, there exists the Persons with Disabilities Act of 2010 of Tanzania, which incriminates all forms of discrimination and mistreatment against the disabled while at the same time providing for the rights and duties of the same (Uromi & Mazagwa, 2014). Another structure that exists to promote the welfare and rights of people with disabilities in Tanzania is the Federation of Disabled People's Organisation (FDPO), in Kiswahili, known as Shirika la Vyama vya Watu wenye ulemavu Tanzania (SHIVYAWATA) (Aldersey, 2012).

While having these legislative laws, acts, and policy provisions in place are something to be appreciated, they remain statements. Their intended impacts on the living situation of disabled people in the community are not yet visible. More work needs to be done by the Government and its representative bodies to implement and realise changes, as promised in these policy and legislative documents at the grassroots, community, and national levels.

One of the biggest challenges that the disabled face is stigma. Research has shown that stigmatisation still exists on a large scale and leads to exclusion, continued poverty, and a poor standard of life (Munyi, 2012; Koszela, 2013). People with disabilities in Tanzania face attitudinal barriers, including prejudice, low expectations, and even fear. Negative attitudes about disability impact all aspects of the lives of people with disabilities, including their ability to access education, participate in work, make decisions, live where and with whom they choose, and move about freely within the community (Munyi, 2012). This abuse and discrimination happen at both the domestic and community level. One person with a disability shared her opinion as to why mistreatment and the denial of equal rights happen to the disabled in Tanzanian society:

"I think it is mostly due to the negative attitude attached to people with disabilities. Most people do not respect us as people who deserve to be treated with dignity. When something happens to a disabled person, it is not taken as seriously as when something happens to a nondisabled person. This is not only by the community, even the police, the hospitals, the schools, the churches, parents, everybody." (Mary)

The question that lingers is why discrimination and stigma surrounding disabilities still exist in African society. Studies on this matter attribute this problem to misconceptions. Lack of awareness or knowledge is one reason the negative attitudes manifest as explicit vilification or direct or indirect discrimination (AbleChildAfrica, 2013; Stone-MacDonald and Butera, 2014). AbleChildAfrica (2013) observed that stigma against children with disabilities arises for various reasons in sub-Saharan Africa and Tanzania. One reason is a lack of information regarding what causes disabilities and what a child with a disability can achieve. Indeed, not being aware of how physical disability occurs and thus having an incorrect mindset leads people to come to the wrong conclusions. Mostert (2016:9) observed that misconceptions about the cause of disabilities often result from cultural or religious beliefs. Disability is often blamed on the misdeeds of ancestors or parents, the transgressions of the person with disabilities, or supernatural forces such as demons, spirits, witchcraft, or punishment from God (Mostert, 2016:9). In a circumstance where a baby is born with disabilities, often the blame is placed on the mother for having a child with a disability, but the impairments can be caused by poor maternal health or a lack of prenatal services during pregnancy (AbleChildAfrica, 2013; Uromi and Mazagwa, 2014). Besides, in some families and communities, disabled children are hidden away because of the stigmas placed on them and the embarrassment or harassment that the mother may encounter. Hence, societies have minimal experience and few examples of what children with disabilities can accomplish, leading them to assume that they are incapable and should not be included in daily life (AbleChildAfrica, 2013).

Disabled people may face significant challenges in overcoming the negative views held by the community and society, making it difficult for them to achieve self-acceptance and a sense of pride in their lives. The stigmatisation of people with disabilities can lead to exclusion from society and from developmental programmes that could help improve a person's quality of life and future. Stone-MacDonald and Butera (2014:6) explained that: "Inequalities not only lead to their exclusion… but combined with the general absence of social protection measures, almost unavoidably lead persons with disabilities (and their families) to situations of poverty and extreme poverty, which can even result in a risk to their lives."

The discussion in this section indicates the social status of women and people with disabilities in Tanzanian society. It reveals the harmful impact that inequality has on the reality of life for women, girls, and the disabled. Inequalities create many barriers, including physical and institutional communicational obstacles and attitudinal barriers. These barriers often lead to women and disabled people being invisible and considered to lack the ability to participate in society and decision-making processes.

At the grassroots level, local non-governmental organisations address gender inequality, welfare, and the rights of disabled people in Tanzania. One of the organisations involved in this research is the Social Mainstreaming for Gender Equality Organisation (SMGEO). This organisation is based in Morogoro and works around the Morogoro, Dodoma, and Tabora regions. The researcher was interested to learn what issues this organisation tackles.

The next section looks at the origins and formation of the Social Mainstreaming for Gender Equality Organisation (SMGEO). It explains when and why this organisation was formed.

9.2 Origins and Formation of SMGEO

SMGEO is a non-governmental organisation working at a national level in mainland Tanzania. It was established on 10th August 2015 and received permission from the United Republic of Tanzania to carry out its tasks under the Ministry of Community Development, Gender, and Children (MCDGC). The emergence of SMGEO was rooted in evidence-based research about the prevalence of social inequality in Tanzanian society.

SMGEO believes that gender discrimination and imbalance are challenges that jeopardise society's stability and well-being for the present and future generations. Thus, SMGEO, as a non-profit organisation, attempts to restore and promote the equal integration of men, women, and disadvantaged groups in developing projects that benefit the community. SMGEO was formed to deal with the present socio-economic problems in different areas in Tanzania. However, currently, its work focuses more on the Morogoro-Chamwino community area, where its main office is located. It aims to achieve its goals by understanding the issues, sharing them, and solving them through free discussion in different projects.

SMGEO's mission is to promote gender equality and freedom effectively and efficiently from discrimination and segregation for all people (male and female) in society in general. The purpose of SMGEO is:

- to provide teaching and information that promotes the equal integration of both men and women as well as disadvantaged groups, including people with impaired vision, physical disability, albinism, and deaf people, in the process of development.
- to help society and individuals willing to create equal opportunities in ownership, access, and control.
- to provide information that reveals the current situation surrounding gender issues, and the impact that this has on society.

- to propagate ideas that promote gender relations within the community.
- to provide necessary knowledge regarding gender matters within society. (SMGEO Profile Information October 2018,)

During an interview, James, a male respondent from the managerial level, explained how this organisation started, saying:

"This organisation was started in 2015 by Mr Eric Kuhoga. Mr Kuhoga received education in gender-related issues and social development from the university. Through his education, Eric saw a need to set up an organisation that would address gender inequality and women's mistreatment problems in our society, which is apparent at all levels of our society. The Chamwino community is a place where gender inequality is visible." (James)

Another respondent, Matthias, from the managerial level, described the formation of the organisation in these words:

"SMGEO is a local organisation established to address the attitudes, traditions, and cultures that oppress women, girls, people with disabilities, and those with special needs. We felt it was important to educate communities about gender equality, women's rights, and disabled human rights. Women, as human beings, have the potential to bring about social and economic development." (Matthias)

SMGEO operates in the Chamwino district in eastern Tanzania, west of Dar es Salaam. Chamwino is three kilometres from the city and is distinguished from the Morogoro inner-city area. It seems to have been built without proper planning, and its residential outlook appears disorganised. Its proximity to the Morogoro city centre attracts many people looking for employment from the surrounding villages, who come and set up some forms of shelter, including mud houses.

Some people who live in the area commute back and forth for work in the city centre. Previous social studies about the Morogoro-Chamwino area estimated its population to be around 100,000

(Lyimo-Macha et al., 2002), although figures on the current total were unavailable. When visiting the organisation, I saw a heavily congested area bustling with people at every angle. There were primary schools, a health dispensary centre, and various small businesses, shops, and agricultural activities. It was confirmed during the interviews that poverty is widespread, there are not many job opportunities in this area, and many of the residents are unemployed.

Neither the provincial nor the local government seems to be doing enough to help the inhabitants of this area improve their social and economic conditions. According to SMGEO, most families in the area are headed by single mothers as many families are abandoned by men, with social problems and poverty ripping families apart. This organisation is a voluntary local social welfare organisation engaging in activities relevant to social work. I interviewed a total number of twenty participants. The identities of the respondents who participated in this investigation are pseudo-anonymised to protect their identity. I translated the respondents' answers into English from the audio recordings, which were made during the interviews undertaken in the Kiswahili language.

According to their constitution, the organisational structure of SMGEO follows this order:
- Members/General Assembly
- The Board of Directors
- The Executive Committee

The General Assembly meets at least once a year with a plan set according to the Constitution. Voting on some issues is part of the assembly. Also, this general assembly determines the Board of Directors. The organisation has few employees and relies heavily on volunteers to fulfil its mission. This dependency on volunteers raises questions of commitment, reliability, and how realistic an organisation can accomplish its objectives by relying mainly on honorary members and voluntary workers. In an official document, SMGEO indicates having 9–26 Field Worker Volunteers working part-time. This is quite a large range. However, during the period in which this research took place, the researcher witnessed five individuals representing the organisation at the managerial level and three field workers.

Another vital aspect to consider concerning the organisation's functioning is its source of resources and funds. The organisation needs resources and funds to function and carry out its social service mandate. Support comes from the following sources:

- Contributions from members statutory registration fees
- Fundraising events
- Donation and grants
- Charitable individuals
- Compulsory annual SMGEO membership contributions as may be determined.

Let me elaborate more on the compulsory annual SMGEO membership contributions as a finance source of the organisation. To become a member, a person needs to pay an initial 100,000 TSH (equivalent to approximately £32) or $550 if a non-Tanzanian. Then, the annual fee for members is 50,000 TSH (equal to about £16). Any member can pay more if they wish to.

The organisation invites those who wish to undertake a research study about the organisation's work; however, they must pay a fee to the organisation. Thus, I paid TSH 100,000 before prior to my involvement studying the work of the organisation. The organisation stipulates that:

"Anyone who wants to volunteer as part of their training or field study in the organisation should contribute TSHs 100,000 for Tanzanians while USD 550 for non-Tanzanians. Those basic needs such as accommodation and meals shall be their own cost during training time. Still, the organisation will support volunteers to meet their targeted goal where necessary." (Constitution of Social Mainstreaming for Gender Equality Organisation (SMGEO)2015:6). The organisation put in place a members' statutory registration fee to ensure some inflow of funds for its operation. The employees are mandated to pay TSH 50,000 annually as a statutory registration fee. However, during my time with the organisation, the leadership made it apparent that this type of fund does not come in regularly as it is supposed due to the financial difficulties that individual workers have. Having no steady inflow of finance means there will always be a deficit in the organisation's budget for its program. Elaborating further on the issue of staff contributions, Matthias, chairman of the organisation, said:

"Employees are also members of the organisation. The decision and order of employees to contribute was established and accepted as an appropriate procedure by the organisation practically based on the actual economic and financial situation. Also, the decision considered the broader environment around us, socially and economically. So, this is an organisational process. Our organisation, for the most part, is almost exclusively a volunteer; the membership form explains it. Employees donate these donations to develop the organisation only. But if a person fails to give because he is not in good financial condition, he is not obliged to contribute, there is no problem, he is not bothered, but the day he gets it he will bring it. The organisation is considering alternative projects, various projects that will generate income for its support and community service projects." (Matthias, April 30th, 2021).

What this quote reveals about the organisation's finances is essential because it shows the constraints under which it operates, which have implications for its overall strategy. This response also helps to explain why the organisation might struggle to offer the kinds of material assistance for which its 'clients' might be hoping.

9.3 Gender inequality and discrimination and the way it affects women's social well-being and experience of life

In an interview, a respondent, James of managerial level, described some of the cases they deal with in the organisation: "We have received female clients complaining about the lack of support, neglect and abuse from their husbands. For example, one woman, a mother of three children, came to us. She told us she is among those women who received a loan for a vegetable business. Still, her husband has made it difficult for her to set up a business, and sadly, he has taken the money that was meant for the vegetable business, claiming that he can use it on an important matter. She is frustrated by her husband's behaviour, who has stopped her from using the loan for her vegetable business. She doesn't know what her husband has done with the money." (James)

This account illustrates the challenges faced by a woman who experiences discrimination and is denied her basic rights to earn a living by her spouse. James also highlights the instances of domestic abuse that women encounter when they seek assistance. What becomes evident here is the power dynamics that directly affect the economic well-being of women. This issue of power, predominantly associated with decision-making, is firmly rooted in a patriarchal culture characterised by patronising and devaluing attitudes towards women in their homes. Additionally, patriarchal culture's pervasiveness means that this problem experienced by females stems from within society. The unhelpful traditions and customs dictate and direct the social and interpersonal relations and functioning of men and women in society. Studies on female empowerment in the developing world highlight the challenges women who desire to run small businesses face. Access to finance is just one of the female entrepreneurs' many challenges (Kuschel et al., 2017). Other barriers stem from deep-rooted socio-cultural values and strong family orientations that tend to influence women's choices (Ituma and Simpson, 2009; Cabrera and Mauricio, 2017).

In an interview, a respondent, James, who represents the managerial level, stated:

"Gender inequality is a phenomenon whereby a person is discriminated against based on gender. In our context, women are the most discriminated against, and in some situations, they even experience violence, bullying and mistreatment." (James)

James outlines two key issues here. One of them lies in the domestic abuse category, which has an immediate impact on women's mental, psychological, and physical well-being. The other one is gender inequality. Both issues seem to stem from the general social-cultural discriminatory mindset of society.

Another respondent, a female social worker, Janet, described the problems affecting women's well-being and functioning in the community:

"In Morogoro's community, women have no say and no power, and their voices are squashed continuously both at domestic settings and social levels. There have been some incidents where a woman is domestically abused, intimidated, or suppressed by a husband or a male colleague. Here at our office, we have had women come to report abuse, a husband taking all the money for his drinking habit and leaving his wife nothing, and yet she is supposed to be caring for the children. When she has dared to question him, the only reply consists of beatings and insulting words." (Janet)

Janet's account describes the general social context. There is a culture of abuse and the oppression of women's rights at domestic and societal levels. The husband's behaviour in this story indicates the influence of the patriarchal culture. One of its characteristics is the undervaluing of women. It is a culture that does not seem to regard women as entitled to equal rights. This account also indicates that the woman is suffering and unable to care for the children due to a lack of money. It is almost a paradox: on the one hand, women are suppressed and restricted in decision-making, and on the other hand, they are expected to care for the family when they are denied their right to make a livelihood.

A female respondent, Rahel, a service user, described the difficult situation she experienced domestically:

"There was a time when I got the opportunity to go into management and leadership training. The problem came when I was assigned to teach a women's seminar in another place, away from home, to teach other women about what I had learned. The idea of me going to conduct a women's seminar away from my home area was a big problem for my husband. My husband disagreed despite explaining how important participating in the seminar was to us as a family. He stopped me, forcing me to stay home, but I decided to go because I felt my education would help many other women and my progress... When I returned, the situation got worse in my home. I received harsh, insulting remarks from my husband. He decided that I should never go to teaching seminars again. He did not have any underlying reasons to stop me, but oppression tended to see the woman as a mere passive instrument and follower of a husband. So, I often get in touch with women here in this area. I desire to know what I know, and I would like others to know too." (Rahel)

Rahel's narrative reveals how male control suppresses women's freedom and affects women's rights, status, and social progress. This observation indicates how women are denied the power and liberty in decision making, significantly when it involves their progress. Rahel's actions show an attitude of someone determined not to give in, who tries to stand up to her husband's oppressive behaviour and takes bold effort to accomplish what she sees to be of benefit for herself and her family without her husband's consent.

9.4 How does SMGEO address gender-based problems and support women victims of discrimination and domestic abuse?

The organisation offers counselling to help women who are victims of gender-based violence, domestic abuse, and discrimination. It works with clients to understand their situation and provide options to support them. This procedure featured in James' response in an interview:

"When such a case comes to us, we listen to the client. We, together with the client, seek a way forward. If the client has been subjected to a life-threatening experience, we then would advise to take her to the police and follow legal advice, the legal pathway to secure justice." (James)

James' account indicates how the organisation provides options appropriate to the problem described. In the case of assisting the victims of social and domestic abuse, the involvement of the police and the legal system is the correct course of action. The organisation listens to female victims of domestic abuse and journeys with them throughout the recovery and acquisition of justice. One of Dominelli's models, this therapeutic approach, focuses on the individual situation and emphasises the need to provide the individual with skills. Giving someone skills as a means for recovery is also emancipatory.

To address the issue of making a livelihood to avert poverty and lack of finances and resources and improve women's progress and living standards, SMGEO undertakes some activities, including helping female clients interested in starting a small business by organising business training workshops. A respondent, a female social worker named Janet, described this service:

"Many female clients are interested in starting a small business, so they come to us looking for ways to get a loan and start a business. We, as an organisation, organise entrepreneurship education. We look for the right facilitator to provide empowering women seminars." (Janet)

Janet's account indicates that the organisation facilitates entrepreneurship workshops to equip women with the knowledge and skills to start small businesses in their communities. This essential training seems vital for women to grasp the idea of business and gain enough understanding to boost their confidence. Again, the organisation's activities in response to their client's situations reflect the therapeutic approach. Regarding Janet's quote, Janet uses the phrase "empowering women seminar" to describe the activity. I want to develop the concept of empowering women further.

Studies on women's empowerment provide insights into what the word 'empowerment' means in this context. Accordingly, women's empowerment emphasises their participation, for example, in political structures, informal decision-making, and the ability of female members of society to obtain an income, enabling their participation in social and economic decision-making (Mosedale, 2005; Aminur, 2013). Equally, Gupta et al. (2006) explained that women's empowerment is necessary for the very development of a society since it enhances both the quality and the quantity of human resources available for development. Another perspective construes empowerment to mean accepting and allowing people (women) who are outside of decision-making processes into it. Others consider women's empowerment (or female empowerment) to mean accepting women's viewpoints or making an effort to seek them, raising the status of women through education, awareness, literacy, and training (Bayeh, 2016:38).

The women's empowerment agenda may be focused solely on facilitating the realisation of women's potential and their contribution to society's social, political, and economic development. On the other hand, the emancipatory response to a problem delves deeper into unravelling the social structural root causes of the social issues that affect individuals' well-being and functioning in society. Nevertheless, there are connections between women's empowerment and the emancipatory response to social problems. As the few studies cited here show, in some way and to some degree, the empowerment of women is an emancipatory issue as it addresses the factors that keep women in poverty and deprive them of freedom and equal access to social and economic opportunities in Tanzanian society.

The organisation also endeavours to educate various social groups in the community on the impact of gender inequality and the culture of discrimination on a woman's life experience. A respondent, James, in an interview, explained:

"The organisation involves educating the various groups in our community, such as women's group (women forum), seminars attended by men only, and seminars attended by both men and women. Also, the organisation carries out workshops in primary schools and secondary schools." (James).

James's account indicates the organisation's effort to change the cultural mindset and held attitudes that perpetuate discriminatory behaviour against women must involve the various people that make up society.

Asked why SMGEO decided to carry awareness seminars to schools, James, a respondent at the managerial level, replied: "We felt that without engaging with both primary and secondary schools, the realisation of a society characterised by gender equality would be a distant dream in our community. The future progress of our society depends on the girls and boys who are currently in schools. Suppose they are well educated on these issues. In that case, they may avoid and challenge the wrongly held traditions about the place of men and women in society and the roles woman and man potentially fulfil and create a culture that equally values both men and women. They would seek to create a society that holds equal right for both genders." (James)

As this account shows, SMGEO's vision aims to transform society. It sees the students, girls, and boys currently in education as key social change agents. If adequately educated on the harmful impacts that gender inequality and social discrimination have on women's well-being, the young generation can be instrumental in change. One area of life crucial in realising gender balance is sharing chores domestically—men and women collaborating and partnering together in running family life. Women in Tanzanian culture are overwhelmed by domestic responsibilities. This aspect of domestic life is included in SMGEO's awareness programme, which is carried out in the community.

The organisation's actions and activities demonstrate that their targets and structural responses to social issues affecting women mainly reflect the emancipatory approach. The usefulness and application of the emancipatory approach arise from the realisation that the problems that affect individuals have their root causes at the heart of society's structures. Gender inequality and how it manifests itself through male control, abuse, the suppression of women's freedom, the exclusion of women from decision-making, and the deprivation of women's equal access to social and economic opportunities are all problems structurally caused. They happen because the existing traditions and customs sanction them. SMGEO's involvement with various social groups and people at multiple levels helps emancipate the whole community from these problems.

9.5 Impact of SMGEO's Activities on gender discrimination and women victims of domestic abuse: From a Perspective of Service Users

The discussion here focuses on the impact of SMGEO's work on their clients' problems and situations (women). In order to understand the effect that the service provider has, we have considered the service users' perspectives collected from the women who participated in this study.

The first reflection is provided based on a female respondent's feedback regarding her experience of domestic abuse and discrimination. When asked to describe what help she has received from the organisation, Aliya replied:

"The organisation is vital in our Chamwino area because it educates us. I have received education on gender equality and women's rights. Education is a significant contribution. It would be great if they could find us the capital and other equipment." (Aliya)

Aliya acknowledges that, on a personal level, she has benefited from the organisation's awareness and education programme on gender equality and women's rights provided in the community. However, in her response, she asks for money and equipment, most likely to make a livelihood.

Another female respondent, Rahel, gave this perspective on the service provision:

"There are many women and mothers in this community whose life is full of challenges like mine, but they do not have any help. Most women do not dare to fight against oppression or harassment by men, especially in family settings. SMGEO's organisation, in one of its campaigns, has put forth a lot of effort into the issue of sexual harassment and gender-based discrimination and in protecting women's rights and children's rights. Their work has helped women like me to know ourselves, our place in society, and to have the courage and to stand up against abuse and discrimination and get justice." (Rahel)

This narrative positively reflects the service provided by the organisation in the community. Accordingly, women seem to grow in self-awareness and confidence and understand that they have a role to play in combating gender-based discrimination. Another female respondent, Eriety, gave this reflection:

"Up until now, the organisation has been able to help us women, widows with ideas. The organisation has helped us understand the concepts of women rights, self-awareness, and women's self-esteem. The importance of using mental abilities and opportunities in improving our lives and our families." (Eriety)

Eriety's account positively reflects the organisation's impact on social issues at the community level. The women in this community have gained knowledge that is vital to women's progress. Consequently, women know their rights and have their confidence boosted with regards to decision-making. There is a sense that the respondent feels empowered by this knowledge. Another female respondent, named Dilek, spoke of what the organisation had done for her:

"This organisation gives us many ideas on how to improve our social and economic life. Counselling can be enough to help, because someone may give you some money, but if they cannot give you some ideas on spending that money, you can waste that money." (Dilek)

Dilek acknowledged having received counselling services and ideas from the organisation, and she seems to value this type of service much more than receiving money. Observing the respondents' reflections on the service of the SMGEO closely, one can see that the organisation focuses more on informing and increasing awareness of the impact of gender inequality and discrimination on women's experience of life, emphasising the importance of women knowing their human and legal rights. Given that the organisation focuses on training and education, it can be said that the organisation requires qualified members. The ones interviewed were university graduates; some have community development discipline education. There is hardly any mention of material support for basic needs. This way of serving is advocacy work addressing the underlying causes of gender inequality and discrimination against women.

9.6 People with disabilities and the challenges of their welfare

In an interview, a male respondent described the personal challenges he faced. Rashid, a service user, has a physical mobility limitation. He cannot stand on his feet and uses his hands to walk. Describing the problems that he faces in life, Rashid said: You find that neighbours sometimes do not help you or bring something you need. Since I am disabled, my life is dependent on the support of people who are not disabled. Maybe you need water to wash your clothes. Sometimes, you need someone to hang the clothes on the dryline to dry them in the sun. Because of my disability, my own life depends heavily on other people to help me in various ways. But sometimes the neighbours around me do not help me at all. Some even prevent their children from helping me fetch water and other necessities. This situation hurts me. You feel that because you are disabled, then you have no value in the eyes of others. You are considered a burden. (Rashid)

In this account, Rashid describes a situation in which he has a personal difficulty exacerbated by other people's unwillingness to help him. His limited physical mobility impacts his daily living negatively and makes him dependent on his community. The lack of support from the people around him complicates his everyday practical living experience. The unwillingness of people to help him seems to be rooted in broader social and cultural negative attitudes towards people with disabilities.

Another respondent, a female older person with a disability named Fatima, described the challenges she faces in life:

"Hunger is a great challenge. Also, I am old, and life is harder. I do not have work. And on top of that, you see I have disfigured fingers. … My legs do not have the strength to allow me to stand for a long time or hours, so I cannot do much work either." (Fatima).

Responding to a follow-up question on how she meets her basic needs, Fatima replied: "I live by begging people to help; whoever is willing and able to help. That is how my day goes by. My legs do not have the strength to allow me to stand for a long time or hours, so I cannot do much work either. Life, for me, is extremely hard." (Fatima)

Fatima's daily life is complicated by a physical disability that does not sufficiently allow her to use her legs or fingers. Her physical situation restricts her from getting involved in any activity that could enable her to earn a living. She also points out that being disabled and old, without reliable support, is even more challenging for an individual.

All the people with some form of impairment who participated in this investigation shared that they experience difficulties undertaking physical tasks to support their daily living. Therefore, an individual must rely on the kindness and support of the people around them.

Another respondent at the organisation's managerial level, named James, described the issues and needs that the disabled face:

"People with some form of disability experience neglect at the family level and community level. One thing you notice here is that it is hard to see a person with a disability mingling with other people publicly. At the family level, you find a person with a disability kept inside, just staying home, not much thought given about his or her future life prospect. The language people use when talking about a person with disability implies as if he or she is less human, or it is his or her fault that is born in that way or involved in an accident."(James)

James' account indicates the entrenched culture of stigma and social discrimination of the disabled at the structural and societal level, impacting their life experience at a familial level. Negative attitudes from family members and people around them act as barriers to social equality and promoting their social wellbeing. The word 'neglect' in James' account could mean that no one is paying positive attention to the wellbeing of the person with a disability or thinking constructively about things that could further their personal, social, and economic welfare. Another respondent, a male service user named Mohamed, has a physical mobility problem and cannot move without a mobility aid. Mohamed has a wife and three children and is involved in polishing and mending shoes as his source of income. He described the challenges he faces and the challenges that the disabled in general encounter in his community:

"A disabled person is put at a very lower rank person in our society. People in our community see me not as a person, but they see the disabilities I have. Disabled people in our society are denied work opportunity and other rights. When you look for work, the way you are looked at, judged is different from a person without a disability. Disabled people in our society are always looked at pitifully but not dignified, enhancing way." (Mohamed)

Mohamed's account presents the social challenges that affect the disabled' social wellbeing and functioning in the wider social context. While other factors are considered in the employment processes, such as academic qualifications and relevant experience related to the post, Mohamed's account indicates a negative attitude and cultural mindset. According to this observation, a stigma breeds discriminatory attitudes that affect people socially, hampering their dreams of personal progress. Mohamed further indicated other aspects of the challenges the disabled experience daily at the societal level, affecting their practical living reality and general social well-being. Mohamed explained:

"The problem that people with disabilities experience here is the challenge of getting a place to live. Renting a room for a person with a disability is challenging. People with disability experience discrimination. Rent charges are higher. Even when you get a place to rent, you are constantly harassed, belittled, and debased, by landlords and fellow tenants living in the same house. When you delay paying the rental payment, you receive a lot of threats, and abusive words. Being a disabled person feels isolated, like you are not part of the rest of the community. It is a big problem. For example, I do not have a big job giving higher income; my daily job is mending old shoes and torn shoes." (Mohamed)

Mohamed's narrative indicates an embedded culture of discrimination, exclusion, and stigma, which exhibits itself in the way that landlords and people, in general, treat disabled people regarding renting and housing, among other matters.

Data findings indicate that misconceptions and lack of knowledge about disability in the community create unfavourable conditions which cause a problematic living experience for disabled people. James' response reflected this fact:

"The language people use when talking about a person with a disability implies as if they are less human, or it is their fault that is born in that way or involved in an accident. 'Oooh... there must be a curse in their family, or they might have wronged God to be born like this. They are too lazy to work." (James)

James' narrative indicates that misunderstandings concerning disability lead to discrimination. The reasoning and type of language employed to understand disability demonstrate that stigma runs deep in the community mindset.

Using public transport is a complicated affair for disabled people. This problem featured in the response of Mohamed, who described the situations that the disabled face in society:

"Public transport is not friendly towards people with disabilities. In buses and Trains, you are overlooked, harassed, and criticised by the transport conductors for being slow. As you can see, I cannot walk; I use my hands in movement. Sometimes, fellow travellers want you to speed up, push you around, want you to act or move like you have no disability. I thank God very much because one person in the community has seen me struggling a lot and decided to buy me this bicycle. Now I use this bicycle to journey." (Mohamed)

Public transport should be for everyone; however, Mohamed's account indicates that people with disabilities are unfairly treated. Such attitudinal behaviour by the public seems to confirm that a person with a disability is not welcome in that social sphere, often facing discrimination and harassment. This raises questions about the role of the government in ensuring the application and enforcement of policies to enable and protect people with disabilities.

Another male respondent, Rashid, described how he thinks his community perceives disabled people:

"Every human being has the right to be respected, recognised, and loved by the community around him. The community around me is not in this way; the community around me does not treat people with disabilities with respect. People with disabilities almost do not exist as people in the eyes of our society. Some individuals in the community are nice and show concern towards us." (Rashid)

This account depicts a concerning portrayal of the interaction between individuals with disabilities and their community. Rashid discusses the qualities that define a supportive neighbourhood with a positive attitude towards people with disabilities—qualities such as respect, recognition, and compassion. He emphasises that these essential human rights should also apply to individuals with disabilities. Nevertheless, the reality seems to contradict this ideal. There's a palpable sense of sadness as Rashid expresses his longing for social acceptance as an equal member of society. Nonetheless, he acknowledges that some members of his community exhibit more compassionate attitudes and behaviours.

9.7 Addressing of Problems of The disabled People by SMGEO

Data findings indicate that the organisation does attend to their client's immediate needs.

Rashid, when asked about the help that he has received from the organisation, replied:

"This organisation has only helped me once. They have given me laundry soap. It has been a long time since I saw them. Today, they again invited me to meet you." (Rashid)

Rashid's reflection on service concerning his problems indicates the provision of a material item but suggests that such provision does not occur regularly. Besides his invitation to attend this study, there also seems to be no regular contact with the organisation. In answering the question about how the organisation addresses the needs of its clients, James explained,

"When we can, we provide laundry Soap, and sugar for those struggling. Mostly, we provide advice and encourage people to get involved in some form of work." (James)

This response indicates that the organisation directly supports people with disabilities. However, this help is only available to clients when the organisation has the resources.

A point worth highlighting is that the organisation's effort to respond and directly bring solutions to support clients reaffirms the maintenance approach to solving problems within Dominelli's social work practice model. Through this process, social workers always strive to help individuals regain social normality and control of their situations. However, the immediate problems and needs do not always receive sufficient attention and response from the organisation, a challenge that the organisation faces due to its limited resources and the issues being out of its original remit. The organisation's focus is more on factors that seem to underlie social problems and structural defects. Hence, broader social circumstances underlie stigma, discrimination, and misunderstanding regarding disability and the life of a disabled person.

A male respondent, Matthias, at the managerial level, described the action they take:

"We tell the community to value people with disabilities, regard them as part of a community, and that people with disabilities have the right to live, be heard, and have the same basic needs as anyone else in the community. People with disabilities have the intellectual capacity, knowledge, and effort to make progress. Many people in the community believe that the disabled person cannot even participate in economic activities. This view is incorrect, and it results in a breakdown." (Matthias)

The responses reveal that SMGEO focuses very much on the emancipatory approach to problem-solving concerning issues affecting disabled people. The key is educating the wider community and creating an awareness of problems faced by people with disabilities.

9.8 Impact of SMGEO's Activities on The Disabled People's welfare Concerns: Perspective of Service Users

This section considers the impact of SMGEO's responses and service to the issues and clients' situations. The discussion is based on understanding the impact of service provision from the users' perspectives. The data findings portray a contradictory picture concerning the service provision and the effects of the service. For example, a male respondent, Mohamed, said:

"Support, like things, I have never received. Sometimes they only give you advice on how to make progress, how to improve your life." (Mohamed)

This reflection on the service provided suggests that he has not received any tangible support from the organisation. However, he did receive some help in the form of counselling. This type of support fits within Dominelli's "therapeutic" response category, which involves working with the individual by listening to their concerns, understanding their story, and giving advice to help individuals solve their problems.

He went on to suggest what he wished to see happening concerning the organisation's service provision:

"I pray that this organisation also cares about us and gives us the services it promises. Visit us regularly at our homes and at the places where we work. If possible, provide us with money or enable us to live our lives in other ways. My most significant request for the organisation is to help me find a transportation tool, like a bicycle. This tool will be a great help to me in life." (Mohamed).

Mohamed's account of the service and his experience indicate a mixed picture. He expresses dissatisfaction about the service due to not receiving tangible things and materials that could help his immediate needs and improve his living conditions. Mohamed would most value the types of service by visiting staff members and money, tangible and material support fitting Dominelli's maintenance response category. In addition, he would like to get a bicycle, reflecting Dominelli's therapeutic approach, as it would improve his position through professional intervention.

Mohamed's account reveals another aspect worth noting here. In his reflection, he uses the phrase "support like things I have never received." Here, the respondent appears to feel that his pressing needs to change his immediate circumstance are not addressed.

This perception that respondents do not see rapid changes in their circumstances is apparent because the organisation focus on broader structural issues.

Another respondent, Fatima, gave her reflection on the service provision:

"The organisation shows interest in helping, but only in words. I have never seen any material support from them. The only thing they do is send people around to register names of people like us who need help, but help is nowhere to be seen."(Fatima)

She then went further to say: "I have never been helped anything, and they never visited me. But yesterday, someone gave me one kilogram of sugar."(Fatima)

Fatima's narrative also indicates a sense of dissatisfaction. Fatima points out that the organisation has expressed interest in helping but has remained only in the form of words and has not been translated into direct support for her immediate needs in the form of material items.

Another respondent, Rashid, expressed what he wishes to see the organisation doing for him: "I would advise the organisation to remember us, to help us regularly, for example, flour, soap, even a little money to relieve the difficulty of life". (Rashid)

All respondents' reflections on the service provision they have received indicate one aspect: the association of "help" with receiving or being given something tangible or of a material nature to address their immediate needs. Both women and disabled people, clients of SMGEO, indicate consistent reflections on the service experience and the impact of the organisation's work on their situations and broader society.

SMGEO has positioned itself in the public sphere and has taken a vital responsibility to intervene in people's social situations and address social needs. When an organisation puts its vision and mission into practice and meets its client's needs, changes, in reality, become visible. In the case of SMGEO, addressing issues affecting its clients' social well-being has not been straightforward. The participants acknowledge the impact of SMGEO at the societal and structural level, but at the individual level, its effect appears to be not very noticeable.

The clients who took part in this investigation are facing immediate problems. The organisation's limited impact on its clients' immediate problems stems from its limited financial capacity and limited personnel. This fact is featured in the response of Matthias, a representative of the managerial level. In reflecting on the organisation's performance, he refers to the shortage of resources and finance, saying:

"Due to our limited capacity and challenges, we are reaching out to a few people. Indeed, we have no money, but it is a great resource to have. In general, we do not have anything other than what we are using in our performance individual capacity."

Indeed, the shortage of funds and other necessary resources could potentially affect the organisation's overall performance and specific decisions. For example, recruiting qualified full-time workers might be complex, and adequately reaching clients and meeting their needs may not be possible.

The data revealed that the organisation focuses much more on advocacy work than addressing its clients' immediate needs. This discrepancy could be rooted in a mismatch of expectations. SMGEO set out to challenge society on the matter of inequality. However, they would like to see their immediate issues addressed when engaging with clients. So, as an organisation, SMGEO must think about communication and collaboration with their direct clients to ensure a fruitful interaction with and satisfaction of their clients. Data findings indicated that participants/clients linked to this organisation considered issues that have immediate impacts essential and wish to see them addressed. However, the organisation's responses seem to be directed at the societal and structural levels. Considering both problems that directly impact clients and those emanating from societal and structural levels appears to be challenging for the organisation.

The following chapter indicates what I have learned from the data and demonstrates how the data provided evidence for the thesis' findings. It concludes by specifying some research implications and suggesting future research and recommendations.

10 Conclusion

The original study featured in this book sought to comprehensively understand the pivotal role played by local non-governmental welfare organisations in addressing the far-reaching social problems affecting the well-being of people in Tanzania. This was achieved through detailed case studies examining the operations of these organisations across three distinct regions of the country. The original studies were meticulously carried out in both rural and urban settings, meticulously examining the issues addressed, strategies deployed, and the substantial impact on the well-being of clients and the broader communities they serve.

The discussion in this section comprises aspects from (i) the history of the country regarding social welfare development, (ii) findings that emerged from the data and the usage of Dominelli's social work practice model, (iii) Intersectionality understanding of problem-solving organisations may learn. (iv) Perspectives on social work's role in problem-solving from within Africa; (v) a re-thinking of the use of Dominelli's model in light of the gathered data findings; (vi) The demand and necessity of social protection policy measures to protect vulnerable populations groups; and (vii) criticism of the study including limitations of its contribution and issues worthy of further investigation.

10.1 Lessons Learnt from the History of Social Welfare Development

It seemed essential to have a historical chapter in this work to provide insights into the social welfare development in Tanzania because by looking at the past, we can understand why certain things are in a certain way in the present. This historical examination has shed light on some efforts and development of social welfare in Tanzania, especially non-governmental welfare organisations, including the three organisations in this study. In chapter six, the historical development of social welfare in Tanzanian society was examined. Similar to many traditional societies in Sub-Saharan Africa, the responsibility for addressing social welfare issues historically fell within the domain of the family and community. There were no independent private organisations or state provisions for those in need. Despite the support offered by the extended family network and communities, certain segments of society continued to face challenges due to entrenched traditional attitudes, such as those towards women within the patriarchal system and perceptions of disabled individuals. Notably, the interference of external forces, particularly colonial invasions, disrupted the traditional ways of life and problem-solving mechanisms within African societies. The country of Tanzania went through different stages of colonial occupation. The historical examination indicated that Germany's colonial government first invaded and occupied the Tanzanian territory from 1884 to 1919. The colonial invasion and occupation meant that native societies were no longer free to conduct their lives and economic activities, as the humanity and social welfare of the native people were irrelevant to the colonial regime. They became enslaved people and subjects of the colonial master, who demanded that these people work for the economic interests of the colonial 'home' country. The regime's focus was to exploit raw materials. In the regime's eyes, local people were cheap labour and could be exploited to benefit German society's economic and social development back in Europe.

History also revealed that German missionaries carried out Christian mission work when the German colonial power occupied Tanganyika. Missionary work focused on the social welfare development of indigenous people; however, the main aim was to convert them to the Christian faith. Unlike the ruthless attitude that marked the German colonial regime's involvement with the indigenous population, German missionaries seemed to be more engaging, at least on the surface, though, as indicated by literature, this, in turn, was used by the colonial administration to fulfil its agenda. Missionaries carried out activities, including literacy-education programmes and providing health-related services. However, it should be noted that these activities were not aimed at liberating native people and enhancing their social welfare development, but those activities were instead a means to convert Africans.

The presence of the Lutheran Christian denomination in Tanzania today represents the German missionary work. The German missionaries, and later on the British missionaries, introduced and formalised the voluntary sector approach to addressing people's welfare issues in Tanzania. Though there may have been other voluntary organisations and international non-governmental welfare organisations working in Tanzania, the work of Western mission organisations laid the foundation for the subsequent emergence of the voluntary sector. The German administration was forced out of Tanzania after losing World War I in 1918. During this period, German missionary activities across Tanzania were also forced out of the country.

From 1919 to 1961, Tanzanian society was once again occupied by another colonial regime: this time, the British. Like the German administration, the British colonial's move to Tanzania was motivated by acquiring raw materials and increasing African economies' output to compensate for Britain's economic weakness. Upon taking over the Tanzanian colony, the British regime chased out all German military and mission organisations.

Even though this was a challenging time for the native Tanzanian people, a more formalised social welfare system developed. Non-governmental welfare organisations were involved with native people's social concerns while the colonial regime reigned over people. British missionaries and voluntary mission organisations operated, and the British colonial government acknowledged their work. Thus, non-governmental welfare organisations from the United Kingdom, whose work focused more on tackling the problems that affected native people's social wellbeing, provided medical and health-related services, education in the form of schools, and spiritual services through established churches for the native people. While the voluntary sector was focused on tackling the issues affecting local communities' social wellbeing, the British colonial regime continued with its subjugating agenda. There were efforts by the government to address a limited number of social concerns; for example, they attempted to set up social welfare centres for returning ex-native military servicemen who were fighting abroad. It was hoped that through educational activities in these social welfare centres, native people would be enlightened and prepared to enter the 21st century, characterised by a civilised modern lifestyle and leadership; however, such attempts were unsuccessful. The colonial regime struggled with implementing a social welfare system sponsored by the state for the Tanzanian people. There was no mutual, respectful, working relationship between the colonial regime and indigenous people; the administration made no effort to determine how native communities thought and felt about addressing social issues. In the end, the British regime decided not to implement a general social welfare system for indigenous people.

In 1961, the British colonial government relinquished Tanganyika (which became the United Republic of Tanzania in 1964 after unity with Zanzibar) and allowed native people to form a national government. At that time, the social and economic situation of the country was not at all good. High levels of poverty, illiteracy, poor living conditions, and health-related issues affected many native people. Provisions to deal with these issues were not readily in place for the new government as they began their job. The newly appointed government under the premiership of Julius Nyerere decided that one of its main priorities would be to address the social problems affecting its citizens. During Nyerere's era, many Tanzanians benefited from free social welfare provision. These services relied on international hand-outs rather than the country's own capabilities, which rendered these provisions unsustainable in the long-run.

Additionally, as indicated in the historical chapter, the national regime, guided by its socialist agenda, barred the operation and contribution of the private and voluntary sectors. The government's attitude and approach, primarily influenced by the negative impact of the colonial legacy, was to present itself as the only body able to deal with the social and economic problems affecting its people. However, as the historical chapter has made apparent, such a position and approach were inappropriate. The government's efforts in addressing social issues and social welfare service provision met numerous challenges. Factors such as corruption, a low level of economic production in agriculture, a low level of industries' performance, and a lack of adequate finance hampered the government's efforts to provide free social welfare services to all Tanzanians. In the 1980s, it became clear that the social and economic contributions of the private and voluntary sectors were indeed needed. The appointed governments that followed after Nyerere recognised the importance of the private and voluntary sectors' contribution to people's economic and social welfare.

In contrast to the Nyerere era, the leadership of President Mwinyi from 1985 to 1995 enabled the country to collaborate with outside economic institutions. It allowed local and international NGOs to operate and address social welfare needs. Consequently, after opening up, the voluntary sector, especially non-governmental welfare organisations, began actively addressing and supporting those affected by social problems in the country. Indeed, the emergence and the operation of the three organisations selected for this research could not have been possible if the government had not allowed NGOs to take an active role in the social welfare concerns of its citizens.

Tanzania is an evolving nation; however, it is still relatively weak in providing its citizens with a full, formalised social welfare service. Thus, in the 21st century, Tanzania must continue to grapple with social welfare provision questions, especially helping disadvantaged people. Social problems still affect most people, and those from socially deprived areas and backgrounds who lack support are most affected, and their well-being and social functioning are impaired. In this context, the work of the voluntary sector is significant.

The Tanzanian government is currently focusing more on improving infrastructures, with expensive, extensive projects happening across the country constructing roads, bridges, new hospitals, and healthcare centres. A new, large water dam that will have the capacity to generate and supply a considerable amount of electricity across the country is underway, as well as a new oil pipeline project shared between Tanzania and Uganda. The government is also reviving industries and the manufacturing sector across the country. It is hoped that by restoring old sectors and setting up new ones in various regions according to each region's agricultural products, livestock, and natural resources, a large population in these regions will benefit from increased job opportunities in the private and public sectors. Some literature emphasises that industrialisation is critical to economic development (Martorano et al., 2017; Mufuruki et al., 2018).

Similarly, commenting on this development in Tanzania, Kweka (2018: 2) wrote, "as Tanzania gears towards its vision of becoming a middle-income economy by 2025, the National Five-Year Development Plan 2016/17–2020/21 (FYDP II), published in 2016, identifies industrialisation as the main policy objective and a key driver of economic transformation". Indeed, the 5th Phase Government is relentlessly pursuing industrialisation as an overriding priority in the implementation of FYDP II.' Despite the importance and priority of industrialisation, Kweka (2018) noted that progress on the ground has been slow, significantly hampered by the overwhelmingly large amount of finance needed to push progress in many of the FYDP II flagship projects. However, this focus has meant that the social issues critical to citizens' everyday social living are being overlooked, and welfare concerns, especially the concerns of those from disadvantaged backgrounds and areas, are not being addressed by the government.

To a certain extent, the voluntary sector can bridge this gap in service provision. NGOs can act more rapidly as they are typically more flexible and less bureaucratic than government bodies. They can challenge the government in advocating the people's needs, as not everybody will benefit from the government's economic initiatives. NGOs should also support initiatives in the deprived areas of the country.

One point worth noting is that the presence and the impact of missionaries' activities in Tanganyika during the colonial era left an indelible mark. Though changes in the voluntary sector have occurred over time, this sector continues to grow in Tanzania. There are different types of organisations, faith-based and secular, involved in tackling people's social welfare concerns. An example of this continuity is the Dogodogo Street Children Trust, formed in 1992 by Sister Maryknoll Jean Pruitt. The Maryknoll Sisters are a group of Roman Catholic religious women, initially based in New York, involved in missionary work. Though today, this is an entirely secular, locally registered non-governmental organisation.

This investigation and the subsequent data findings indicate that certain social groups in Tanzania are more affected by social issues, including older people in rural settings, street children, women, and people with disabilities. Local non-governmental welfare organisations focus on these social groups; however, what they do and their contribution to improving people's welfare has been under-researched. The current research sought to learn more about these organisations' roles and impact on individuals and society.

10.2 Summary of Data Findings and its Implication on Applicability of Dominelli's Social Work Model

I conducted this research in Tanzania with the three selected social welfare organisations, MAPERECE, Dogodogo Street Children Trust, and SMGEO. As the data findings have shown, each organisation that took part in this study has taken the responsibility to intervene and address issues affecting some of the most disadvantaged social groups in Tanzania.

Each organisation participating in this study is involved with critical social problems that the government has not sufficiently tackled. Though the government has put in place various policies, its involvement and implementation at a practical level towards different vulnerable social groups remain weak. As indicated in this study, the government enacted the "National Ageing Policy" in 2003. This policy expresses the importance of intervening to help older people realise their essential welfare needs and protect their fundamental human rights. However, the government fails to adhere to this policy and provide tangible support to older people; thus, this social group in rural areas remains vulnerable.

Additionally, the government has enacted the 'Persons With Disabilities Act No. 9 of 2010' at the policy level. This Act aims to make provision for the health and social wellbeing of disabled people in the country. However, the government's involvement in supporting disabled people remains weak. Disabled people continue to face problems that affect their wellbeing and personal progress, both economically and socially.

Regarding gender inequality and discrimination against women, the country has gender policies and legislation. The constitution of Tanzania promulgated in 1977 and the amendments that followed both forbid biases based on gender. Additionally, Tanzania formulated the Women and Gender Development Policy (WGDP) in 2000 and the National Gender Development Strategy (NGDS) in 2005 to implement the WGDP. These policies aimed to mainstream gender perspective into policies, programs, and strategies and create opportunities for women to participate in poverty reduction and development. The Tanzanian government also committed to supporting the increased involvement of women in governmental decision-making by re-enforcing the quota system for female representatives at the national parliamentary and local council levels. Despite having these policies in place, women and girls in Tanzanian society continue to experience abuse, mistreatment, and the deprivation of their fundamental rights. As indicated in this study, the acceptance of customary laws (Customary Law Declaration Order: CLDO of 1963) based on the traditions and customs of communities and the practice of traditional African religion hampers the efforts to eliminate gender inequality. Additionally, religion-based laws (such as Islamic Law) often prevail over statutory laws. Consequently, the rights stipulated in statutory laws often go unprotected (Tanzania Women Lawyers Association-TAWLA, 2014).

This social contextual reality in which these vulnerable social groups and others in this study live makes the work and contribution of non-governmental welfare organisations towards improving the wellbeing of the disadvantaged people in Tanzania very significant.

The study's empirical process involved interviewing people connected to the three selected local non-governmental welfare organisations. People who participated in the interviews included those involved in addressing and providing social support. This category comprised individuals at the managerial level and employees/social workers. The other participants were those who received the social service associated with the respective organisations. Interviewing the people who receive and experience services across the three organisations allowed the researcher to obtain information showing the involvement and activities of local non-governmental welfare organisations in response to social problems. More importantly, this study revealed knowledge concerning the contribution of the voluntary sector—local non-governmental welfare organisations—in social problem-solving in the context of Tanzania.

The data findings from the sampled population indicate problems affecting people's wellbeing and social functioning. Issues that have an immediate effect on the wellbeing of individuals stem from broader circumstances as source-foundation of difficulties. Within the three organisations that I worked with during this investigation, all respondents shared issues in common, as follows:

- Respondents-service users experience Health-related challenges across the three organisations. For example, whilst spending time in an unhealthy environment, street children contract physical injuries and illness. Due to cost and distance, older people living with illnesses cannot access treatment.
- Respondents lack a reliable means of income and the knowledge to facilitate the understanding and ability to engage in income-generating business.
- The respondents indicated they face deficiencies in accessing immediate daily basic needs, such as food, water, a safe living environment, a safe place to sleep, and medical-related services.
- Respondents across the three case studies indicated that they experience stigma, discrimination, and mistreatment.

For example, the data showed that street children are neglected and shunned by the community. In this environment, they experience harassment and endure beatings. The negative and uncaring attitudes of government and society have condemned these children to live in a hazardous environment, lacking all basic needs, leaving them susceptible to harmful situations that impact their physical, mental, and social wellbeing.

The data also indicated that older people, especially older women in rural communities, experienced victimisation, stigmatisation, and discrimination due to allegations of witchcraft. As a result, older women have faced beatings, and some have lost their lives. On top of that, older people in rural areas lack the necessities to sustain their general wellbeing. Older people also face a problem of self-management and the inability to take care of their living surroundings.

- The respondents indicated that they experience the deprivation of their human rights and the social and economic opportunities to which they are entitled.
- Data revealed that women participants experience discrimination and abuse in domestic /family settings; they have been deprived of their human rights to freedom of expression, making choices, and pursuing their career goals.
- The data findings have also revealed that people with disabilities are stigmatised, socially discriminated against, and lack social support.

Society's condescending and discriminatory attitudes create an unhealthy social living environment for disabled people. They feel socially unwanted. The mistreatment and uncaring attitudes of the community stem from misconceptions about disability and disabled people.

In understanding why these problems occur, it is essential to note that they have underlying causes within society, at a structural level and in the general cultural attitude. For example, when the government lacks any authentic interventional system at the central and local government levels to support its citizens, especially socially disadvantaged groups, it creates more problems at an individual level. Additionally, the general cultural perceptions and attitudes characterised by misconceptions towards disability and street children, ageing, as indicated in this study, contribute further to the problematic living experience facing these individuals. Addressing these issues is vital, as it would bring about positive attitudes and changes in enhancing vulnerable individuals' social and physical wellbeing.

The reviewed literature for this study revealed social science scholars' perspectives on the above problems shared across the case studies. For example, in Chapter Two, Lerisse et al. (2007) examined people affected by problems and classified them into a category they named "extremely vulnerable groups." Those in this category include individuals with high-risk exposure and a low capacity to cope. Street children, older people in rural areas, the disabled and many women represent vulnerable groups in Tanzanian society. Mesaki (2016) pointed out that the population in disadvantaged areas are vulnerable and at risk of a diverse set of outcomes such as impoverishment, ill health, and social exclusion. The vulnerable populations in Tanzania refer to but are not limited to street children, older people in rural areas, disabled people, and many women representing vulnerable groups in Tanzanian society. I used 'the phrase' many women' and not just 'women' to emphasise that there are exceptions to women whose experience of life is affected by discrimination and the prevalence of the culture of inequality in Tanzania (Mtambalike, 2013; Refworld-Canada, 2015).

Because of space, time, and size, the current study has concentrated on discovering the lived experience of older people, street children, women, and disabled people concerning problems and service receipt in Tanzania. However, the researcher knows that many other vulnerable population groups in Tanzania are disadvantaged and need social services and protective interventions equally. For example, People with albinism, People living with a long-term illness, such as HIV/AIDS, sexual minorities, homeless people, children, drug addicts, and alcoholics (Hamisi, 2019).

One aspect that surfaces in the literature is how gender is related to vulnerability. When one looks at gender concerning social problems, welfare services, and people in vulnerable life situations, women are defined as being more vulnerable than men within communities in Africa. The vulnerability of female members of societies is related to women's weaker and less protected economic circumstances in certain life situations and lack of support for their needs (Lombe and Sherraden, 2008; Hamisi, 2019). However, one cannot generalise that all women are vulnerable. Hamisi (2019) observed that in Tanzania, widows and many women who cannot support themselves but depend on their husbands' provision and yet experience abuse at the hands of abusive partners are vulnerable. Hence, according to Hamisi's observation, vulnerable women include widows who experience marginalisation and women unable to support themselves due to various economic and social processes (Hamisi, 2019). This observation means that not every woman in Tanzania can be considered vulnerable, but many are.

Significant progress has been noticeable at political and leadership levels, as many women are currently in leadership positions in Tanzania. There is apparent positive evidence of progress concerning gender inequality in society, as the current president of Tanzania is a female. Indeed, on the one hand, having a female president is an indication that one cannot generalise that all women are vulnerable or treated discriminatorily. However, on the other hand, having a female president and some females in different prominent leadership positions does not mean that there are no gender and inequality issues within the broader society of Tanzania. Still, many women in rural and urban areas face particular hardship and are disadvantaged in many vital areas of their lives (Zambelli et al., 2017; Idris, 2018). Literature concerning vulnerability recognises that social groups are a mix of social variables. Thus, placing people in one group leads to generalised conclusions or, even worse, stigmatisation (Kuran et al., 2020). Tierney (2019) explained that the degree of vulnerability does not depend on any one-dimensional attribute (e.g., to a demographic group, such as the elderly or children) but results from the complex relationship between different factors, like social class, race, sex, and age (Tierney 2019, quoted in Kuran et al. 2020:2). Furthermore, Tierney (2019:127) emphasised that:

"People are not born vulnerable; they are made vulnerable... different axes of inequality combine and interact to form systems of oppression – systems that relate directly to differential levels of social vulnerability, both in normal times and in the context of disaster. This perspective on vulnerability calls attention to the need to avoid statements like "women are vulnerable" in favour of a more nuanced view."

This view compels us to have a broader assessment of how individuals might be experiencing problems. Hence, considering elements of a person's identity in understanding an individual's vulnerability is vital in engaging and effectively helping individuals.

However, it is also essential to consider the role social structures and institutions play in causing the vulnerability of individuals and social groups, as indicated by some literature (Koch, 2015; Hamisi, 2019). It is essential to be mindful of the structural and social processes and institutions that initially created and sustained this very vulnerability (Koch, 2015). This insight marks out the difference between vulnerability and inherent vulnerability. Someone is made vulnerable by the structure around them. In this case, it is right to argue that women are not necessarily inherently vulnerable, but they tend to be marginalised by the social structure in society (MacIntyre et al., 2019). Indeed, the current study has proven this reality to be the case in Tanzanian society. Problems that, for example, older people and street children face do not result from being a child or an older person but from structural defects. The structure's defects underpin the situations facing these groups.

This study revealed that the disabled, street children, and the elderly experience stigma. Stigma against people with disabilities in the Tanzanian context arises from a misunderstanding about impairment and its causes (AbleChildAfrica, 2013). However, the consequences of experiencing stigma on a person's life are highly damaging. According to Mostert and Weich (2017), stigma profoundly affects the people who experience it. It can result in a lowering of status within the community. Stigma and discrimination by society against the disabled can create a barrier to the disabled exercising their right to full participation in society (Mostert and Weich, 2017).

This study also found that gender inequality and discrimination against women in society are caused by tradition and customs at work in the community, particularly the pervasiveness of patriarchal culture. The physical and psychological abuse many women experience in domestic settings is primarily caused by a culture of male control (Olatunji, 2013). Society must critically examine and challenge the traditions and customs that create a negative living experience for female community members, potentially affecting their personal and social development.

Dominelli's social work model was used to consider how the organisations respond to the identified problems. The model offers three possible approaches that social workers or organisations might use in social problem-solving and helping people with problems: the maintenance, therapeutic, and emancipatory approaches. These three approaches have different purposes that aim to achieve different outcomes for a client's situation. Depending on the understanding of the nature of the problem, the effort to solve it can be directed at individual cases or the social or societal levels.

Briefly, let me recap what the three approaches in this model entail. According to Dominelli (2009), social workers who utilise the maintenance approach see the primary purpose of social work as maintaining society's social order and social fabric. Maintenance responses seek to provide the necessary support that is appropriate for an individual to function again. Social workers who take a maintenance approach are also more likely to focus simply on an individual (and family relationships) without noticing that many individuals with similar problems expose broader social issues. This approach and response do not ask a practitioner to consider the impact of policies on resource availability for certain needs or the appropriateness of eligibility criteria for groups of people who might be routinely excluded (Dominelli, 2009:12). The second approach to social work practice is the therapeutic approach. Dominelli (2002c) explained that in therapeutic interventions, the primary, although not only, the focal point is interpersonal relations. This approach focuses primarily on how individuals can improve their position through targeted professional interventions. A principal aim is to enhance psychological and emotional functioning so that a person can handle their affairs (Dominelli, 2002c:12). Counselling is part of the therapeutic approach. Through listening and Counselling, a social worker can explore a client's difficulty, distress they may be experiencing, or perhaps their dissatisfaction with life or loss of a sense of direction and purpose (Dominelli, 2002c). The therapeutic response is interested in understanding the individual's situation by listening to a person while considering the social interactional factors and understanding a wide picture of the social environment surrounding the individual.

The third approach is the emancipatory approach. The emancipatory approach covers a broader spectrum of practice than either the maintenance or therapeutic procedures (Adams et al., 2009). This approach is associated with radical social work and questions the balance of power in society and resource distribution. It identifies the oppressive nature of social relations and argues that social workers are responsible for doing something about these while helping people as individuals (Dominelli, 2002c). Dominelli (2002c:85) also clarified, "Practitioners who follow emancipatory approaches seek to achieve anti-oppressive practice by focusing on the specifics of a situation in a holistic manner and mediating between its personal and structural components."

Dominelli's emancipatory approach is clearly featured in the three organisations' work as they attempt to address issues affecting their clients' social wellbeing. For example, SMGEO's efforts to address gender inequality and discrimination against women in the community indicate an awareness that problems that affect women's personal and social wellbeing emanate from within society. Their awareness programme helps primary and secondary schools think about issues related to gender inequality, prompting recognition of the underlying cause of discrimination and mistreatment women experience in domestic and social settings. They aim to explain unhelpful cultural notions and attitudes that are influenced by patriarchal culture and carry the notion that men occupy a special social status and are entitled to all privileges. A respondent, James, a manager at SMGEO, said:

"We felt that without engaging with both primary and secondary schools, the realisation of a society characterised by gender equality would be a distant dream in our community... Suppose they are well-educated on these issues. In that case, they may avoid and challenge the wrongly held traditions about the place of men and women in society and the roles women and men potentially fulfil and create a culture that equally values both men and women." (James)

The study revealed that the social wellbeing of disabled people is affected by stigma and discriminatory attitudes in society, damaging their lives, particularly as some traditional African beliefs about disability are construed on the wrong premises. These misconceptions are, for example, that having a disability is the result of a curse, 'ancestors' punishment, or an indication that a person has wronged God, or that disability is a sign of the laziness of a person not wanting to work. All these fallacies concerning disability yield negative social interactions and discriminatory attitudes in the community towards a disabled person. Data findings from respondent interviews (of people with physical disabilities linked to SMGEO) made similar observations concerning daily social challenges. They pointed out that stigma, discriminatory attitudes in society and social structure, dislike, and abuse prevent them from living like any other person in their community and progressing socially and economically. Misunderstanding disability plays a large part in creating these unwarranted social attitudinal barriers in communities. Emancipatory efforts by SMGEO in addressing the problems involve raising awareness of the rights of a person with a disability and challenging any entrenched harmful misunderstanding and attitudes associated with disability and person with a disability at the community and structural level.

A lack of education is a problem that most street children face. Data shows that Dogodogo assesses the person and arranges for the individual to access formal education, such as primary education, reflecting an emancipatory approach to solving this issue. What Dogodogo Street Children Trust does is emancipatory, including campaigning to tackle stigma, advocating for street children to attend school, and challenging negative perceptions and attitudes concerning who street children are at the society's level.

Also, the Dogodogo Street Children Trust, in their efforts to help, consider situations with an immediate impact on a street child. For example, children and youth living and working in the streets face physical and health problems. Data shows that Dogodogo responds to these issues by sending staff members to assess the children's health conditions and offer first-aid services. If a street child/youth has a serious health condition, the organisation responds by taking the individual to the hospital for further medical treatment. This sort of response reflects the maintenance approach to problem-solving of Dominelli's model. The maintenance response addresses an individual's immediate situation to recover and continue life.

The data findings suggest a mismatch between the problems faced by service users and their views on how these can best be addressed and the focus of the three organisations who seem to take a longer-term perspective, a structural picture of social problems. Indeed, respondents described their experiences of problems that immediately impacted their lives. For example, a male respondent with a physical disability explained how difficult it is to undertake simple yet necessary tasks such as fetching water. Thus, he relied entirely upon other people's mercy to support him, but often, no one was available or willing to assist him. Findings indicate no actions or suggestions from SMGEO on how to help a person in this situation. Likewise, female respondents (older people) living alone, linked to MAPERECE, expressed daily difficulties due to a lack of assistance with practical tasks. They stressed the need for a person or care worker to be with them daily and help with heavy tasks such as fetching water, cleaning the house, and cooking. However, MAPERECE's managerial staff do not say how they help older people in this situation. Only one female respondent, a social worker, indicated that she helps maintain an older person's house and living environment when she pays a visit to clients. This observation raises important questions about how local NGOs manage their problem-solving role in Tanzania, particularly how they understand issues affecting clients' functioning and well-being and organisations' capacity to cover their needs sufficiently.

10.3 An Intersectionality Perspective on Understanding Problems

Intersectionality is a fundamental theoretical perspective acknowledged in social science research as a useful conceptual tool to understand the impact of problems. This concept stresses the intersectionality nature of social identities and how multiple social identities of a person potentially contribute to an individual's experiencing disadvantages. Lessons from this theoretical perspective could benefit individuals and organisations in addressing social problems in Tanzania.

The term intersectionality traces its origin to the work of Crenshaw (1989). A female black law professor in the USA, Crenshaw introduced and developed the intersectionality theory. Her research examined how intersecting social identities, especially those from minority identities, are related to systems and structures of oppression and prejudice in American society (Crenshaw, 1989). Also, Crenshaw's research work focused on intersectional feminism. She applied the intersectionality concept within her legal studies discipline to address Black women's experiences. Crenshaw examined the overlapping systems of discrimination that women face because of their ethnicity, sexuality and economic background (Crenshaw 1989; Crenshaw 2011). Many other discussions and research on social issues by contemporary scholars have utilised and built on Crenshaw's intersectionality theory (Emmett and Alant, 2006; Adewunmi, 2014; Wisner, 2016; Miller, 2017; MacIntyre et al., 2019; Hamisi, 2019; Hafford-Letchfield and Cocker, 2022; to mention but a few).

Other studies have construed the concept of intersectionality to describe how different elements of a person's identity can be discriminated against, resulting in adverse outcomes (MacIntyre et al., 2019; Emmett and Alant, 2006). Depending on the number of elements of a person's identity, an individual can experience multiple disadvantages or vulnerabilities. This concept intrinsically stresses the need to understand different ways individuals might be vulnerable. The notion of vulnerability is complex because it involves many characteristics of people and groups that expose them to harm and limit their ability to anticipate, cope with, and recover from harm (Wisner, 2016, quoted by Hamisi, 2019:609).

Indeed, the intersectionality model is helpful. It may inform academicians, social work practitioners, or organisations involved in addressing issues about how the different aspects of someone's identity can result in poorly treated in society or increase their chances of being disadvantaged. It is natural for any organisation involved in social problem-solving to have a fixed gaze on a particular kind of need or focus their attention on a specific aspect, the thing it is going to address. An established focus on organisational aims can be perceived as a strength because it gives an organisation something straightforward to focus on. However, having a fixed focus can also be a weakness because it encourages organisations to abstract some difficulties from broader problems and leaves other issues out of focus.

From an intersectionality perspective, we briefly examine the multi-dimensional nature of the impact of problems on people's well-being examined in this study. The study revealed that some individuals (clients) are doubly disadvantaged regarding the impact of problems because of the multiple aspects of identities that characterise their lives. The intersectionality perspective believes that experiences can be exacerbated depending on the different characteristics of an individual (MacIntyre et al., 2019). For example, if you look at the population sample that I have worked with, you will find that there are older people who are also women who also have disabilities. These multiple layers of disadvantage based on different aspects of an individual's identity intersect, resulting in an even more significant burden for particular groups. To elaborate further, in this case, what happens is that by being a woman, an individual already experiences discrimination and is often denied such fundamental rights as the right to self-expression and access to social and economic opportunities in society. However, her life is further complicated by being disabled or having disabilities. The stigma attached to disability puts her in a more disadvantaged position that impacts the social aspect of her existence and personal well-being. Women with disabilities face more significant levels of poverty. Women in this culture are not being listened to and constantly struggle to be heard and respected. Emmett and Alant (2006) revealed insights into the social living situation of women with disabilities in African communities, especially from the point of view of the interface of multiple disadvantages. They observed that 'women with disabilities are at greater risk of physical, mental, and sexual abuse, and because of stigmatisation, have lower marriage prospects. There are more barriers to access and participation for women than for men (Emmett and Alant, 2006:445). Individuals or organisations committed to social service provision helping women or older women must be aware of different ways clients experience disadvantageous situations.

Another standout example that illustrates the intersectionality nature of problems is the victimisation, persecution, and killing of older women because they are alleged to be witches in rural communities. MAPERECE's view on this problem is that they see the persecution and killing of older women as primarily a problem of old age and misunderstandings about the physical signs of ageing. However, from an intersectionality perspective, more factors underpin these disadvantageous situations and harmful conditions older women face. MAPERECE must do more to consider the different ways in which older women (clients) are disadvantaged in their social settings.

For example, one characteristic of this group is that they are women, and already, women in the community experience unequal treatment and discrimination emanating from held traditional prejudices against them. Women are likely to be significantly disadvantaged because of their gender. An additional characteristic is that these are older women and, by virtue of being old, older women have an added disadvantageous situation, as they are vulnerable and an easy target. The intersectionality concept teaches us that old age is only one social aspect of identity that marks out the older population; one cannot focus on only one part of the person's identity. For example, it is not just old age affecting this group. Older women suffer disadvantages; this reality is reflected in the imbalances in witchcraft-related murders. This situation is happening not simply because there are more women in the elderly population but because women in these communities are disproportionately disadvantaged and severely affected by issues.

Concerning this study, the whole idea of intersectionality acknowledges commonly lived experiences shared across groups. Although the three organisations appear to be geographically distant from each other, each of these populations seems to exhibit the same lived experience of issues. Hence, this study focused on experiencing common problems across the groups, older people, street children, women, and people with disabilities: stigma, discrimination, marginalisation, poverty, neglect, and lack of social protection.

The intersectionality perspective on understanding the impact of problems can help us understand the diverse ways people might experience difficulties influenced by the multiple characteristics of their identity. Indeed, there are various lessons the organisations may learn from this study; one of them may be to understand further how different sources of disadvantages intersect and interact and, therefore, impact individuals. Various contemporary literature emphasises the importance and relevance of intersectionality in studying vulnerabilities. For example, Kuran et al. (2020:1) wrote:

"We promote the application of intersectionality...as a guiding principle in risk and crisis management to provide a better and more nuanced picture of vulnerabilities and vulnerable groups. This can help national and local authorities and agencies formulate specific guides, hire staff with the skills necessary to meet particular needs, and inform vulnerable groups in a particular way, taking into account the differences that may coexist within the same group. Intersectionality allows us to read vulnerability, not as the characteristic of some socio-demographic groups. It is rather the result of different and interdependent societal stratification processes that result in multiple dimensions of marginalisation."

Indeed, organisations involved in helping clients address their living situations must, in their deliberation and actions, consider closely the different ways clients might be experiencing social problems due to the multiple dimensions of their identities.

10.4 The Role of Social Work and NGOs in Problem-Solving: African Perspectives

There are several different ways in which social work can be undertaken, and the culture largely influences this. Within Africa, a particular focus has been on the developmental social work approach to resolving social problems. Chapter Four has explained this matter in detail.

This debate centred on finding the right approach to social work practice in East Africa and Tanzania, leading to the emergence of the social developmental approach. Embracing the social developmental model was partly a reaction against the idea of taking on Western, personal-centred social work approaches, such as 'maintenance, therapeutic, remedial, casework,' and applying them in an African context. This stance, the decision to use the social developmental approach, and the rejection of individual-oriented methods considered 'non-African' influenced the thinking and social work practice of non-governmental welfare organisations, including the three organisations that took part in this investigation.

Consequently, the emphasis placed on using the social developmental approach and undertaking social work that concentrates only on structural problems could result in a gap in service provision by rejecting individual-focused approaches to problem-solving. Many service users – respondents reported that their immediate needs were not being addressed, as the NGOs focus on the emancipatory approach attempting to tackle broader structural issues, though there is some evidence of using maintenance and therapeutic approaches alongside this. One possible explanation for the emancipatory focus of the organisations with its emphasis on structural issues rather than immediate needs lies in the organisations' initial formulation of services and social problems outlined in their mission and vision statements. Since their formation, it is also likely that they have encountered the necessity to tackle issues of an immediate nature, but this has proven difficult due to resource limitations. The current study has demonstrated the existence of issues with immediate impact and at a broader structural level, therefore emphasising the need to reconsider traditional approaches to understanding social work. Thus, this study utilised Dominelli's model, which represents different ways of thinking and undertaking social work that focuses on immediate and structural issues through the maintenance, therapeutic, and emancipatory approaches.

This does not undermine the importance of using the social developmental approach in problem-solving. It is a method that significantly impacts issues stemming from within a broader social-cultural structure. Nevertheless, when I consider how this social developmental approach works in practice on the ground, it is essential to look at people's immediate needs that are not being addressed. This method almost entirely focuses on social structural, and cultural changes, thus creating a disconnect between clients' immediate needs and their perception of services and service providers' perceptions.

Organisations providing social services in Tanzania must prioritize addressing individuals' immediate needs while also recognizing the profound impact of social structures and cultural factors on disadvantaged groups. Factors such as stigma, discrimination, domestic abuse, victimization, and cultural attitudes, as well as the absence of consistent government intervention programs, contribute to the suppression of rights among disadvantaged groups, often perpetuated by patriarchal dominance. Understanding these complexities is essential for organisations to effectively tackle societal issues at a structural level, fostering empathy and a deeper understanding of the challenges faced by these marginalised groups.

10.5 Social Protection Policy Measures for the Vulnerable: A Long-term solution

Addressing critical social issues in Tanzania requires the introduction of social protection measures for vulnerable populations as a long-term solution. Currently, there is increased attention on this solution in the ongoing debate about resolving problems affecting older people and other social groups in Africa and Tanzania. The lack of social protection provisions, particularly statutory policy related to social protection, is a fundamental issue underlying the problems faced by disadvantaged social groups. There is limited social security coverage for specific groups, such as few older people in public employment being covered by statutory social protection provisions. In Tanzania, the social insurance system primarily serves current urban workers, leaving out older people living in rural areas. The lack of statutory social protection coverage leaves many people unprotected and vulnerable to diverse situations, making their recovery a struggle.

The question and demand for general statutory social protection provided for all older people regardless of one's economic status have been at the centre of academic discussion and advocated by social work practitioners for almost twenty years. During the 2000s, international NGOs, the ILO, and some international donors initially promoted a non-contributory old-age pension. Only later did the Ministry of Labour in Tanzania seriously investigate the matter. However, in the end, the Ministry of Finance promised to introduce a social pension for older people. Nevertheless, it is still unclear whether this promise will turn into actual delivery (Ulriksen, 2016), as the government has not taken any significant steps to resolve this critical issue.

The current living conditions for many elderly individuals in rural areas present a number of difficulties. One potential long-term solution is for the Tanzanian government to ensure that all elderly individuals, including those in marginalised rural agricultural-based communities, receive equal social protection. According to one study in the early 2000s, older people are the least supported, with the International NGO, HelpAge, drawing attention to the impoverishing forces facing the elderly (Lerisse, Mmari & Baruani, 2003:69). Also, there are local non-governmental welfare organisations, included MAPERECE in the Mwanza region and REPSSI (Regional Psychosocial Support Initiative), founders of the KwaWazee pension fund in the Nshamba villages in the Muleba District, north-western Tanzania, to mention but a few, that are dedicated to addressing social welfare needs of older people.

The conversation among scholars and social work professionals has brought attention to the fact that due to the lack of a formal social protection system and necessary government interventions, many elderly individuals in Tanzania and other sub-Saharan countries rely on assistance from family and community networks to address their challenges. In their research on the availability of social protection mechanisms, especially the absence of statutory social security in Tanzania, Mallya and Mwankanye (1987:227) found that:

"social protection, to a large extent, embraces mutual assistance mechanisms traditionally embodied in the extended family and kinship systems. These mechanisms are based on in-built values of mutual aid and protection with characteristic emphases on interdependence between the family, clan, and village members. In this view, support to older people is given essentially in recognition of their past contribution to society during their active years, and it is bound by a moral rather than a legal force."

However, twenty-four years later, Spitzer and Mabeyo's study (2011) raised the same issue again: the need for comprehensive statutory social protection coverage for all older people in Tanzania. Their observation attributed the decline in the traditional family network support system for older adults in present-day Tanzania to the erosion of *social structures* and a weakening of cultural norms and obligations (Spitzer and Mabeyo, 2011). They wrote:

"One of our key intentions was to determine to which extent these support mechanisms and structures are in place and how they translate into social protection in old age. A general observation in both study sites [urban Dar es Salaam and rural communities in Lindi District] was that these structures are in the process of being eroded and affected by different factors, such as the effects of liberalised and free market economies as well as the impact of HIV/AIDS. Although the supporting power of families and relatives is obviously still a strong force in social protection for older people, we can also state that its scope seems to be weakening daily" (Spitzer and Mabeyo, 2011:106).

The above observation reinforces a key point worth emphasising. There is a realisation that reliance on traditional family network support as a social protection mechanism for people in old age and the general vulnerable population is not guaranteed in the long future. Therefore, this reality necessitates statutory social protection measures as an alternative solution to ensure older people's welfare needs. Likewise, Morisset (2013a) observed that most Tanzanians have no access to social protection provisions and rely only on informal support systems. When confronted with financial distress or some other difficulty, over 80 per cent of Tanzanian families say they count on relatives and friends for the support needed (Morisset, 2013a).

Equally, Ulriksen (2016:3) observed that social protection for poor and vulnerable groups in Tanzania was woefully inadequate, with few programmes existing. There were, for instance, programmes that targeted vulnerable children by advocating children's rights, improving their access to essential services and assisting orphans. There were also credit schemes, counselling and assistance for needy women and people with disabilities (Lerisse, Mmari & Baruani, 2003). Emergency food aid programmes were also in place to temporarily help particularly vulnerable groups (poor households during food shortages and refugees) (World Bank, 2011). Nevertheless, a common observation was that most programmes were small-scale, covering only specific geographical areas or moments (e.g., in times of poor harvest), and were primarily externally funded (Ulriksen, 2016). Literature has cited a general lack of financial resources and capacity within government as factors that hinder the full social protection provision to its citizens. However, others have highlighted a lack of political will as an underlying explanation for the state's failure to provide adequate social protection to people experiencing poverty (Mchomvu et al., 2002; Lerisse, Mmari & Baruani, 2003). Efforts to find solutions to social problems and improve the living conditions of most Tanzanians have a history in the country. For example, the Development Vision 2025 was started under President Mkapa in 1995 and unveiled in 2000. The Vision was developed through discussions with domestic stakeholders including "Honourable Members of Parliament, all political parties, leaders of various religious denominations, women and youth organisations, chambers of commerce and industry, farmers, professional associations, renowned personalities in our nation's history and ordinary Tanzanians" (President Mkapa in Foreword to the 2025 Vision-United Republic of Tanzania, 2000, in Ulriksen, 2016:8). Hence, the Vision is a genuinely Tanzanian document. However, it probably reflects more the views of the political-economic elite than the broad Tanzanian population. The 2025 Vision highlights various impediments to development; the first is 'Donor–Dependence Syndrome and a Dependent and Defeatist Development Mindset' (Ulriksen, 2016:8). It further elaborated that "the mindset of the people of Tanzania and their leaders has succumbed to donor dependency and resulting in an erosion of initiative and lack of ownership of the development agenda… the mindset … has neither been supportive of hard work, ingenuity, and creativity." (The United Republic of Tanzania, 2000:8). In suggesting solutions to this state of affairs, the Vision states: "The effective transformation of the mindset and culture to promote attitudes of self-development, community development, confidence and commitment to face development challenges and exploit every opportunity to improve the quality of livelihood is of prime importance. The effective ownership of the development agenda and the spirit of self-reliance at all societal levels are the primary driving force for the realisation of the Vision."(United Republic of Tanzania, 2000: 17, quoted by Ulriksen, 2016:9).

Voluntary organisations such as MAPERECE, SMGEO and Dogodogo Street Children Trust have limitations on what they can achieve. MAPERECE cannot solve the economic disadvantages that underpin the problems of older people in rural settings. These local non-governmental organisations can only raise public awareness of these critical issues, including the need for social protection coverage for older people, to try to achieve further government action. Social protection is essential as it is concerned with preventing, managing, and overcoming situations that adversely affect people's well-being—the absence of social protection impacts drivers of poverty and vulnerability (Babajanian, 2013). To improve clients' wellbeing older people who are at the heart of MAPERECE's concerns, the organisation must do more to strengthen its involvement, especially establishing a stronger direct connection with individual clients in their living circumstances. At the same time, the organisation must strongly continue pushing the government to provide social protection for all older people, especially those in rural areas left out of the current social protection policy scheme.

One may ask, what is the solution to these issues? It seems to me that the responsibility to change the situation lies with the national government. The practical solution is to find transport, a vehicle that can serve as a local ambulance and be dedicated to helping older people by taking them to hospitals. The government administration should facilitate the funding for such transport. The local community should organise the services running and ensure that older people get to hospitals in time for treatment. An alternative solution to this problem would be for the government health welfare ministry to create what I may call a 'mobile healthcare service unit' associated with governmental hospitals in each region and district. This healthcare service unit could have doctors and nurses whose task is to take medical and health-related services to older people in rural communities. Turning the focus to the problems related to the welfare of street children in Dar es Salaam, let me express some general thoughts concerning intervention.

One general issue concerning the welfare of street children in Dar es Salaam is that street children are without parental guidance. One may argue that this lack of parental guidance and involvement with children is a natural result of them moving away from the home settings. However, in knowing the importance and benefits of street children maintaining a social connection with people and the community around Dar es Salaam and other cities, it was evident that more could be done to foster social interaction and support toward street children.

One way to foster social interaction and community's support towards street children would be to involve the government in establishing a formal guardianship programme in cities where street children are present. This solution could be in some form of foster care. Families or adults could take children under their wing and support them until they can stand on their own feet. Such a plan could increase understanding and accepting attitudes toward street children. It could also encourage families from within city communities to become more involved and possibly take a guardianship role to support vulnerable children living in these hazardous environments.

The situation of street children in Dar es Salaam has highlighted the significant influence of Tanzanian police officers on their daily challenges. This emphasises the need for further research into the attitudes and interactions of police officers with street children. The current study lacks the perspectives of the police on the welfare of these children, making it important to address this gap. Additional training for police officers, including sensitivity training and conflict resolution workshops, is recommended to address the challenges faced by street children and the potential positive role of the police in resolving these issues effectively.

Further investigation is required to produce research-based evidence addressing the perspectives of governmental bodies on these matters. Financial planning and responsibility are crucial considerations for the funding of such measures, and strategies for financing these programs should be developed if the government is committed to taking action.

Local non-governmental social welfare organisations play a significant role in addressing the issues faced by disadvantaged groups in Tanzania. However, there is room for improvement in the support provided by these organisations. Research-based knowledge could guide these organisations in rethinking their approaches to social work activities, focusing on service users in various settings within Tanzania. Dominelli's social work practice model could serve as a valuable tool to reshape the organisations' practices and approach to social problem-solving, thereby aiding individuals and communities in addressing issues effectively. Collaboration between social workers and their clients is essential in understanding the situations impacting the well-being of clients in their respective settings, allowing for responsive actions based on reality and mutual expectations. The discussion in this book has emphasised that issues affecting older people, street children, women, and disabled individuals stem from complex root causes. The social work programs carried out by local non-governmental welfare organisations must operate at different levels—micro, meso, and macro— and within broader spheres of influence to meet the unique needs of their clients. While each organisation demonstrates determination in supporting their clients, their limited capacity necessitates the implementation of a collaborative model involving various stakeholders. A multidimensional approach is essential to addressing cultural and structural factors underpinning the problems faced by older people, street children, gender-based discrimination impacting women, and issues affecting the well-being of disabled individuals. However, this cannot be achieved without the crucial collaboration between local NGOs and the government. This emphasises the necessity of unity and collective action to bring lasting impact to vulnerable social groups in Tanzania.

Reference

AbleChildAfrica – (Organisation works with disabled children and young people in Africa) Report on stigma and discrimination surrounding disabilities in African societies (2013).

Aboderin I. (2006). Intergenerational Support and Old Age in Africa. New Brunswick: Transaction.

Aboderin, I. (2010) "Global Ageing: Perspectives from Sub-Saharan Africa," in The SAGE Handbook of Social Gerontology, (eds.) Dannefere D. & Phillipson C (eds). (London, Thousand Oaks, New Delhi: SAGE Publications.

Adams, R., Dominelli L. & Payne M. (2009) Social Work: Themes, Issues and Critical Debates (3rd ed.), Red Global Press.

Adams, R., Dominelli, L. & Payne, M. (2009) Critical Practice in Social Work, 2nd ed. Basingstoke: Palgrave Macmillan.

ADD International, Tanzania (2012) Education for all-supporting disabled children.

Adewunmi, B (April 2, 2014). "Kimberlé Crenshaw on intersectionality: 'I wanted to come up with an everyday metaphor that anyone could use'". www.newstatesman.com. Retrieved January 19, 2022

Adichie, C.N. (2014) , "I decided to call myself a Happy Feminist", in The Guardian For 200 years- we should all be feminist-Culture. Information accessed on April 2020, at https://www.theguardian.com/books/2014/oct/17/chimamanda-ngozi-adichie.

Afolabi, B. (2013) Street Children Phenomenon in Nigeria: The challenges and Way Forward. In *Social Science Research Network (SSRN) – Electronic Journal*, Research Gate.

Agarwala, R. & Lynch, S. M. (2006). Refining the measurement of women's autonomy: An international application of a multi-dimensional construct. *Social Forces*, 84(4), 2077–2098.

Ahmed N. (2017) Factors influenced Gender Based Violence among Women in Tanzania. (Unpublished Paper)—Institute of Social Work.

Ajayi, J.F. (1965) Christian missions in Nigeria, 1841-1891: the making of a new élite. London: Longmans.

Akuma J. M (2015) Socio–cultural and family change in Africa: Implications for adolescent socialization in Kisii County, South Western, Kenya. In *The East Africa Review 50, Open Edition Journals*.

Aldersey, H. (2012) Disability and Work: The United Republic of Tanzania's Workplace Policies in the Persons with Disabilities Act of 2010. *Disability Studies Quarterly*, Volume 32, No 3.

Alem, H.W. & Laha, A. (2016) Livelihood of Street Children and the Role of Social Intervention: Insights from Literature Using Meta-Analysis, in *Child Development Research* Volume 2016, Article ID 3582101: Hindawi Publishing Corporation.

Aley, R. (2016). An Assessment of the Social, Cultural and Institutional Factors that Contribute to the Sexual Abuse of Persons with Disabilities in East Africa. *Advantage Africa*.

Ali, N. (2011) The Vulnerability and Resilience of Street Children, Global Studies of Childhood Volume 1 Number 3 2011: COLLOQUIUM.

Ali, T.S., Karmaliani R., Mcfarlen J., Khuwaja H.M. A, Somani Y., Chirwa E D., & Jewkes (2017) Attitude towards gender roles and violence against women and girls (VAWG): baseline findings from an RCT of 1752 youths in Pakistan, in *Global Health Action,* 2017; 10(1), Taylor & Francis Group.

Al-Rossan, F. (2003). Introduction to Special Education. Dar Al-fker, Amman, Jordan.

Amani Children Home: why are there street children/ Accessed at http://www.amanikids.org/why-are-there-street-children/, on 16 November 2020).

Amin, A., Cameron, A. & Hudson, R. (1999) Welfare as Work? The potential of the UK Social Economy, Paper presented at the RGS/IBG Annual Conference, Leicester.

Aminur, R. (2013) Women's Empowerment: Concept and Beyond. In *Global Journal of Human Social Science Sociology and Culture,* 13(6):9.

Andrews, T. (2012) What is Social Constructionism? *The Grounded Theory Review,* Volume 11, Issue 1, pages 39-46.

Anheier, H.K. (2014). Nonprofit Organizations theory, management, policy. New York: Routledge.

Apt, N.A. (2000). Rapid urbanization and living arrangements of older persons in Africa. Legon: Centre for Social Policy Studies, University of Ghana.

Apteker L. & Stoecklin, D. (2014) Street Children and Homeless Youth: A Cross-Cultural Perspective. Springer Science & Business media Dordrecht.

Aronson, J. (1995) A Pragmatic View of Thematic Analysis. *The Qualitative Report*, 2(1), 1-3. https://doi.org/10.46743/2160-3715/1995.2069.

Arora S.K., Shah D., Chaturvedi S., & Gupta P. (2015) Defining and Measuring Vulnerability in Young People. *Indian Journal of Community Medicine*, Jul-Sep; 40(3):193-197. doi: 10.4103/0970-0218.158868

Asante, M.K. (2007) The history of Africa: The quest for eternal harmony. Florence, KT: Routledge.

Asha-Rose Migiro (2012) The National Strategy for Gender Development: Tanzania ministry of Community Development, Gender, Children, and old people.

Ayandele, E.A. (1966) The Missionary Impact on Modern Nigeria. London: Longman. Google Scholar.

Ayuku, D., Kaplan, C. & Baar, H. (2004). Characteristics and personal social networks of the on-the-street, of-the street, shelter, and school children in Eldoret, Kenya. International Social Work. 47(3): 293-311.

Babajanian B., (2013) Social Protection and its Contribution to Social Inclusion. Paper presented at the UNDESA expert group meeting New York, 10-11 September 2013. AusAID.

Baggott, R. (2004) Health and Healthcare in Britain, 3rd edn, Basingstoke: Palgrave Macmillan.

Barrientos, A., & DeJong, J. (2004). Child poverty and cash transfers. London: Chronic Poverty Research Centre.

Bassey, M. (1999): "Missionary Rivalry and Educational Expansion in Nigeria 1885– 1945," Studies in the History of Mission, vol. 15. Lewiston, NY: E. Mellen Press.

Baxi, A., & Saikia, D. (2003) Challenges the NGOs Face. Retrieved May 25th, 2021, from http://articles.economictimes.indiatimes.com/2003-10-11/news/27559891_1_indian-ngos-ngos-face-ashok-khosla.

Baxter, K., Courage, C. & Caine, K. (2015) Understanding Your Users: A Practical Guide to User Research Methods, (2nd Edition), Amsterdam: Morgan Kaufmann.

Bayeh, E. (2016) The role of empowering women and achieving gender equality to the sustainable development of Ethiopia. Pacific Science Review B: Humanities and Social Sciences, Volume2, Issue 1, pages 37-42.

Becker, S., Fonseca-Becker, F. & Schenck-Yglesias, C. (2006). Husbands' and wives' reports of women's decision-making power in Western Guatemala and their effects on preventive health behaviours. *Social Science and Medicine*, 62(9), 2313–2326.

Benjamin, C.R. (1976) African Religions: Symbol, Ritual, and Community, Englewood Cliffs: Prentice-Hall.

Berman, E.H. (1974) African Responses to Christian Mission Education. *African Studies Review* 17, no. 3 (1974): 527-540.

Betron, M. & Doggett, E. (2006). Linking gender-based violence research to practice in East, Central and Southern Africa: a re-view of risk factors and promising interventions. *Publication produced for review by the United States Agency for International Development* (USAID).

Bhalalusesa, E. (2003). Education for all: is Tanzania on track? In Norrag (Ed.), Critical Perspectives on Education and Skills in Eastern Africa on Basic and Post-Basic Levels (pp. 49-53). Norrag: Network for International Policies and Co-operation in Education and Training.

Bhalalusesa, E. & Mboya, M. (2003). Gender analysis to the factors influencing performances management and leadership. Unpublished paper, University of Dar es Salaam, Dar es Salaam, Tanzania.

Bhukuth, A. & Ballet, J. (2015), Children of the Street: Why are they in the Street? How do they Live? Economics and Sociology, Vol. 8, No 4, pp. 134-148.

Bisanda B.W, & Ming W., (2019) Assessing Factors Accelerating Gender Inequality in Tanzania Education System: Mien of Imperative Government Policy for Development. *Public Policy and Administration Research*, Vol.9 (5)26-35.

Blumer, H (1992) Symbolic Interactionism: Perspective and Method. Berkeley: University of California Press.

Boote, D. N. & Beile, P. (2005). Scholars before researchers: On the centrality of the dissertation literature review in research preparation. Educational Researcher 34(6), 3–15

Bossert, A. (1985/1987) Traditionelle und moderne Formen sozialer Sicherung in Tanzania. Eine Untersuchung ihrer Entwicklungsbedingungen, Berlin 1985 – English Translation: Traditional and Modern Forms of Social Security in Tanzania. An Examination of the Conditions of their Development, Augsburg 1987. Berlin. Duncker & Humblot.

Boughelaf, J. (2012). Women of the Egyptian revolution. Credemus Associates
(Retrieved from: http://www.credemus.org/images/stories/ reports/ women-of-the-egyptian-revolution.pdf, on 20 Jun 2020.

Braun, V. & Clarke, V. (2006) Using thematic analysis in psychology. *Qualitative Research in Psychology* 3: 77 – 101.

Brennan, J.R. (2002) 'Nation, race and urbanization in Dar es Salaam, Tanzania, 1916–1976' (Ph.D. thesis, Northwestern University, 2002.

Bridgman, J. & Clarke, D.E. (1965) German Africa: A Selected An notated Bibliography

Brode, H. (1969) British and German East Africa: their economic commercial relations (classic reprint). S.I., Forgotten Books. Accessed at https://dl.wdl.org/11957/service/11957.pdf on 09 July 2018

Brodsky, A.E. & Welsh, E. (2008). Applied Research. Field Notes. Negative Case Analysis and Researcher as Instrument. In *The Encyclopedia of Qualitative Methods*. Sage.

Brookfield, S. (2009) The concept of critical reflection: promises and contradictions. In, *European Journal of Social Work*, 12:3, 293-304, DOI: 10.1080/13691450902945215.

Brown, J. (1999). Why Vygotsky? The role of social interaction in constructing knowledge. In P. Lloyd & C. Fernyhough (Eds.), Lev Vygotsky: critical assessment (volume 3) UK: Taylor & Francis. Bruner, J. (1986). Actual minds, possible worlds. Harvard University Press, Cambridge, Massachusetts.

Bryman, A. (2004) Social research methods, 2nd ed., Oxford; New York: Oxford University Press.

Bryman, A. (2012) Social research methods 4th ed., New York: Oxford University Press.

Buckner, J.C. (2008) Understanding the Impact of Homelessness on Children Challenges and Future Research Directions, in *American Behavioural Scientist* Volume 51 Number 6 February 2008: 721-736: Sage.

Buell, R.L. (1928). The Native Problem in Africa, Vol 1 and 2. New York: MacMillan.

Bujari, P. "Towards Healthy Ageing: A Viewpoint from Tanzania," Quarterly Journal of the International Institute on Ageing Vol.14, No.2 (2004): 11-17.

Burell, G. & Morgan, G. (1979). Sociological and Paradigms and Organizational Analysis. London: Heinemann Educational Books.

Burgman, M. (2005). Risks and decisions for conservation and environmental management. Cambridge University Press, Cambridge, United Kingdom.

Burr, V. (2003). Social constructionism (2nd Ed.). New York, NY: Routledge.

Burton, A. (2003) 'Townsmen in the making: social engineering and citizenship in Dar es Salaam, c. 1945–1960', *International Journal of African Historical Studies*, 36 (2003), 331–65.

Burton, A. (2008) The Eye of Authority: 'Native' Taxation, Colonial Governance and Resistance in Inter-war Tanganyika, in *Journal of Eastern African Studies*, 2:1, 74-94, DOI: 10.1080/17531050701847250

Buske, S.L. (2011). A Case Study in Tanzania. Police Round–Ups and Detention of Street Children as a Substitute for Care and Protection. *South Carolina Journal of International Law and Business*, Vol, 8.

Cabrera, E.M. & Mauricio, D. (2017) Factors affecting the success of women's entrepreneurship: a review of literature, *International Journal of Gender and Entrepreneurship*, Vol. 9 Issue: 1, pp.31-65.

Campbell, A., Taylor, B.J. & McGlade A. (2017) Research Design in Social Work: Qualitative, Quantitative & Mixed Methods, London: Learning Matters—SAGE Publication Ltd.

Carlson, G.J., Kordas, K. & Murray-Kolb, L.E. (2015). Associations between women' s autonomy and child nutritional status: A review of the literature. *Maternal & Child Nutrition*, 11, 452–482. https://doi.org/10.1111/mcn.12113.

Carson, D., Gilmore, A., Perry, C. & Gronhaug, K. (2001). Qualitative Marketing Research. London: Sage.

Chapman, S. (2006) Thinking about language; Theories of English. Palgrave Macmillan, New York.

Cheong, Y.F., Yount, K. & Crandall, A. (2017). Longitudinal measurement invariance of the women's agency scale. *Bulletin of Sociological Methodology*, 134(1), 24–36.

Chidzero, B.T. (1961) Tanganyika and International Trusteeship, Oxford University Press.

Chingonikaya, E.E. & Salehe, F.C. (2019) Contribution of Law Enforcement Institutions in Protecting Street Children's Rights in Dar Es Salaam, Tanzania. Archives of Current Research International 17(1): 1-10, 2019; Article no.ACRI.41733.

Chitereka, C. (2009) Social Work Practice in a Developing Continent: The Case of Africa. In: *Advances in Social Work* Vol. 10 No. 2 (Fall 2009), 144-156.

Cismaru, M. & Lavack, A.M (2011) 'Campaigns targeting perpetrators of intimate partner violence', *Trauma, Violence and Abuse*, vol. 12, no. 4, 2011, pp. 183–97.

Clarke, J. & Cochrane A. (2005), 'The social construction of social problems', in Saraga, E (ed.), *Embodying the social: constructions of difference*, 3-38. Routledge.

Clarke, V. & Braun, V. (2013). Successful Qualitative Research: A Practical Guide for Beginners. London: Sage.

Cleary, S. (1997). The Role of NGOs Under Authoritarian Political Systems. Hampshire, UK: Palgrave Macmillan.

Clubb A.C, & Hinkle, J.C (2015) Protection motivation theory as a theoretical framework for understanding the use of protective measures. *Criminal Justice Studies – A Critical Journal of Crime, Law and Society* Volume 28, Issue 3. Pages 336-355.

Cochrane, A. (1998) 'Globalisation, fragmentation and local welfare citizenship', in Carter, J. (ed) Postmodernity and the Fragmentation of Welfare, Routledge, London, pp. 252-266.

Cohen, O. (2003). The Israeli family. *The International Encyclopedia of Marriage and Family* (Vol. 2, pp. 960–964). New York: Macmillan.

Cohen, L., Manion, L. & Morrison, K. (2006) (5TH ed). Research Methods in Education. London: Roultedge.

Colin, G., Turner, J., Bailey, C. & Latulippe, D. (2000) Social security pensions: development and reform. Geneva: International Labour Office.

Collins, P., (1998) Negotiating Selves: Reflections on "Unstructured" Interviewing. Sociological Research Online, 3 (3). Accessed on 25 January 2018 at:
http://www.socresonline.org.uk/3/3/2.html

Collins, P.H. (2000) Black Feminist Thought: Knowledge, Consciousness, and the politics of Empowerment, 2nd, edn. London: Routledge.

Connolly, M. (1990) Adrift in the City: A Comparative study of street children in Bogota, Colombia and Guatemala, New York: Haworth Press.

Connolly, M. & Ennew, J. (1996) Introduction: Children out of place, London, Thousand& New Delhi: SAGE Publications, Vol. 3(1996) 131-45.

Cooper, F. (1996) "Our strike": equality, anticolonial politics and the 1947–48 railway strike in French West Africa', Journal of African History, 37 (1996), 83.

Cooper, F. (1996) Decolonization and African Society: The Labor Question in French and British Africa, Cambridge

Cooper, H.M. (2010). Research Synthesis and Meta-Analysis. A Step-by-Step Approach. 4th ed. Thousand Oaks, CA: Sage.

Cornwall, A. (2016). Women's empowerment: What works. Journal of International Development, 28, 342–359. https://doi.org/10.1002/jid.

Council of Europe, Convention on Preventing and Combating Violence against Women and Domestic Violence. Strasbourg, Council of Europe, 2011.

Craig, G & Manthorpe, J. (1999) "Unequal Partners? Local government reorganisation and the voluntary sector", *Social Policy and Administration*, 33 (1), 55 – 72.

Crenshaw, K (1989) Demarginalizing the intersection of race and sex: A Black feminist critique of antidiscrimination doctrine, feminist theory and antiracist politics. *The University of Chicago Legal Forum* 140: 139–167.

Crenshaw, K (2011) Postscript. In: Lutz, H, Herrera Vivar, MT, Supik, L (eds) *Framing Intersectionality: Debates on a Multi-faceted Concept in Gender Studies*. Farnham, Ashgate, pp. 221–233.

Crespi, I. (2003) Gender socialization within the family: a study on adolescents and their parents in Great Britain, Paper for BHPS, Catholic University of Milan.

Creswell, J.W., (2003) Research design: qualitative, quantitative, and mixed methods approach, 2nd ed., CA: Sage: Thousand Oaks.

Creswell, J.W. (2014). Research Design: Qualitative, Quantitative and Mixed Methods Approaches (4th ed.). Thousand Oaks, CA: Sage.

Crocker, J., Major, B. & Steele, C. (1998). Social stigma. In Fiske, S., Gilbert, D., Lindsey G *Handbook of Social Psychology*, ed., vol. 2, pp. 504–53. Boston, MA: McGraw-Hill.

Crossman, A. (2020, August 27). Definition of Scapegoat, Scapegoating, and Scapegoat Theory. Retrieved October 10, 2020, from https://www.thoughtco.com/scapegoat-definition-3026572.

Crossman, A. (2020, August 28). The Major Theoretical Perspectives of Sociology. Retrieved July 5, 2021, from https://www.thoughtco.com/theoretical-perspectives-3026716.

Crotty, M. (1998). The foundations of social research: meaning and perspectives in the research process. Sage, London.

Crow, L. (1992) Renewing the Social Model of Disability, *Coalition*, July: 5-9 French, S.

Currie, Rose resource Inc., Sekenke Gold mine accessed on 8th June 2020, at Wikipedia, https://en.wikipedia.org/wiki/Sekenke_Gold_Mine

Davidson, B. (1969) The African Genius, Boston. James Currey.

Davies, M. (2008) The Blackwell companion to Social Work. 3rd edition. UK, Blackwell Publishing Ltd.

Deakin, N. (1996) "The Devil's in the Detail: Some reflections on contracting for social care by voluntary organisations", *Social Policy and Administration*, (30), 20-38.

Devaney J. (2013) Older women living and coping with domestic violence (BA). *The journal of the Community Practitioners' & Health Visitors' Association (Community Pract)*, 86 (2) 28. Reductive Publishing Ltd.

Devaney J. (2014) Male perpetrators of domestic violence: How should we hold them to account? *The Political Quarterly* Volume 85, Issue (4) Pages 480-486.

Dean, H. (2012) Social Policy: Short introductions, 2nd ed, Polity Press.

De Haas, M., & Frankema E. (2018) Gender, ethnicity, and unequal opportunity in colonial Uganda: European influences, African realities, and the pitfalls of parish register data. *Economic History Review* 71, no. 3 (2018): 965-994.

Dempsey L., Dowling M., Larkin P., & Murphy K. (2016) Focus on Research Methods: Sensitive Interviewing in Qualitative Research. Research in Nursing and Health (39), 480-490.

Denscombe, M. (2003) The Good Research Guide: For Small-Scale Social Research Projects. (2nd edition) Buckingham: Open University Press.

Diamond, J. (2012) The World Until Yesterday, UK, Penguin Books: Clays Ltd, St Ives plc.

Dieronitou, I., (2014) The Ontological and Epistemological Foundations of Qualitative and Quantitative Approaches to Research with particular reference to Content and Discourse Analysis of Textbooks. *International Journal of Economics, Commerce and Management,* Vol. II, Issue 10.

Dillip A., Mboma, Z.M., Greer, G. & Lorenz, L.M. (2018) 'To be honest, women do everything': understanding roles of men and women in net care and repair in Southern Tanzania, in *Malaria Journal*, 2018; (17): 459.Published online, doi: 10.1186/s12936-018-2608-7.

Dixon, J. (1987). Social Welfare in Africa. London: Crooms Helm.

Dogodogo Street Children Trust (http://www.dogodogocentre.com, accessed on 27 November 2019).

Dogodogo Centre (2020). https://dogodogocentre.or.tz/about-us/ (retrieved on 07 Aug 2021).

DogodogoStreetChildrenTrust. (http://archive.maryknollogc.org/regional/africa/Together-with Africa/Dogodogo%20Centre.html, on 27 November 2019.)

Dogodogo Street Children Trust, 1992. Mission, Dar es Salaam, Africa Sana

Dolan, C.S. (2001). The "Good Wife": Struggles over resources in the Kenyan horticultural sector. The *Journal of Development Studies*, 37(3), 39–70.

Dominelli, L. (1997) Social Work and Social Development: A Partnership in Social Change, *Journal of Social Development in Africa. Vol. 12. No 1. pp. 29-38.*

Dominelli, L. (1998), 'Anti-Oppressive Practice in Social Work', in Adams, R., Dominelli, L. and Payne, M., Social Work: Themes, Issues and Critical Debates. Basingstoke: Palgrave Macmillan.

Dominelli, L. (2002a) Anti-Oppressive Social Work Theory and Practice. London: Palgrave.

Dominelli, L. (2002b) Anti-oppressive Social Work: Theory and Practice. Basingstoke: Palgrave Macmillan.

Dominelli, L. (2002c) Anti-oppressive practice in context, in Adams, R., Dominelli L., & Payne, M (eds) Social Work: Themes, Issues, and Critical Debates (2nd edn), Basingstoke: Palgrave Macmillan: 3-19.

Dominelli, L. (2004) Social Work: Theory and Practice for a Changing Profession, Cambridge, Polity Press.

Dominelli, L. (2009) Introducing Social Work, Polity Press.

Dougherty, M.I. (1966) Tanganyika during the twenties: a study of the social and economic development of Tanganyika under British mandate, *African Studies*, 25:4, 197-226, Doi: 10.1080/00020186608707244.

East Africa Community – EAC SECRETARIAT (2012): EAC Strategy Plan for Gender, Youth, Children, Persons with Disability, Social Protection and Community Development (2012-2016-). Arusha – Tanzania.

East, C. (2016). A year on: Magufuli's reforms and Tanzania's economic outlook. Availablefromhttp://globalriskinsights. com/2016/11/a-year-on-magufulis-reforms-and-tanzanias-economicoutlook/ Accessed on 27th August 2019.

Eboiyehi F.A, & Onwuzuruigbo I. C. (2014) Care and Support for the Aged among the Esan of South-South Nigeria, in *The Nigerian Journal of Sociology and Anthropology* Volume 12, No. 1.

Eckert, A. (2004) Regulating the Social: Social Security, social welfare, and the state in late colonial Tanzania, in: *Journal of African History*, 45(2004), pp.467-89, UK: Cambridge University Press.

Eger, C., Miller, G. & Scarles, C. (2018). Gender and capacity building: A multi-layered study of empowerment. *World Development*, 106, 207–219. https://doi. org/10.1016/j.worlddev.2018.01.024. Accessed on 15 October 2020.

Eisikovits, Z., Koren C. & Band-Winterstein, T. (2013) The social construction of social problems: The case of elder abuse and neglect, in *International Psychogeriatrics* DOI: 10.1017/ S1041610213000495 · Source: PubMed/ResearchGate

Elder-Vass, D. (2012). The Reality of Social Construction, Cambridge, University Press.

Elkind, D. (2004) The problem with constructivism. *The Educational Forum* 68(4): 306–12.

Elliot, M. L. (2015). "What do you think we should do?" Relationship and reflexivity in participant observation. OTJR: Occupation, Participation and Health, 35(3), 133-141

Elmir, R., Schmied, V., Jackson, D., & Wilkes, L. (2011). Interviewing people about potentially sensitive topics. Nurse Researcher, 19(1), 12–16

Emmett, T & Alant, E (2006) Women and disability: exploring the interface of multiple disadvantages, *Development Southern Africa, Vol.* 23, Issue (4): 445-460

Enock, A., Mensah K A., Adjei R O., Edusei AK., Okyere P. & Appiah-Brempong E., (2015) We are Seen but not Recognized"; Disability Stigma and Disabled People's Exclusion from Community Activities: The Case of Disabled People in a Traditional Community in Ghana, in *Developing Country Studies* Vol.5, No.19. ISSN 2224-607X (Paper) ISSN 2225-0565 (Online).

Ernest, P. (1998) Social Constructivism as a Philosophy of Mathematics: Radical Constructivism. State University of New York Press, Albany.

Essien A. M, & Ukpong D.P. (2012) Patriarchy and Gender Inequality: The Persistence of Religious and Cultural Prejudice in Contemporary Akwa Ibom State, Nigeria. In *International Journal of Social Science and Humanity*, Vol. 2, No. 4.

Evans, R. (2002) Poverty, HIV, and Barriers to Education. Street Children's Experiences in Tanzania. *Gender and Development*, Vol 10, No. 3

Evans, R. (2005) Social networks, migration, and care in Tanzania. In *Journal of Children and Poverty,* 11 (2). pp. 111- 129. ISSN 1079-6126 doi: https://doi.org/10.1080/10796120500195527Available at http://centaur.reading.ac.uk/24445/

Ezedike, E.O. (2009) African Culture and the African Personality. From Footmarks to Landmarks on African Philosophy. Somolu: 0baroh and 0gbinaka Publishers.

Farmer E., & Callan, S. (2012) Beyond Violence: Breaking Cycles of Domestic Abuse, London, Centre for Social Justice, 2012.

Feinstein, S, Feinstein R, & Sabrow S. (2010) Gender inequality in the division of household labour in Tanzania, *African Sociological Review*. 2010;(14):98–109.

Ferguson, I. (2008) Reclaiming Social Work: Challenging Neo-liberalism and Promoting Social Justice. London: Sage.

Ferguson, K.M. (2007) Implementing a Social Enterprise Intervention with Homeless, Street-Living Youths in Los Angeles, *Social Work*, Volume 52, Issue 2, Pages 103–112, https://doi.org/10.1093/sw/52.2.103.

Fernandez-Castilla, R. (2008). "Panel discussion." Evidence-based policy making to implement the Madrid International Plan of Action on Ageing. The United Nations Department of Social and Economic Affairs and UNESCO'S Management of Social Transformation (MOST) Programme.

Ferreira, M (2005) Elder Abuse in Africa: What Policy and Legal Provisions Are There to Address the Violence? *Journal of Elder Abuse & Neglect*, Volume 16, 2005 –Issue 2. Taylor & Francis Online.

Fikowski, T. (2013) Police officers accused of raping street children in Tanzania, accessedon28February2021 https://terifikowski.wordpress.com/2013/07/15/ police-officers-accused-of-raping-street-children-in-tanzania/.

Flick, U. (2009). An introduction to qualitative research (4th ed.). Sage Publications Ltd.

Forrester, K. (1998) Older people in Tanzania – a research report from HelpAge International. Dares Salaam: HAI.

Foster, P.J. (1965) Education and Social Change in Ghana. Chicago: University of Chicago Press.

Fox, L. (2016). Gender, Economic Transformation and Women's Economic Empowerment in Tanzania. Overseas Development Institute. Accessed at https://set.odi.org/wpcontent/uploads/2016/03/Gender-application-to-Tanzania-paper_March_Final.pdf, on 25 April 2021.

Frankema, E. (2012) The origins of formal education in sub-Saharan Africa: was British rule more benign? *European Review of Economic History* 16, no. 4 (2012): 335-355.

Franklin, A., Lund, P., Bradbury-Jones, C., & Taylor, J. (2018). Children with albinism in African regions: their rights to 'being' and 'doing'. In *BMC International Health and Human Rights*, 18:2, 1-8.

Franzen, B. (1990). Attitudes towards the disabled in Kenya and Zimbabwe. School for International Training, Nybro.

Fredrick, K. (2010). Sexual business affects street children in Mwanza. *Mwananchi, Issue No. 03769,* Mzumbe University.

Freeman, M. & Mathison, S. (2009) Researching Children's Experiences, Guilford Publications.

French, S. (1993). Disability, impairment or something in between? Sage Publications, Inc; Open University Press.

Friberg, A., & Martinsson V (2017) Problems and Solutions when Dealing with Street Children: A qualitative study based on experience from social workers in Bloemfontein, South Africa. School of Health and Welfare, Jönköping University.

Friedland, W.H. (1969) Vuta Kamba: The Development of Trade Unions in Tanganyika *(Stanford, 1969)*.

Fuchs M., (1985) Social security in the Third world: a case study Kenya, (Baden Baden, (1985), 100–3. In Eckert, A. (2004) Regulating the Social: Social Security, social welfare, and the state in late colonial Tanzania, in: *Journal of African History*, 45(2004), pp.467-89, UK: Cambridge University Press.

Galbin A., (2014) An Introduction to Social Constructionism, in *Social Research Reports*, 2014, vol. 26, pp. 82-92. Expert Projects Publishing House. Accessed on 17 Feb 2021 at www. researchreports.ro

Gammage, S., Kabeer, N. & Rodgers, Y. V. D. M. (2016). Voice and agency: Where are we now? *Feminist Economics*, 22(1), 1–29.

Gellately, R. & Kiernan, B. (2003), The Specter of Genocide: Mass murder in historical perspective; Cambridge University Press.

Gergen, K. J. (1985). Theory of the self: Impasse and evolution. In Galbin A. (2014) An Introduction to Social constructionism,

Social Research Reports, 2014, Vol.26, pp.82-92, Expert Projects Publishing House.

Gergen, K J. (1991) The saturated self-dilemmas of identity in contemporary life, New York, Basic Books.

Ghuman, S. J., Lee, H. J. & Smith, H. L. (2006). Measurement of women's autonomy according to women and their husbands: Results from five Asian countries. *Social Science Research*, 35(1), 1–28.

Godda, H. (2018) Free Secondary Education and the Changing Roles of the Heads of Public Schools in Tanzania: Are They Ready for New Responsibilities? *Open Journal of Social Sciences,* 6, 1-23. https://doi.org/10.4236/jss.2018.65001.

Goffman, E. (1963). Stigma. London–Penguin.

Government of the United Republic of Tanzania and USAID Kizazi Kipya Project (2018). Street-Connected Children in Tanzania: Headcount Findings 2017. Dar es Salaam, Tanzania: Government of the United Republic of Tanzania, Railway Children Africa, Ipsos, and Pact Tanzania.

Gracey, M. (2002). Child health in an urbanizing world. ACTA Paedeatrica, 91(1), 1–8. doi:10.1080/080352502753457842.

Gray, D.E. (2009) Doing Research in the Real World, second edition, London; SAGE Publications Ltd.

Gray, M. (2002) Developmental Social Work: A "Strength" praxis for social development, *Social Developmental Issues, 24(1),* pp. 4-14.

Gray, M. (Ed.), (2016) Handbook of Social Work and Social Development in Africa. Routledge, London.

Gredler, M.E. (1997). Learning and instruction: Theory into practice (3rd ed). Upper Saddle River, NJ: Prentice-Hall.

Green, J., Willis K., Hughes E., Small Rh., Welch N., Gibbs L. & Daly J., (2007) Generating best evidence from qualitative research: the role of data analysis. *Australian and New Zealand Journal of Public Health*. 2007; 31(6): 545-50. PMid:18081575 http: //dx.doi.org/10.1111/j.1753-6405.2007.00141.x

Green, S. (2008). Perspectives of some non-governmental organizations on progress towards developmental social welfare and social work. *The Social Work Practitioner-Researcher*, 20(2), 174-191.

Groce, N., & McGeown, J. (2013). Witchcraft, Wealth and Disability: Reinterpretation of a folk belief in contemporary urban Africa (Working Paper Series: No. 30). Leonard Cheshire Disability and Inclusive Development Centre, UCL.

Grown, C., Rao Gupta, G. & Kes, A. (2005) Taking Action: Achieving Gender Equality and Empowering Women, UN Millennium Project Task Force on Education and Gender Equality, London and Sterling, VA: Earthscan http://www.unmillenniumproject.org/documents/ Gender-complete.pdf

Guba, E.G., & Lincoln, Y.S. (2005). Paradigmatic Controversies, Contradictions, and Emerging Confluences. In N. K. Denzin & Y. S. Lincoln (eds.), The Sage handbook of qualitative research (p. 191–215). Sage Publications Ltd.

Gupta, K. & Yesudian P.P. (2006) Evidence of Women's empowerment in India: A study of socio-spatial disparities. In *GeoJournal*, 65(4):365-380, Springer. Doi:10.1007/s10708-006-7556-z.

Hafford-Letchfield, T. & Cocker, C. (2022), 'Feminisms and intersectionalities' in Cocker C. & Hafford-Letchfield, T (eds.), Rethinking Feminist Theories for Social Work Practice, Basingstoke: Palgrave Macmillan.

Hagues, R. (2017) The Girl Is Brought Up Knowing She's Nothing: Listening to Voices of Tanzanian Women and Girls, in: *Children & Schools* Volume 39, Number 2 April 2017.

Hai, A., (2014) Problems Faced by the Street Children: A Study on Some Selected Places in Dhaka City, Bangladesh. In *International Journal of Scientific & Technology Research* Vol.3, Issue 10, October 2014. ResearchGate.

Hailey, L. (1938) An African Survey: A Study of Problems Arising in Africa South of the Sahara. Oxford: Oxford University Press

HakiElimu. (2008). Do Children with Disabilities Have Access to Education? A Research Report on Accessibility to Education for Children with Disabilities in Tanzanian Schools. Dar es Salaam: HakiElimu.

HakiElimu (2017) The Impact of the Implementation of Fee-Free Education Policy on Basic Education in Tanzania: A Qualitative Study. HakiElimu, Dar es salaam.

Halfpenny, P, Reid, M, 2002, Research on the voluntary sector: *An overview, Policy & Politics,* (30), 533-50.

Hamel, J., (2016) Domestic Violence Perpetrator Programs Around the World. In *Partner Abuse*, Volume 7, Number 3. Springer Publishing Company.

Hamisi S.H., (2019) Understanding Vulnerabilities in Tanzania. In. *Global Scientific Journals*: Volume 7, Issue 5, May 2019, online: ISSN 2320-9186 www.globalscientificjournal.com.

Hammersley, M. & Atkinson P. (2007) Ethnography principles in practice 3rd Edition, London & New York, Routledge: Taylor & Francis Group.

Hannan, C. (2001). The United Nations commitment to gender mainstreaming – a global strategy for promoting equality between women and men. Paper prepared for the 2001 ODCCP Field Representatives Seminar. Office of the Special Advisor on Gender Issues and Advancement of Women, New York.

Harris J (ed) (2003) Civil Society in British History: Ideas, Identities, Institutions, Oxford University Press.

Harris M (2016) Where did we come from? The emergence and early development of voluntary sector studies in the UK. *Voluntary Sector Review*, Vol 7 (1) 5–25. PolicyPress.OnlineISSN20408064. http://dx.doi.org/10.1332/204080516X14552851619827.

Harrison B (2003) Civil Society by Accident? Paradoxes of Voluntarism and Pluralism in the Nineteenth and Twentieth Centuries, in Harris J (ed) (2003) Civil Society in British History: Ideas, Identities, Institutions, Oxford University Press.

Hart, C. (1998) Doing Literature Review: Releasing the Social Science Research Imagination, SAGE Publications.

Hartz, L. (1948) Economic Policy and Democratic Thought: Pennsylvania, 1776-1860. Cambridge: Harvard University Press.

Haupt, W. (1984). Deutschlands Schutzgebiete in Übersee 1884–1918. Friedberg: Podzun-Pallas Verlag. Translated: Haupt, W. (1984) Germany's overseas protected areas 1884–1918. Friedberg: Podzun-PallasVerlag. Accessed on 9th June 2020, at https://en.wikipedia.org/wiki/German_East_Africa#cite_note-Haupt-16.

Heberlein, T. A. (1988). Improving interdisciplinary research: integrating the social and natural sciences. *Society & Natural Resources* 1:5–16.

Hedley, R. & Smith, J.D. (1992) Volunteering and Society: principles and practice, Bedford Square Press, London.

Heggenhougen, K. & Lugalla J. (ed) (2005) Social change and health in Tanzania, Dar es Salaam, Tanzania: Dar es Salaam University Press.

Heise, L. & Garcia-Moreno, C. (2002). Violence by intimate partners. In E. Krug, L. L. Dahlberg, & J. A. Mercy et al. (Eds.), World report on violence and health. Geneva: WHO.

Heise, L., Ellsberg, M., Gottmoeller M. (2002) A Global Overview of Gender-based Violence. in *International Journal of Gynecology and Obstetrics* 78 Suppl. 1 S5–S14.

Heise, L., Green M.E., Opper N., Stavropoulou M., Harper C. & Nascimento M. (2019) Gender Inequality and restrictive gender norms: Framing the challenges to health. *In Gender Equality, Norms, and Health,* Volume 393, Issue 10189, pp 2440-2454.

HelpAge International, (2002) State of the world's older people, London, HelpAge International.

HelpAge Tanzania. (2014) "Tackling witchcraft accusations," Sauti Ya Wazee Issue 05.

HelpAge International, (2016) "Amplifying voices of older women" *Sauti ya Wazee,* Issue 06.

HemaMehta, Hollis, (1954), Social Work, Retrieved June 30, 2020, from wikipedia.org/wiki/Caseworker

Henderson, W.O (1935) Historical Revision: LXXIX. —The German Colonial Empire, 1884–1918. In, History New Series, Vol. 20, No. 78 (September, 1935), pp. 151-158.

Henn, M., Weinstein, M., & Foard, N. (2009) A critical introduction to social research. Sage Publications.

Henslin, J.M. (2006). Essentials of Sociology: A down-to-earth approach (6th e.d.). Boston: Pearson/Allyn and Bacon.

Herbert H.W. (1974) Governing an African City: A Study of Nairobi. London: Africana Publishing Co.

Heslop, A., Agyarko R., Adjetey-Sorsey E. & Mapetla T. (2000) The contribution of older people to society: evaluation of participatory research methodology employed in studies in Ghana and South Africa, in *Southern African Journal of Gerontology* (2000), 9(2): 6-12.

Hitchcock, G. & Hughes, D. (1995) (2nd ed). Research and the Teacher. London: Routledge.

Holt, J. (2008) Addressing Gender-Based Violence Through Community Empowerment, Namibia: Legal Assistance Centre/ John Meinert Printers.

Hudson, M.F. (1991) Elder mistreatment: taxonomy with definitions by Delphi. *Journal of Elder Abuse and Neglect*. 1991; 3: 1–20.

Hudson, L. & Ozanne, J. (1988) Alternative Ways of Seeking Knowledge in Consumer Research. *Journal of* Consumer *Research*, 14(4), 508–521.

Ibhawoh, B. & Dibua, J. (2003). Deconstructing Ujamaa: The legacy of Julius Nyerere in the quest for social and economic development in Africa. *African Journal of Political Science*, 6(1), 59-83

Ibrahim, A. (2012) Characteristics of Street Children. *E-International Relations accessed at* https://www.e-ir.info/2012/12/11/characteristics-of-street-children/ on 20th January 2021.

Ibrahima, A.B. & Mattaini, M.A. (2019) Social work in Africa: Decolonizing methodologies and approaches, in *International Social Work* 2019, Vol. 62(2) 799 –813.

Idris, I. (2018). Barriers to women's economic inclusion in Tanzania. K4D Helpdesk Report. Brighton, UK: Institute of Development Studies.

IDEO.org (2015) The Field Guide to Human-Centered Design-Design KIT, IDEO.org.

Iliffe, J. (1969) Tanganyika under German Rule 1905-1912, Publisher: CUP London.

Iliffe, J. (1979). *A Modern History of Tanganyika*. Cambridge: Cambridge UP.

Iliffe, J. (1987) *The African Poor: A History.* (African Studies Series, number 58.) New York: Cambridge University Press.

Ingelaere, B. (2016) Inside Rwanda's /Gacaca/ Courts: Seeking Justice after Genocide- Critical Human Rights, University of Wisconsin Press.

Ingham, K. (1962) A History of East Africa. London, Longmans, Green.

Ituma, A. & Simpson, R. (2009) The 'boundaryless' career and career boundaries: Applying an institutionalist perspective to ICT workers in the context of Nigeria. *Human Relations*, Volume 62(5): 727–761, SAGE Publications.

Jackendoff, R. (2009) Language, consciousness, culture: essays on mental structure. The MIT Press, Cambridge.

Jackson, M. (2010). From anxiety to method in anthropological fieldwork: An appraisal of George Devereux's enduring ideas. In Davies J. & Spencer D.(Eds.), Emotions in the field: *The psychology and anthropology of fieldwork experience* (pp. 35-54). Stanford, CA: Stanford University Press.

Japhet, B. (2017) Is Tanzania's Urban Street Child Population Increasing? in *the Citizen-Tanzania*, Dar es Salaam.

Jennings, M. (2013) Common Counsel, Common Policy: Healthcare, Missions and the Rise of the 'Voluntary Sector' in Colonial Tanzania, in *Development and Change,* Volume 44, Issue 4, (2013), pp 939-963.

Jennings, M. (2014) Bridging the Local and the Global: Faith-Based Organisations and the Emergence of the Non-State Provider Sector in Tanzania. Cornell University Press.

Jennings, M. (2015) The precariousness of the franchise state: Voluntary sector health services and international NGOs in

Tanzania, 1960s e mid-1980s, *Social Science & Medicine* 141 (2015) 1-8. ELSEVIER.

Jepson, P. (2005). Governance and Accountability of Environmental NGOs. *Environmental Science and Policy,* 8, 515-524. Retrieved May 26, 2021, from Sciencedirect Databases.

Jivani, R. (2010) What are the Impacts of Non-Governmental Organisations on the Lives of the Citizens of Tanzania? *Social Impact Research Experience* (SIRE) 4.

Jordan, B. (2004) Emancipatory Social Work? Opportunity or Oxymoron. *The British Journal of Social Work, 34*(1), 5-19. Retrieved May 10, 2021, from http://www.jstor.org/stable/23719980.

Joubert, J., Lindgren, P. & Bradshaw, D. (2005). Elder abuse in South Africa: Responding to a changing world. Global Ageing: Issues and Actions. *Journal of the International Federation on Ageing)*, 3(1), 53–76.

Juma, S.K. (2008). Social and psychological problems facing orphaned children in Zanzibar. Published research paper MAASP. *Papers in Education and Development* No. 28, pp 139-160.

Kabeer, N. (1999). Resources, agency, achievements: Reflections on the measurement of women's empowerment. *Development and Change*, 30, 435–464.

Kabeer, N. (2005). Gender equality and women's empowerment: A critical analysis of the third millennium development goal 1. *Gender & Development,* 13(1), 13–24.

Kabeer, N. (2011). Between affiliation and autonomy: Navigating pathways of women's empowerment and gender justice in rural Bangladesh. *Development and Change*, 42(2), 499–528.

Kaiser, P.J. (1996). Structural Adjustment and the Fragile Nation: The Demise of Social Unity in Tanzania. *Journal of Modern African Studies* 34(2): 227-237.

Kandiyoti, D. (1988). Bargaining with patriarchy. *Gender & Society*, 2(3), 274–290. Kenya National Bureau of Statistics (KNBS) & ICF International. Demograp

Kanuha, V.K. (2000) "Being" Native versus "Going Native": Conducting Social Work Research as an Insider, *Social Work*, Volume 45, Issue 5, October 2000, Pages 439–447, https://doi.org/10.1093/sw/45.5.439

Kanyandago, P. (ed.) (2002) Marginalized Africa: *An International Perspective*. Nairobi, Kenya: Paulines Publications Africa.

Kaseke, E. (1991) Social Work Practice in Zimbabwe in *Journal of Social Development in Africa,* Vol. 6. No. 1. pp. 33-45.

Kaseke, E. (1998) "Social Welfare in Southern Africa: The Need for Transformation." *Social Work/Maatskaplike Werk* 34 (2): 144–149.

Katemba M.S Registration of NGOs in Tanzania According to the NGO Act No.24/2002 As Ammended by ACT NO.11/2005. The United Republic of Tanzania: Ministry of Community Development, Gender, older people and Children, (2005).

Kaufmann, O. (1982) Social security in relations between France and the African countries south of the Sahara (Frankfurt am Main, 1982), 86–9. In Eckert, A. (2004) Regulating the Social: Social Security, social welfare, and the state in late colonial Tanzania, in: *Journal of African History*, 45(2004), pp.467-89, UK: Cambridge University Press.

Kibassa C.G. & Lugalla, J.L.P (2003) Urban Life and Street Children's Health Children's Accounts of Urban Hardships and Violence in Tanzania. Transaction Publishers, Hamburg.

Kibuga, K.F. & Dianga A. (2000) Victimisation and killing of older women: witchcraft in Magu district, Tanzania, in: *Southern African Journal of Gerontology* (2000), 9(2): 29-32.

Kilbride, P.L., Suda, C. & Njeru, E. (2000) Street Children in Kenya: voices of children in search of a childhood. Westport: Greenwood Press.

Kim, B. (2001). Social Constructivism. In Orey M (Ed.), Emerging perspectives on learning, teaching, and technology. Retrieved Feb 14, 2021, from http://projects.coe.uga.edu/epltt/ http://epltt.coe.uga.edu/index.php?title=Social_Constructivism Researchgate

Kingma B.R. (1997) Public good theories of the non-profit sector: Weisbrod revisited. Voluntas: *International Journal of Voluntary and Non-profit Organizations*, Vol. 8, No. 2, Economic Theory (June 1997), 135-148. Springer.

Kiondo, A. S. Z. (1993). Structural adjustment and non-governmental organisations in Tanzania: a case study. Social change and economic reform in Africa. P. Gibbon. Uppsala, Nordic Africa Institute.

Kisembo, P. (2012). Recognise Street Children. In National Programmes-Study. The Guardian, Monday, 2nd March. Dar es Salaam.

Kishor, S. (2000). Empowerment of women in Egypt and links to the survival and health of their infants. In H. B. Presser & G. Sen

(Eds.), Women's empowerment and demographic processes: Moving beyond Cairo. Oxford: Oxford University Press.

Kitoka, J. (2011) The Dilemma of the Rural Elderly in Tanzania: Social Protection: Protecting whom against what! LAP LAMBERT Academic Publishing.

Klasen, S. & Lamana F, (2008). The Impact of Gender Inequality in Education and Employment on Economics Growth in Development Countries.

Klasen, S. & Schüler, D. (2011) Reforming the Gender-Related Development Index and the Gender Empowerment Measure: Implementing Some Specific Proposals, *FeministEconomics*, 17: 1, 1-30, DOI: 10.1080/13545701.2010.541860

Klugman, J., Gaye, A., Chang, P., Krishnan, A., Dahl, M., & Kishi, R. (2017). Women, peace and security index 2017/18: Tracking sustainable peace through inclusion, justice, and security for women. Washington, D.C.: GIWPS and PRIO.

Knappert, J. (1992). A short history of Zanzibar. Annales Aequatoria, 13, 15-37. Retrieved July 6, 2021, from http://www.jstor.org/stable/25837045.

Knappert, J. & Midgley, J. (2010) Developmental social work and the disabled. In: Midgley, J. & Conley, A. (eds.), Social work, and social development: theories and skills for developmental social work. New York: Oxford University Press.

Koch, E. (2015). Protracted displacement in Georgia: Structural vulnerability and 'Existing not Living'. *Human Organization*, 74(2), 135–143. doi:10.17730/0018-7259-74.2.135

Kopaka, P.A, (2000) The problem of street children in Africa: an ignored tragedy, in *Proceedings of the International Conference on Street Children and Street Children's Health in East Africa*, Dar-es-Salaam, Tanzania, April 2000.

Koponen, J. (1988) *People and Production in Late Precolonial Tanzania: History and Structures. Monographs of the Finnish Society for Development Studies*, No. 2; Transactions of the Finnish Anthropological Society, No. 23; Studia Historica, 28. Uppsala: *Scandinavian Institute of Africa Studies*.

Koponen, J. (1994) Development for Exploitation: German Colonial Policies in Mainland Tanzania, 1884-1914. Helsinki: *Finnish Historical Society*/Lit Verlag.

Koszela, K. (2013) The Stigmatization of Disabilities in Africa and the Developmental Effects. *Independent Study Project (ISP) Collection*. 1639.

Kramer, R. (1986) "the future of voluntary organisations in social welfare", in Independent Sector Inc. and United Way Institute (ed), Philanthropy, voluntary action, and the public good, Independent Inc. Washington DC.

Krauss, S.E. (2005) Research paradigms and meaning making: A primer. *The Qualitative Report*. 2005; 10(4): 758-770.

Kukla, A. (2000). Social Constructivism and the Philosophy of Science. New York: Routledge.

Kunhiyop, S.W. (2008) African Christian Ethics, Nairobi: WordAlive Publishers.

Kuran H.C A, Morsut C, Kruke B.I, Krüger M., Segnestam L., Orru K., Nævestad T.O., Airola M., Keränen J., Gabel F., Hansson S., & Torpan S., (2020). Vulnerability and vulnerable groups from an intersectionality perspective. In: *International Journal of Disaster Risk Reduction* 50 (2020) 101826. published by Elsevier Ltd. http://www.elsevier.com/locate/ijdrr https://doi.org/10.1016/j.ijdrr.2020.101826.

Kuschel, K., Lepeley, MT., Espinosa, F. and Gutiérrez, S. (2017) Funding Challenges of Latin American Women Start-up Founders in the Technology Industry, Cross Cultural & Strategic Management, 24(2), 310-331.

Kusmanto F. X. P. (2013) An Insight into NGO Challenges and the Need for Organisational Capacity Building for Malaysian NGOs: *International Conference on Business, Economics, and Social Sciences Proceeding*-Bangkok, 4-5 November 2013.

Kvale, S. & Brinkmann, S., (2009). Interviews: Learning the Craft of Qualitative Research Interviewing 2nd ed., Thousand Oaks, CA: Sage Publications, Incorporated.

Kweka, J. (2018) Monitoring Policies to support Industrialisation in Tanzania, an update and policy recommendations. *Supporting Economic Transformation, UK aid. Retrieved July, 5, 2021. From* https://r.search.yahoo.com/_ylt=AwrE19Vgdelgg.AAT29XNyoA;_ylu=Y29sbwNiZjEEcG9zAzEEdnRpZANDMjAwM18xBHNlYwNzcg--/RV=2/RE=1625941473/RO=10/RU=https%3a%2f%2fset.odi.org%2fwp-content%2fuploads%2f2018%2f11%2fMonitoring-Tanzania-policies-industrialisation_JKweka_Final.pdf/RK=2/RS=NVnIKse62nyn9tixIzgrlaKow2w-

Lakoff, G. & Johnson, M. (1980) Metaphors we live by. The University of Chicago Press, Chicago.

Lalor, K (1999 Street children: A comparative perspective. *Child Abuse and Neglect.* 25(8): 759-770. ResearchGate.

Lange, S., Wallevik H. & Kiondo, A. (2000) Civil Society in Tanzania, in *Development Studies and Human Rights*, Chr. Michelsen Institute, Norway.

Larkin, E, Friedlander D, Newman S & Goff R (2012) Intergenerational Relationships: Conversations on Practice and Research Across Cultures, New York, London: Routledge, Taylor & Francis Group.

Larsen, U. & Hollos M. (2003) Women's empowerment and fertility decline among the Pare of Kilimanjaro region, Northern Tanzania. *Social Science & Medicine* Vol. 57, Issue 6, Pages 1099-1115.

Lawi, Y.Q, Bech, M., Rekdal, O. & Massay, D. (2013). Changing Policies and their Influence on Government Health Workers in Tanzania 1967-2009: Perspectives from Rural Mbulu District, *The International Journal of African Historical Studies*.

Le Grand J. (1991) The Theory of Government Failure. *British Journal of Political Science*, Vol. 21, (4), 423-442. Cambridge University Press.

Leininger, M.M. (1985). Ethnography and ethnonursing: Models and modes of qualitative data analysis. In M. M. Leininger (Ed.), *Qualitative research methods in nursing* (pp. 33-72). Orlando, FL: Grune & Stratton.

Lekorwe, M., & Mpabanga, D. (2007). Managing Non-Governmental Organisations in Botswana. *The Innovation Journal: The Public Sector Innovation Journal*, 12(3), 1-18. Retrieved May 15, 2021, from http://www.innovation.cc/scholarly-style/lekorwe10final1draft.pdf.

Lenski, G. & Lenski, J. (1974) Human Societies: An Introduction to Macrosociology, New York, McGraw-Hill.

Lerisse, F., Mmari, D. & M. Baruani.(2003). Vulnerability and Social Protection Programmes in Tanzania. Dar es Salaam: Research and Analysis Working Group.

Lerisse, F., Mmari, D. & Baruani M (2007) Vulnerability and Social Protection Programmes in Tanzania, in: *Study on Social Protection Programmes on Vulnerability*. Dar es Salaam.

Leubuscher, C. (1944) Tanganyika Territory: A Study of Economic Policy under Mandate. London, Oxford University Press.

Lewis, D., & Kanji N. (2009). Non-Governmental Organisations and Development. London, UK: Routledge.

Liamputtong, P., & Ezzy, D. (2005). Qualitative Research Methods. Oxford: Oxford University Press.

Linda Z. (2014) Factors causing Gender inequality in Education in Tanzania: A Case of Korogwe District secondary School. Morogoro.

Link, B.G., Struening E l., Neese-Todd S., Asmussen S., & Phelan J C. (2001) Barrier to Recovery: The Consequences of Stigma for the Self-Esteem of People with Mental Illnesses, in Psychiatric Services, 2001 Vol.52 No.12.

Lombard, A. (2007) The impact of social welfare policies on social development in South Africa: an NGO perspective. Social Work/Maatskaplike Werk, 43(4): 295-316.

Lombard, A. & Wairire, G. (2010). Developmental Social Work in South Africa and Kenya: Some Lessons for Africa. *The Social Work Practitioner- Researcher Special Issue* April 2010:98-111.

Lombe, M., & Sherraden, M. (2008). Inclusion in the policy process: An agenda for participation of the marginalized. *Journal of Policy Practice*, 7(2–3), 199–213. doi:10.1080/15588740801938043.

Louis, M.R., & Bartunek, J.M. (1992) Insider/Outsider Research Teams: Collaboration Across Diverse Perspectives. In, Journal of Management Inquiry, Vol. 1 No.2, June 1992, 101-110.

Low, D.A. & Lonsdale J. (1976) 'Introduction: towards the new order, 1945–1963', in D. A. Low and A. Smith (eds.), History of East Africa, III (Oxford, 1976), 12.

Lowenstein, A., Eisikovits, E., Band-Winterstein, T. and Enosh, G. (2009). Is elder abuse and neglect a social phenomenon? Data from the First National Prevalence Survey in Israel. *Journal of Elder Abuse and Neglect,* 21, 253–277. doi:10.1080/08946560902997629.

Luena F. (2011) The problem of street children in Africa: An ignored tragedy. In: *Proceedings of International Conference on Street Children and Street Children's Health in East Africa.* Dar es Salaam, Tanzania; 2011.

Luena, F. (2011) Assessment of Child Abuse among Street Children: A Case Study of Dar es Salaam City, Tanzania. Sokoine University.

Lugalla, J. (1995) Crisis Urbanization and Urban Poverty in Tanzania: A Study of Urban Poverty and Survival Policies, University Press, America Lanham.MD.

Lugalla, J. (2005) The impact of structural adjustment policies on women's and children's health in Tanzania. In Heggenhougen, K.H. & Lugalla, J.L.P. (Eds.) *Social change and health in Tanzania* (pp. 243–256). Dar es Salaam University Press. Google Scholar.

Lugalla, J. & Kibassa, C.G. (2003). Urban Life and Street Children's Health: Children's Accounts of Urban Hardships and Violence in Tanzania. Berlin/Hamburg/Muenster: Lit Verlag.

Lugalla, J. & Mbwambo, J. (1999). Street children and street life in urban Tanzania: The culture of surviving and its implications for children's health. *International Journal of Urban and Regional Research, 23*(2), 329-344.

Lugalla J. & Mbwambo J.K. (2002) Street Children and Street Life in Urban Tanzania: The Culture of Surviving and its Implications for Children's Health. *International Journal of Urban and Regional Research,* Vol.23, Issue 2, (2002) pages 329-344.

Lusk, M.W., (1992) Street Children of Rio de Janeiro. In: *International Social Work*, 35 (3), 293-305.

Mabeyo, Z.M., Ndung'u, E. M., & Riedl, S. (2014). The role of social work in poverty reduction and the realization of millennium development goals in Tanzania. Kampala: Fountain publishers.

MacIntyre, G., Stewart, A., & McGregor, S. (2019). The double-edged sword of vulnerability: explaining the persistent challenges for practitioners in supporting parents with intellectual disabilities. *Journal of Applied Research in Intellectual Disabilities, 32*(6), 1523-1534. https://doi.org/10.1111/jar.12647

Maduga, F.C. (2015) Public Communication and Social security delivery in Tanzania; West London.

Magesa, L. (1997). African religion: The moral traditions of abundant life. New York: Orbis.

Magu-guide, (2002) Muelekeo wa haki kwa ajili ya jamii endelevu- MAPERECE.

Mair, L.P. (1936) Native Policies in Africa. London

Makhubu, L.P. (2009). Traditional medicine and healing in Swaziland. Kwaluseni: University of Swaziland Research Centre, Kwaluseni.

Mallya, W.J & Mwankanye, H.A., (1987) Tanzania, in Dixon J. (ed) (1987) Social Welfare in Africa, Beckenham: Croom Helm Ltd., pp.218-246.

Malunga, C. (2006) Learning Leadership Development from African Cultures: A Personal Perspective, *International NGO Training and Research Centre.*

Manara, K. (2009) Civil Society Voluntarism in Tanzania – kepa's working papers no 29, Helsinki: Kepa.

Manji, F. & O'Coill (2002) The missionary position: NGOs and development in Africa, *International Affairs (Royal Institute of International Affairs* 1944-), Vol. 78, No. 3 (Jul.2002) 567-583. Oxford University Press.

Manyama, W. (2017) Can Tanzania achieve social and economic development without the state provision of social welfare services? A systemic review, in *International Journal of Liberal Arts and Social Science* Vol. 5 No. 8 November 2017.

Manyama, W. (2018) Where Is Developmental Social Work as Social Work Practice Method in Tanzania? The Case of Dar es Salaam Region, in *International Journal of Social Work* 2018, Vol. 5, No. 2.

Manyama W (2017) Dynamics in Family Patterns in Tanzania: The Case of Kijitonyama Ward, Kinondoni District, Dar Es Salaam Region, Tanzania. In *Journal of Sociology and Social Work* Vol. 5, No. 1, pp. 68-79. Published by American Research Institute for Policy Development DOI: 10.15640/jssw.v5n1a7.

Marsh, Z. & Kingsnorth, G.W. (1957) An Introduction to the History of East Africa, Cambridge University Press, Cambridge.

Marshall, C. & Rossman, G.B. (2011). Designing Qualitative Research (5th ed.). Thousand Oaks, CA: Sage Publications.

Martin, C.L., Ruble, D.N., Szkrybalo, J. (2004) Recognizing the centrality of gender identity and stereotype knowledge in gender development and moving toward theoretical integration: Reply to Bandura and Bussey, P*sychological Bulletin*. 2004;130(5): 702–710.

Martorano, B., Sanfilippo, M. & Haraguchi, N. (2017) What factors drive successful industrialization? Evidence and implications for developing countries. Inclusive and Sustainable Industrial Development Working Paper. Vienna: UNIDO.

Maryknoll Office for Global Concerns (2011). A story of hope: The Dogodogo Centre. https://archive.maryknollogc.org/regional/africa/Together-with-Africa/Dogodogo%20Centre.html (retrieved on 07 Aug 2021)

Mascia, M. B., J. P. Brosius, T. A. Dobson, B. C. Forbes, L. Horowitz, M. A. McKean, and N. J. Turner. 2003. Conservation and the social sciences. *Conservation Biology* 17:649–650.

Mason, K.O. & Smith, H.L. (2003). Women's empowerment and social context: results from five Asian countries. Washington, D.C.: The World Bank.

Massie, B. (2006) 'Participation – have we got an Attitude Problem?' Paper presented in the NDA 5th Annual Conference Civic, Cultural and Social Participation: Building an Inclusive Society (paper available at www.nda.ie) Dublin, Ireland, 16th November.

Matotay E. (2014) Inequalities and Structural Transformation in Tanzania: Local/global encounter, in *Society for International Development*, 57(3–4), (591–600).

Matthews, J.R., (2017). Understanding indigenous innovation in rural West Africa: challenges to diffusion of innovations theory and current social innovation practice. *Journal of Human Development and Capabilities* 18 (2), 223–238. https://doi.org/ 10.1080/19452829.2016.1270917.

May, T. (2003) Social Research: Issues, Methods and Research 3rd ed., Buckingham: Open University Press.

May, T. (2011). Social Research: Issues, Methods and Process. 4th Edition. Maidenhead, Berks: Open University Press/Mc Graw-Hill.

May, T. & Powell J.L. (1996) Situating Social Theory, McGraw-Hill Education.

Mayadas, N.S. & Elliott, D. (2001). Psychosocial approaches, social work, and social development. *Social Development Issues*, 23(1), 5-13.

Mays, N. & Pope, C. (1995) Qualitative Research: Rigour and qualitative research, in *British Medical Journal*, 1995:311:109.

Mbepera, J. (2017). The organizational factors influencing women's underrepresentation in leadership positions in Community Secondary Schools (CSSs) in rural Tanzania. *KEDI Journal of Educational Policy*, 14(2), 79-101.

Mbilinyi, D.A. & Omari, C.K. (1996) Gender relations and women's images in the media, Tanzania, Dar es Salaam University Press.

Mbiti, J. (1969) African Religions & Philosophy (2nd ed.), Heinemann Educational Publishers.

Mbiti, J. (1970) African Religions and Philosophy, New York: Doubleday and Company.

Mbunda, T.A.F. (2011) Street Children Economic Empowerment: A Case Study of Street Children in Kigamboni Ward Temeke Municipal Council Dar es Salaam Region. MCED- The Open University of Tanzania, Dar es Salaam.

McAlpine, K., Henley, R., Mueller, M. & Vetter S. (2010) A Survey of Street Children in Northern Tanzania: How Abuse or Support Factors May Influence Migration to the Street. *Community Mental Health Journal* (46), 26–32. https://doi.org/10.1007/s10597-009-9196-5.

McCleary-Sills, J., Namy, S., Nyoni, J., Rweyemamu, D., Salvatory, A., & Steven, E. (2013). Help-Seeking Pathways and Barriers for Survivors of Gender-Based Violence in Tanzania: Results from a Study in Dar es Salaam, Mbeya, and Iringa Regions. Dar es Salaam, Tanzania: EngenderHealth/CHAMPION.

Mchomvu, A., Tungaraza, F. S. K. & S. Maghimbi. (2002). Social Security Systems in Tanzania: Phase I Overview of Social Security in

Tanzania. *Journal of Social Development in Africa* 17(2): doi:10.4314/jsda.v17i2.23831.

McCloskey, L.A., Williams, C., & Larsen, U. (2005). Gender inequality and intimate partner violence among women in Moshi: Tanzania. International Family Planning Perspectives, 31, 124–140.

McCrann, D., Lalor, K., & Katabaro, J. K. (2006). Childhood Sexual Abuse among University Students in Tanzania. *Child Abuse & Neglect*, 30, 1343-1351.
https://doi.org/10.1016/j.chiabu.2006.05.009

McFarlane, A. H., Bellissimo, A. and Norman, G. R. (1995) Family structure, family functioning and adolescent wellbeing: the transcendent influence of parental style. *Journal of Child Psychology and Psychiatry,* 36, 847-864

McLleod, J (2003) An Introduction to Counselling. Buckingham: Open University Press.

McMahon, M. (1997, December). Social Constructivism and the World Wide Web – A Paradigm for Learning. Paper presented at the ASCILITE conference. Perth, Australia.

Merriam, S. B., Johnson-Bailey J., Lee M., Kee Y, Ntseane G., & Muhamad M. (2001) Power and positionality: Negotiating insider/outsider status within and across cultures, *International Journal of Lifelong Education,* 20:5, 405-416.

Mesaki S (2010) Witchcraft and Law in Tanzania, ResearchGate, https://www.researchgate.net/publication/228668099

Mesaki S. (2016) Social Protection of Persons with Disabilities in Tanzania: Policies, Legislations and Framework. Dar es Salaam.

Midgley, J., (1981). Professional Imperialism: Social Work in the Third World. Heinemann, London.

Midgley, J. (1995) *Social Development: The Developmental Perspective in Social Welfare*. London: Sage.

Midgley J. (2010) The theory and practice of developmental social work. In: Midgley J and Conley A (eds) Developmental social work and social development: Theories and skills for developmental social work. New York: Oxford University Press, 3-28.

Midgley, J. & Conley, A. Eds. (2010). *Social Work and Social Development: Theories and Skills for Developmental Social Work*. New York: Oxford University Press.

Midgley, J. (2014) *Social Development: Theory and Practice. London: SAGE*.

Midgley J. (2014), 'Professional Social Work in East Africa: *A Foreword*. In Spitzer H., Twikirize J.M., & Wairire G.G (editors) (2014) Professional Social Work in East Africa: Towards Social Development, Poverty Reduction and Gender Equality. Kampala: Fountain Publishers.

Miedema, S.S., Haardörfer, R., Girard A.W. & Yount K.M. (2018) Women's empowerment in East Africa: Development of a cross-country comparable measure, *World Development Journal*, volume 110, pages 453-464, Published by Elsevier Ltd.

Miguel, E. (2005). Poverty and Witch killing. in *Review of Economic Studies*. Vol. 72, No. 4.

Millar, A., Devaney, J. & Butler, M. (2019) Emotional Intelligence: Challenging the Perceptions and Efficacy of 'Soft Skills' in

Policing Incidents of Domestic Abuse Involving Children. *Journal of Family Violence* (2019) 34: 577–588. https://doi.org/10.1007/s10896-018-0018-9.

Miller, H. (August 11, 2017)."Kimberlé Crenshaw Explains The Power Of Intersectional Feminism In 1 Minute".*Huffington Post.* (Retrieved January 19, 2022).

Mills, C.W. (1959) *The sociological imagination.* London/New York: Oxford University Press.

Minde, J.J. (2015) Analysis of Gender Roles within Chagga Households that Practice Ripe Banana Street Selling in Moshi Rural, Tanzania, in *Journals of Developing Country Studies,* Vol 5, No8 (2015)9-14.

Minkler, M. (2004) Ethical challenges for the "outside" researcher in community-based participatory research, in *Health Education & Behaviour,* Vol. 31 (6): 684-697 DOI: 10.1177/1090198104269566.

Minkler, M., Fadem P., Perry M., Blum K., Moore L., & Judith Rogers J. (2002) Ethical Dilemmas in Participatory Action Research: A Case Study from the Disability Community, *Health Education & Behavior,* Vol. 29 (1): 14-29 (February 2002)

Mistry, R., Galal, O. & Lu, M. (2009). Women's autonomy and pregnancy care in rural India: A contextual analysis. *Social Science and Medicine,* 69(6), 926–933.

Mkalawa C.C. & Haixiao, P. (2014) Dar es Salaam city temporal growth and its influence on transportation, Urban, Planning and Transport Research, 2:1, 423-446, DOI: 10.1080/21650020.2014.978951. Publisher: Taylor & Francis.

Mkenda, B.K. (2005a), "The Impact of Globalisation on the Labour Market: A Case Study of Tanzania", Research Report submitted to the ESRF-Economic & social Research Foundation.

Mnyampala, M.E. (1954) Historia, Mila na Desturi za Wagogo wa Tanganyika. Translated by Maddox G.H (ed.), (1995) Introduction: The Ironies of History, Customs, and Traditions of Wagogo, Armonk.

Moghadam, V.M. & Senftova, L. (2005). Measuring women's empowerment: Participation and rights in civil, political, social, economic, and cultural domains. *International Social Science Journal*, 18, 389–412.

Molohan, M.J.B. (1959) Detribalization (Dar es Salaam, 1959), 67.

Moon K., & Blackman D., (2014) A Guide to Understanding Social Science Research for Natural Scientists, Review. In *Society for Conservation Biology*, Volume 28, No. 5, 1167–1177 DOI: 10.1111/cobi.1232

Moncrieffe, J. (2006) The Power of Stigma: Encounters with 'Street Children' and 'Restavecs' in Haiti. Institute of Development Studies Bulletin Vol.37 (6)34-46.

Mooney, A., Oliver, C. & Smith, M. (2009) Impact of Family Breakdown on Children's Wellbeing: Evidence Review, in *Research Report No DCSF-RR113*.

Morris, J. (1991) Pride Against Prejudice, Women's Press, London.

Morisset, J. (2013a). Should Government Give Money to Tanzania's Poor? December 12.

http://blogs.worldbank.org/futuredevelopment/
should-government-give-moneytanzania-s-poor.

Morisset, J. (2013b). Tanzania Economic. Update Raising the Game:
Can Tanzania Eradiate Extreme Poverty? Issue 4. Washington
DC: World Bank Group.
http://documents.worldbank.org/curated/en/2013/12/18620924/
tanzania-economicupdate-raising-game-can-tanzania-eradicate-
extreme-poverty.

Mosedale, S. (2005) Assessing Women's empowerment: towards a
conceptual framework, in Journal of International Development,
17(2):243-257. https://doi.org/10.1002/jid.1212.

Mostert, M.P. (2016) Stigma as a barrier to the implementation
of the Convention on the Rights of Persons with Disabilities in
Africa. In *African Disability Rights Yearbook*, 2-24.

Mtaita, F. (2015) Perception of Street Children and the Role of
Community in Supporting their access to Education: A Case
study of Ilala Municipality, Dar es Salaam, Tanzania. *A Dissertation
submitted in partial fulfilment of the requirement for the degree of
Master of Education in Administration, Planning and Policy studies
(MED APPS) of the Open University of Tanzania.*

Mtambalike, M.J (2013) Domestic Violence Against Women in
Tanzania, the never-ending story, wewrite for rights, available at:
https://wewriteforrights.wordpress.com/2013/08/11/domes-
tic-violence-against-women-in-tanzania-the-never-ending-sto-
ry/ [accessed 25 December 2021].

Mtshali, P.H. (2004). The power of the ancestors: The life of a Zulu
traditional healer. Mbabane, Swaziland: KaMhlaba Publications.

Mufuruki, A., Mawji, R., Kasiga, G. & Marwa, M. (2018) Tanzania's industrialisation journey, 2016–2056: from an agrarian to a modern industrialized state in forty years. Dar es Salaam: Moran Publishers.

Mungóngó, C.G. (2003) Social transformation and political empowerment in the age of globalization: looking beyond women's empowerment in Tanzania. *Nordic Journal of African Studies*. (12):119–33.

Munyi, C.W. (2012) Past and Present Perceptions Towards Disability: A Historical Perspective, in *Disability Studies Quarterly*, Vol 32, No 2.

Mupedziswa, R. (2005). Challenges and prospects of social work services in Africa. in: *Journal of Social Development in Africa,* Vol 7, No 2.

Muro, A. (2003) The empowerment of women, in Chachage, C.E. & Mbilinyi M., (2003) Against Neo-Liberalism: Gender, Democracy and Development. Dar-Es-Salaam, Tanzania: E&D Limited.

Mushi, P.A.K. (2009) History and Development of Education in Tanzania, Dar es Salaam University Press.

Mutume, G. (2011) African Women Battle for Equality. *African Review* 19.2 (2011): 6-9.

Mwansa, L.K.J. (2012) 'Social Work in Africa', in Healy L.M. & Link R.J. (eds) Handbook of International Social Work: Human Rights, Development, and the Global Profession, pp. 365–71. Oxford: Oxford University Press.

Mwanyangala, M. A., Mayombana C, Urassa H, Charles J, Mahutanga C, Abdullah S & Nathan R (2010) Health status and quality of life among older adults in rural Tanzania, in *Global Health Action,* Taylor & Francis Group.

Mwenzwa, M.E. & Waweru, S.M. (2016). The Oscillating State's Role in the Provision of Social Welfare Services in Kenya *International Journal of Humanities and Social Science* Vol. 6, No. 5; May 2016

Myers, S. & Milner, J. (2007) Working with Violence: Policies and Practices in Risk Assessment and Management, Palgrave.

Myers, S. & Milner, J (2007) Sexual Issues in Social Work, Bristol: Policy Press.

Napu, N. & Hasan, R. (2019) Translation Problems Analysis of Students' Academic Essay, in *International Journal of Linguistics, Literature and Translation (IJLLT) ISSN: 2617-0299:* ResearchGate.

Nasir, M., Khalid A. & Shoukat, A. (2014) Maslow Theory of Human Development and Emergence of Street Children Phenomenon in Pakistan, *Consortium for Street Children.*

National Bureau of Statistics: Tanzania Disability Survey Report (2008). Dar es Salaam.

Ndjovu, C.E. (2015) Compulsory Land Acquisitions in Tanganyika: Revisiting the British colonial Expropriation Principles and Practices. In *International Journal of Scientific and Technology Research*, Vol 4, Issue 12, Dec 2015.

Ndlovu, H.L. (2016) African Beliefs Concerning The disabled: Implications for Theological Education, in *Journal of Disability & Religion* 2016, Vol. 20, Nos. 1-2, 29-39 http://dx.doi.org/10.108 0/23312521.2016.1152942, Routledge: Taylor & Francis Group.

Ndulo, M. (1985) Widows Under Zambian Customerly Law and the Response of the Courts, in *Comparative and International Law Journal of Southern Africa*, Volume 18, Issue No 1, pp 90-102. https://hdl.handle.net/10520/AJA00104051_755

Ndulo, M. (2011) African Customary Law, Customs, and Women's Rights, *Indiana Journal of Global Legal Studies* Vol. 18 No 1 (Winter 2011) available at https://heinonline.org/HOL/License. Accessed on 24th July 2019.

Neuman, L.W. (2000). *Social Research Methods: Qualitative and Quantitative Approaches (4th Ed.)*, USA: Allyn and Bacon.

Newing, H. (2010). Conducting research in conservation: social science methods and practice. Routledge, Milton Park, Oxfordshire, United Kingdom.

Ngowi, H.P. (2009) Economic development and change in Tanzania since independence: The political leadership factor, in *African Journal of Political Science and International Relations* Vol. 3 (4), pp. 259-267.

Niboye, E.P (2013) Effectiveness of Non-governmental Organizations in the Rehabilitation of Street Children – Experiences from Selected NGOs in Dar es Salaam, Tanzania. *Journal of Education and Practice* www.iiste.org (Online) Vol.4, No.1.

Njuki, J. (2020) Tackling the root causes of gender inequality through research, *in Africa Times*, 10 March 2020.

Njuki, J., Kaaria, S., Chamunorwa, A. & Chiuri, W. (2011). Linking smallholder farmers to markets, gender, and intra-household dynamics: Does the choice of commodity matter? *European Journal of Development Research*, 23(3), 426–443. https://doi.org/10.1057/ejdr.2011.8.

Njunwa. P (2005) Public Sector Reforms in Tanzania, Mzumbe University.

Nolan, B. & Whelan, C.T. (2007) On the multidimensionality of poverty and social exclusion. Inequality and poverty re-examined (Part II): 146–165. OUP Catalogue, Oxford University Press.

Nolan, B. & Whelan, C.T. (2011) Poverty and deprivation in Europe. OUP Catalogue, Oxford University Press.

Nolan, L., McCarron, M., McCallion, P. & Murphy-Lawless, J. (2006). Perceptions of stigma in dementia: An exploratory study. Alzheimer Society of Ireland.

Norozi, S.A. & Moen, T. (2016) Childhood as a Social Construction, *Journal of Educational and Social Research* Vol. 6 No.2 May 2016, MCSER Publishing, Rome-Italy.

Ntamanwa, F. L. (2015) Factors leading to low employment rate of people with physical disability in Tanzania: A Case study of Temeke Municipal Council, Dar es Salaam region, Tanzania: The Open University of Tanzania.

Nyakwesi, M. (2012) Makini Organisation-Street Children, NGO-Dar es Salaam.

Nyaundi, N.M. (2005) The Contemporary African Family in the Light of Rapid Social Change Theory, Nairobi, Paulines Publications Africa.
Nyerere, J. (1966) 'First speech in Legislative Council', in J. Nyerere, Freedom and Unity / Uhuru na Umoja: A Selection from Writings and Speeches 1952–65 (Dar es Salaam, 1966), 30–4.

Nyerere, J. (1967) The Basis of African Socialism in Ujamaa: Essays on Socialism, Dar es Salaam: Oxford University Press.

Nyerere, J. (1968) The Arusha Declaration: Freedom and Socialism. Dar es Salaam, Oxford University.

Nyoni, E.J (2007): Street Children and Capacitation: A Case Study in Songea Municipal Council, Ruvuma Region, Tanzania. Ruvuma.

Ocheni, S. & Nwankwo, B.C. (2012). Analysis of Colonialism and Its Impact in Africa. In *Cross-CulturalCommunication*, 8(3), 46-54, doi: 10.3968/j.ccc.1923670020120803.1189.

O'Donell, G. (2002) Mastering Sociology 4th Edition, New York: Palgrave Publishers Ltd.

O'Donoghue, K. (1999) Safety Nets for Vulnerable Groups; A research Report for HelpAge International.

Ohnuki-Tierney, E. (1984) Illness and Culture in Contemporary Japan: An Anthropological View, Cambridge University Press.

Okon E.E. (2014) Christian Missions and Colonial rule in Africa: Objective and contemporary analysis. *European Scientific Journal* Vol.10. No.17.

Okorley, E.L., Nkrumah, E. E. (2012). Organisational factors influencing sustainability of local non-governmental organisations: Lessons from a Ghanaian context. *International Journal of Social Economics*, 39 (5), 330 – 341. Retrieved June 10, 2021, from Emerald Databases.

Olatunji, C.M.P. (2013) "An Argument for Gender Equality in Africa." *CLCWeb: Comparative Literature and Culture* 15.1 (2013).

Oliver, M. (1983). Social Work with Disabled People. Basingstoke: Macmillan.

Oliver, M. (1990). The Politics of Disablement. Basingstoke: Macmillan.

Oluwabamide, A.J. (2005). The Aged in African Society. Lagos: Nade Nigeria Ltd and F.B. Ventures.

Oluwabamide, A.J. & Eghafona K.A. (2012) Addressing the Challenges of Ageing in Africa.Anthropologist, 14(1):61-66. ResearchGate. Accessedat: https://www.researchgate.net/publication/266229980, on 29th April 2021.

Organisation for Economic Co-operation and Development (OECD) report 2010. Gender equality situation-Tanzania. UN.

Ott, J. S. & Dicke, L.A. (2016). The Nature of the Nonprofit Sector, 3rd Ed. Boulder: Westview Press.

Ottka, U. (2010). Small Organisations, Big Challenge. Retrieved June 18, 2021, from http://www.icsw.org/doc/2011-01-The- Situation-of-NGOs-in-Tanzania.pdf

Padmore, G. (1949) Britain's Third Empire. London, Dobson.

Pakenham, T. (1992). The scramble for Africa: The white man's conquest of the dark continent from 1876 to 1912. New York, NY: HarperCollins.

Parker, R. & Angleton, P. (2003) HIV and AIDS-related stigma and discrimination: a conceptual framework and implications for action. Social science & Medicine 57(2003)13-24, Elsevier Science Ltd.

Parveen, S. (2014) Conceptual Meaning and Definition of Street Children: Worldwide. Sociology International Journal, 118, Vol – XII, (11) Pages 78-80.

Patel, L. (2005). Social welfare and social development in South Africa. Cape Town: Oxford University Southern Africa.

Patel, L., Perold, H., Mohamed, S.E. & Carapinha, R. (2007). Five-country study on service and volunteering in southern Africa (CSD Research Report 07–19). St. Louis, MO: Washington University, Centre for Social Development.

Patton, M.Q. (1990). Qualitative evaluation and research methods (2nd ed.). Beverly Hills, CA: Sage.

Patton, M.Q. (2002). Qualitative research and evaluation methods (3rd ed.). Thousand Oaks, CA: Sage Publications.

Payne, M. (2005) Modern Social Work Theory. 3rd ed. London: Palgrave.

Payne, M. (2006) "The Origins of Social Work. *The Journal of Sociology & Social Welfare*: Vol.33: Iss.4, Article 21. Available at: https://scholarworks.wmich.edu/jssw/vol33/iss4/21.

Pease, B. & Fook, J. (1999) Transforming Social Work Practice: Postmodern Critical Perspectives. London: Routledge.

Pedersen, S. (1993) Family, Dependence, and the Origins of the Welfare State: Britain and France, 1914–1945, Cambridge University Press.

Perry, F. (2019) Social Model of Disability: who, what and why, in *Disability Horizons-Giving You a voice*, https://disabilityhorizons.com/2019/05/social-model-of-disability-who-what-and-why/, accessed 20th July 2020.

Polkinghorne, D.E. (2005). Language and meaning: Data collection in qualitative research. *Journal of Counselling Psychology, 52*(2), 137–145.
https://doi.org/10.1037/0022-0167.52.2.137.

Polkinghorne, D.E. (2007) Validity issues in narrative research. Qualitative Inquiry (QUAL INQ) 13:471–478. Publisher: SAGE Publications.

Ponterotto, J.G., Casas J. M., Suzuki, L.A. & Alexander, C.M. (2001) Handbook of Multicultural Counselling, 2 Ed, SAGE Publications, Inc.

Potter, J. & Wetherell, M. (1987). *Discourse and Social Psychology: Beyond Attitudes and Behaviour.* London, U.K.: Sage Publications Ltd.

Powell, W. W. & Steinberg, R. (2006). The Non-profit Sector: A Research Handbook. New Haven: Yale University Press.

Power, M. (2011) The Social Construction of Gender, accessed on 15 December 2020 at http://www.personal.psu.edu/bfr3/blogs/applied_social_psychology/

Pratley, P. (2016). Associations between quantitative measures of women's empowerment and access to care and health status for mothers and their children: A systematic review of evidence from the developing world. *Social Science & Medicine*, 169, 119–131. https://doi.org/10.1016/ j.socscimed.2016.08.001.

Prawat, R.S. & Floden, R.E. (1994). Philosophical Perspectives on Constructivist Views of Learning. *Educational Psychologist*, 29(1), 37-48.

Quarshie, E.N.B. (2011) Public's Perceptions of the Phenomenon of Street children: A Qualitative Study of Students and Shopkeepers in Accra, Ghana. Unpublished Master's Dissertation of Philosophy degree in Human Development, Institute of Psychology, Norwegian University of Science and Technology, Trondheim.

Railway Children Organisation-Street Children (2014) Working with vulnerable children on the streets in Tanzania. SOAS, University of London.

Rankopo, M., & Osei-Hwedie, K., (2011). Globalization and culturally relevant social work: African perspectives on indigenization. *International Social Work* Vol.54 (1), 137–147.

Ravenhill, J. (1988) Politics and Society in Contemporary Africa, London: Macmillan, and Boulder.

Reeves, H. & Baden, S. (2000). Gender on development: Concepts and definitions. Falmer: University of Sussex.

Refworld-Canada: Immigration and Refugee Board of Canada, (2015) Tanzania: Situation of female victims of domestic violence, including legislation and availability of state protection and support services (2012- July 2015), 26 August 2015, TZA105300.E, available at:
https://www.refworld.org/docid/55ffaa004.html [accessed 25 December 2021]

Reid, P.T. (2002). Multicultural psychology: Bringing together gender and ethnicity. Cultural Diversity and Ethnic Minority Psychology, 8, 103–114.

Richards. C.A.C. (Commissioner for social development)- PRO CO 822/675: Minutes of the Colonial Social Welfare Advisory Committee, Reports Sub-Committee, 4 Nov. 1952. In Eckert, A. (2004) Regulating the Social: Social Security, social welfare, and the state in late colonial Tanzania, in: *Journal of African History*, 45(2004), pp.467-89, UK: Cambridge University Press.

Richardson-Foster, H., Stanley, N., Miller, P., & Thomson, G. (2012). Police intervention in domestic violence incidents where children are present: Police and children's perspectives. Policing and Society: An *international Journal of Research and Policy*., 22(2), 220–234.

Ridgeway, C.L. & Correll, S. J. (2004) Unpacking the Gender System. In *Gender and Society Journal* 1 8 (4): 5 1 0-531.

Ridley, D. (2008) The Literature Review: A Step-by-step Guide for Students (SAGE Study Skills Series), SAGE Publications Ltd.

Rieger, M. & Trommlerová, S.K. (2016). Age-specific correlates of child growth. Demography, 53, 241–267.

Riggio, E. (2012). Children in an Urban Tanzania. Digital Library of the Tanzania Health Community.

Rodney, W. (1972). How Europe Underdeveloped Africa. Dar es Salaam: Tanzania Publishing House.

Rodney, W. (1982). How Europe Underdeveloped Africa. Enugu, Nigeria: Ikenga Publishers.

Roelen K., Delap, E., Jones, C. & Chettri, H. K. (2017) Improving child wellbeing and care in Sub-Saharan Africa: The role of social protection. In, *Children and Youth Services Reviews* 73 (2017) 309-318. ELSEVIER.

Rogoff, B. (1990). *Apprenticeship in thinking: Cognitive development in social context.* Oxford University Press.

Root, M.P.P. (ed.). (1996). The Multiracial experience: Racial borders as the new frontier. Thousand Oaks, CA: Sage Publications.

Rugira, J. (2015) Forms, Causes, and Effects of Violence Against Women in Mbulu Tanzania. General Education Journal, Vol.4, Issue 1 (2015), pages 16-31. Mount Meru University Research Unit Publisher.

Rwegoshora, H. (2002) Institute of Social Work Dar-Es-Salaam: The Nature and Extent of Street Children in Arusha Municipal which way ward. Dar es Salaam.

Rwegoshora, H.M.M (2014) Social Security Challenges in Tanzania: Transforming the present protecting the Future. Mkuki na Nyota Publishers, Tanzania.

Rwezaura, B. (2000) The value of a child: marginal children and the law in contemporary Tanzania. International Journal of Law, Policy and the Family, Volume 14, Issue 3, Pages 326–364, https://doi.org/10.1093/lawfam/14.3.326

Sabea, H. (2009). The Limits of Law in the Mandated Territories: Becoming *Manamba* and the Struggles of Sisal Plantation Workers in Tanganyika. In *African Studies*, 68:1, 135-161.

Salamon, L. M. (1984a) "Nonprofit Organizations: The Lost Opportunity." Pp. 261-286 in John Palmer & Isabel Sawhill, eds., The Reagan Record. Cambridge: Ballinger. Google Scholar.

Salamon, L. M. (1984b) "Nonprofits: The Results are Coming In," *Foundation News*. 25(4): 16-23.

Salamon, L. M. (1987). Of Market Failure, Voluntary Failure, and Third-Party Government: Toward a Theory of Government-

Nonprofit Relations in the Modern Welfare State. *Nonprofit and Voluntary Sector Quarterly, 16,* 29-49. https://doi.org/10.1177/089976408701600104.

Salamon, L.M., Anheier, H.K., List, R., Toepler., Sokolowski, S. W., & Associates. (1999). Global Civil Society: Dimensions of the Nonprofit Sector. US: *The Johns Hopkins Centre for Civil Society Studies (CCSS)*

Salifu, Y. J. & Somhlaba, N. Z. (2014). Stress, coping and quality of life: An exploratory study of the psychological wellbeing of Ghanaian orphans placed in orphanages. In *Children and Youth Services Review,* 46, 28–37.

Sandelowski, M. (2004). Using qualitative research. Qualitative Health Research, 14, 1366–1386. doi:10.1177/1049732304269672.

Sanga, E. H (2014) Challenges of Access to Justice in Tanzania to Obtain Legal Assistance for Street Children Facing Physical Violence by Police. The Netherlands: Institute of Social Studies.

Sangale, M.K. (2004) Impact of HIV/AIDS on Older people, Research report, Quality Print, Dar es Salaam.

Santhya, K.G., Ram, U., Acharya, R., Jejeebhoy, J., Ram, F. & Singh, A. (2010). Associations between early marriage and young women's marital and reproductive health outcomes: Evidence from India. *International Perspectives on Sexual and Reproductive Health,* 36(3), 132–139.

Save the Children – Tanzania (2013) Child welfare and Protection in Tanzania. UK Save the Children, Dar es Salaam.

Sayers, G.F. (ed.) (1930) The Handbook of Tanganyika. London, Macmillan.

Schneider, F.W., Gruman, J.A., & Coutts, L.M. (eds.). (2005). Applied social psychology: Understanding and addressing social and practical problems. Thousand Oaks, CA: Sage Publications

Schuleaur, S.R., Hashemi, S.M., Riley, A.P. & Akhter, S. (1996). Credit programs, patriarchy, and men's violence against women in rural Bangladesh. *Social Science and Medicine*, 43(12), 1729–1742.

Schwandt, T. A. (2003). Three epistemological stances for qualitative inquiry: Interpretativism, hermeneutics and social constructionism. In Denzin, N. and Lincoln, Y (Eds.), The Landscape of Qualitative Research: Theories and issues. (pp. 292-331). Thousand Oaks, CA: Sage.

Schwandt, T. A. (1994). Constructivist, interpretivist approaches to human inquiry. Pages 118–137 in Denzin N.K & Lincoln, Y.S. (editors). Handbook of qualitative research. Sage, Thousand Oaks, California.

Schwandt, T.A. (2001). Dictionary of qualitative inquiry (2nd ed.). Thousand Oaks, CA: Sage.

Scotland, J. (2012) Exploring the Philosophical Underpinnings of Research: Relating Ontology and Epistemology to the Methodology and Methods of the Scientific, Interpretive, and Critical Research Paradigm. In *English Language Teaching*; Vol. 5, No. 9; 2012, Published by Canadian Centre of Science and Education.

Scottish Office (1998) The Scottish Compact: the principles underpinning the relationship between Government and the voluntary sector in Scotland, Cm 4083, Scottish Office, Edinburgh.

Scottish Parenting Forum (2003) "It takes a Village to Raise a Child". Edinburgh: Scottish Parenting Forum.

Šešić, M. D. (2011). Strategic Approach in NGO Capacity Building and Professional Development. Retrieved June 10, 2021. From http://www.culturecongress.eu/en/ngo/ngo_bestpractice_sesic.

Settles, J.D. (1996) The Impact of Colonialism on African Economic Development. *Chancellor'sHonorsProgramProjects-TennesseeRes earchandCreativeExchange* Accessedon 10 March 2020 at: https://trace.tennessee.edu/utk_chanhonoproj/182

Shafer, E.F. & Malhotra (2011) The Effect of a Child's Sex on Support for Traditional Gender Roles. In *Social Forces*, Vol. 90, No. 1 (September 2011), pp. 209-222, Oxford University Press.

Shakespeare, T. (2010) The Social model of Disability, in *the Disability Study Reader,* Ed. Davis L J. New York: Routledge, 2010. 266-73.

Shastri, A. (2014) Gender Inequality and Women Discrimination, IOSR Journal of Humanities and Social Science (IOSR-JHSS) Volume 19, Issue 11, Ver. VII (Nov. 2014), PP 27-30.

Shaw, I., Briar-Lawson, K., Orme, J. & Ruckdeschel, R. (2010). The Sage handbook social work research. London: SAGE.

Sheikh, L. (1998) Older women killing: Annual Report of Tanzania Media Women's Association (TAMWA). Dar es Salaam.

Sherif, B. (2001) The Ambiguity of Boundaries in the Fieldwork Experience: Establishing Rapport and Negotiating Insider/ Outsider Status. Qualitative Inquiry. 2001;7(4): 436-447. doi: 10.1177/107780040100700403

Shivji, I.G. (2004). Reflections on NGOs in Tanzania: What We Are, What We Are Not, and What We Ought to Be. In *Development in*

Practice, Volume 14, Number 5, pp. 689-695. http://journalson-line.tandf.co.uk (accessed 20/12/2020).

Shoko, T. (2007). Karanga indigenous religion in Zimbabwe: Health and wellbeing. Ashgate, UK: Aldershot.

Shrestha, P. (2009): Background Paper: Street Children International Conference: Reaching the marginalized – How to Approach Inclusive Education: Street Children Accessing Education in Dar es Salaam: Report on Preliminary Düsseldorf, Germany.

Sida.- Report "Disability Rights in Sub-Saharan Africa," January 2015, www.sida.se

Sightsavers, ADD International, HelpAge International & Ifakara Health Institute-Tanzania (September 2016) Full Report: Hear my Voice: Old age and disability are not a curse, A Community-based participatory study gathering the lived experiences of persons with disabilities and older people in Tanzania. Retrieved on January 3rd, 2019, from at www.sightsavers.org/voices.

SPIRI-Society for Promoting International Research and Innovation, (2013) Impact of Public Sector Reforms on Service Delivery in Tanzania. *International Journal of Social Science Tomorrow*, Vol.2 No.2.

Silverman, D. (1989) Telling convincing stories. In: Glassner B, Moreno J, editors. The Qualitative-Quantitative Distinction in the Social Sciences. London (UK): Kluwer; 1989. p. 57-77.

Skoufias, E. & di Maro, V. (2006). Conditional Cash Transfers, Adult Work Incentives, and Poverty. WPS3973-IE. Washington, D.C.: The World Bank.

Slovic, P. (2000). The perception of risk. Earthscan, London.

Smith J.D, Rochester C. & Hedley R. (1995) An Introduction to the Voluntary Sector, London: Routledge.

Soanes, C. & Stevenson, A. (2003). Eds. Oxford Dictionary of English, OUP Oxford.

Social Mainstreaming for Gender Equality Organization (SMGEO)- Profile 2015. RetrievedonApril, 15, 2018, from https://www.globalhand.org/system/assets/7f8c866e9a81f-0189fd4f0644a4d2149e463d6a5/original/smgeo_short_pofile.pdf?1501105249.

Sondhi-Garg, P. (2004) Street Children Lives of Valor & Vulnerability. Ess Publications.

Spicker, P. (2014) Social Policy: Theory and Practice (3 rd Ed.), Policy Press.

Spitzer, H. (2019) Social Work in East Africa: A Mzungu perspective, in *International Social Work*, Vol.62(2)567–580. Doi: 10.1177/0020872817742696 journals.sagepub.com/home/isw. SAGE.

Spitzer, H. & Mabeyo, Z.M. (2011) In Search of Protection: Older People and their Fight for Survival in Tanzania, Klagenfurt – Wien: Drava Verlag.

Spitzer, H., Twikirize, J. M. & Wairire, G.G. (Eds.), (2014) Professional Social Work in East Africa: Towards Social Development, Poverty Reduction and Gender Equality, Fountain Publishers. Kampala.

Spitzer, H. & Twikirize, J.M. (2014) Breaking New Grounds: Conceptual and Methodological Framework of a Regional Research Project.

In Spitzer H., Twikirize J.M, & Wairire, G.G. (eds), (2014) Professional Social Work in East Africa: Towards Social Development, Poverty Reduction and Gender Equality. Kampala: Fountain Publishers.

Spitzer, H., & Twikirize, J.M.(2021) Social innovations in rural communities in Africa's Great Lakes region. A social work perspective. In *Journal of Rural Studies*, https://doi.org/10.1016/j.jrurstud.2021.10.013.

Spitzer, H., Rwegoshora, H. & Mabeyo, Z.M. (2009) "The (Missing) Social Protection for Older People in Tanzania: A comparative Study in Rural and Urban Areas"- Final Report, Carinthia University of Applied Sciences, Austria and Institute of Social Work, Tanzania.

Squires, A. (2009) Methodological challenges in cross-language qualitative research: a research review. In, International Journal of Nursing Studies, 46(2):277-287.

Stanley, N., Fell, B., Miller, P., Thomson G. & Watson, J (2012) 'Men's talk: men's understandings of violence against women and motivations for change', *Violence against Women*, vol. 18, no. 11, 2012, pp. 1300–18.

Stanley, N., & Devaney, J. (2017). Gender-based violence: Evidence from Europe. Psychology of Violence, 7(3), 329-332. http://dx.doi.org/10.1037/vio0000120.

Stevens, R. (1982) "A Poor Sort of Memory: Voluntary Hospitals and Government Before the Depression," *Milbank Fund Quarterly/ Health and Society*, 60(4): 551-584.

Stone-MacDonald, A. & Butera, G. (2014). Cultural Beliefs and Attitudes about Disability in East Africa. In *Review of Disability Studies*, 8:1, 1-19.

Suleman, S. (2016) Colonial Administrative System, accessed at *Tanzania education blog*, http://itessentials.blogspot.com/ on 13 December 2020.

Sunseri, J. (1997). Development for Exploitation: German Colonial Policies in Mainland Tanzania, 1884-1914. *Afr. Affairs, Book Review* 96(382): 145-147.

Tacoli, C. & Agergaard, J. (2017) Urbanisation, rural transformations, and food systems: The role of small towns, Working Paper, Published by IIED.

Tangayika Labour Department, Annual Report of the Labour Department 1950 (Dar es Salaam, 1951), 29. In Eckert A (2004) Regulating the social: Social security, social welfare and the state in late colonial Tanzania. *Journal of African History*, 45 (2004), Cambridge University Press.

Tanganyika, (1952) The Medical (Grants-in-aid to Mission) Regulations, *Tanganyika Territory Official Gazette*, Dar es Salaam. In Jennings, M. (2015) The precariousness of the franchise state: Voluntary sector health services and international NGOs in Tanzania, 1960s e mid-1980s, *Social Science & Medicine* 141 (2015) 1-8. ELSEVIER.

Tanganyika African National Union-TANU (1967) The Arusha Declaration and TANU's policy on socialism and self-reliance, Dar es Salaam: Publicity Section, TANU, 1967.

Tanzania Daily News, 2016 Children and Youth, Dar es Salaam.

Tanzania National Archives (TNA 540/3: Circular Social Welfare Office, Oct. 1945), in Eckert, A. (2004) Regulating the Social: Social Security, social welfare, and the state in late colonial

Tanzania, *Journal of African History*, 45(2004), pp.467-89, UK: Cambridge University Press.

Tanzania National Archive 34257: Report on Social Welfare for the Year 1945. In: Eckert, A (2004) Regulating the Social: Social Security, social welfare, and the state in late colonial Tanzania, in: *Journal of African History*, 45(2004), pp.467-89, UK: Cambridge University Press.

Tanzania National Archive, 1951. In Eckert, A. (2004) Regulating the Social: Social Security, social welfare, and the state in late colonial Tanzania, in: Journal of African History, 45(2004), pp.467-89, UK: Cambridge University Press.

Tanzanian National Archives (TNA 61/67/5: The British Plan for Mass Education. Circular Nx1. Issued by Information Officer in Dar es Salaam, 11 July 1944). In Eckert, A. (2004) Regulating the Social: Social Security, social welfare, and the state in late colonial Tanzania, in: *Journal of African History*, 45(2004), pp.467-89, UK: Cambridge University Press.

Tanzania National Bureau of Statistics and ORC Macro, (2005) Tanzania Demographic and Health Survey 2004-2005. Dar es Salaam-Tanzania/ Maryland, USA.

Tanzania Gender Networking Programme- TGNP (2006): Gender Mainstreaming in Development Policies and Programmes, Paper presented at Policy dialogue Seminar (ESRF-11 May 2006), http://www.tzonl ine.org/ pdf/gender-mainstreaming in development policies and programmes.pdf. Accessed 9th August 2020.

Tanzania Gender Networking Programme, 2012.

Tanzania Media Women's Association, 2012. Dar es Salaam.

Tanzania Media Women's Association (TAMWA)- Gender Equality and Women Empowerment Programme II – GBV Component. A Report Submitted to the Danish International Development Agency (DANIDA). September – November 2013.

Tanzania Women Lawyers Association (TAWLA) (2004). Review of Gender Discriminative Laws in Tanzania. Dar es Salaam: TAWLA.

Tanzania Women Lawyers Association (TAWLA) (2014). Review of Laws and Policies Related to Gender-based Violence of Tanzania mainland. Dar es Salaam.

Tashakkori, A. & Teddlie, C. (1998). Introduction to Mixed Method and Mixed Model Studies in the Social and Behavioral Sciences. USA:Sage.

Tati, G. (2009). Elderly headed households, markets and consumptions in urban South Africa. Paper presented at the IHDP open global meeting held in Bonn, Germany. Accessedatwww.openmeeting2009.org/pdf_files/Pdf%20papers/Tati%20tati.pdf, on 20th April 2021.

Taylor, B. J., Killick C. & McGlade, A. (2015) Understanding and Using Research in Social Work, – Mastering Social Work Practice, London, Learning Matters: SAGE Publications Ltd.

Taylor, J. C. (1963) The Political Development of Tanganyika. Stanford University Press.

Taylor, S.J. & Bogdan, R. (1989). Introduction to qualitative research methods: The search for meanings. New York: John Wiley & Sons.

Taylor, M. (1992) 'The changing role of the non-profit sector in Britain: moving towards the market', Jossey Bass Publications, San Fransisco.

Taylor, M. (1996) "Between public & private accountability in voluntary organisations", *Policy & Politics*, 24 (1) 57-72.

Tavares, W. (2011) An Evaluation of the Kids Are Kids Disability Awareness Program: Increasing Social Inclusion Among Children With Physical Disabilities. Journal of Social Work in Disability & Rehabilitation, Volume 10, Issue1. Taylor & Francis Online.

T. C. (1943) The Economic Development of the British Colonial Empire. In: Bulletin of International News, Vol. 20, No. 4 (Feb. 20, 1943), pp. 139-145. Publisher: Royal Institute of International Affairs.

Teixeira, A.A.C. & Sharifu, H.A. (2017) Female Entrepreneurship and Access to Bank Loans in Tanzania: A Double-hurdled model Approach. *Journal of Developmental Entrepreneurship* Vol. 22, No. 3. World Scientific Publishing Company.

Temu, P. (1972) British Protestant Missions. London: London.

Tetzlaff, R. (1970) Colonial Development and Exploitation. Economic and social history of German East Africa 1883-1914. *Writings on economic and social history*, Vol. 17. Berlin: Duncker and Humblot.

The Global Gender Gap –Insight Report 2018- Measuring the Global Gender Gap: World Economic Forum.

Therborn, G. (2013) The Killing of Fields of Inequality. *Journal of Social Policy*, Volume 43, Issue 4. Cambridge: Polity Press.

Theron, Petria M. (2013) "Practical theologians' calling to serve in the field of gerontology," AOSIS, *Open Journals* (2013): 1.

The United Nations (1996) Report of the Fourth World Conference on Women – the Beijing Platform for Action 1995.

The United Republic of Tanzania – Customary Law Declaration Order: CLDO of 1963.

The United Republic of Tanzania: The Constitution of the United Republic of Tanzania of 1977.

The United Republic of Tanzania (1982) The Disabled Person (Employment) ACT, 1982.

The United Republic of Tanzania (1992) No.26 OF 1991 I ASSENT, A.H. MWINYI President, 9th April: 1992 An Act to amend the Private Hospitals (Regulation) Act, 1977 – to make provision for the management of private hospitals by individuals and organisations. Enacted by the Parliament of the United Republic of Tanzania.

The United Republic of Tanzania –The National Policy on NGOs, 2001.

The United Republic of Tanzania, (2003a:2); National Ageing Policy, Dar es Salaam: Ministry of Labour, Youth Development and Sports.

The United Republic of Tanzania: *National Policy on Disability of 2004*. Ministry of Labour, Youth Development and Sports. Dar es Salaam.

The United Republic of Tanzania and USAID (2008), Gender-based violence in Tanzania: an assessment of policies, services and promising interventions, *USAID Health Policy Initiative*, DaresSalaam,. Retrieved on December 28, 2020, from www.mcdgc.go.tz/index.php/publications/more/gender-based_violence_in_ tanzania_an_assessment_of_policies_services_a/

The United Republic of Tanzania: Ministry of Health, and Social Welfare- Street Children, 2012.

The United Republic of Tanzania (2013). 2012 Population and Housing Census. Population Distribution by Administrative Areas.

The United Republic of Tanzania-Ministry of Health, Community Development, Gender, Elderly and Children, (2017) Gender-Based Violence and Violence against Children: Facilitator's Guide for Health Care Providers and Social Welfare Officers. Dar es Salaam, Tanzania.

The United Republic of Tanzania (2018). Ministry of Education, Science and Technology, Education Sector Development Plan (2016/17-2020/21).

The World Bank (1989) World Development Report 1989: Financial Systems and Development World Development Indicators, Oxford University Press.

Thomas, G. (2017) How to Do Your Research Project: A Guide for Students, (3 rd Ed.) Los Angeles, London/New Delhi, SAGE Publications Ltd.

Thomas, J. & Harden, A. (2008) Methods for the thematic synthesis of qualitative research in systematic reviews. In *BMC Medical Research Methodology*, 8:45.

Thomas de Benitez, S. (2003). Reactive, protective, and rights-based approaches in work with homeless street youth. Children, Youth & Environments, 13, 1–16.

Thomas de Benitez, S. (2011) State of the World's Street Children: Research, London: Consortium for Street Children.

Tibaijuka, A. (1994). The Cost of Differential Gender Roles in African Agriculture: A Case Study of Smallholder Coffee-Banana

Farms in the Kagera Region, Tanzania, *Journal of Agricultural Economics,* Vol. 45 No. 1, January.

Tibaijuka, A. (1998) (editor); The Social Services Crisis of the 1990s – Strategies for Sustainable Systems in Tanzania. Aldershot, Ashgate

Tierney K. (2019), Disasters: A Sociological Approach, Polity Press, Cambridge.

Trotter, C., Cox, D. & Crawford, K. (2002) Family problem solving: A case study, *Australian Social Work,* 55:2, 119-127, DOI: 10.1080/03124070208410965.

Tsiris, G. & Elliot, M. (2019) Reflexivity: Why does it matter? Scottish Graduate School of Social Science – Summer School 2019.

Tsoka-Gwegweni, J. & Cumber Nambile, S. (2016) The Health Profile of Street Children in Africa: A Literature Review. In *Journal of Public Health in Africa*: ResearchGate.

Twikirize, J.M., & Spitzer, H., (2019a). Indigenous and innovative social work practice: evidence from East Africa. In: Twikirize, J.M., & Spitzer, H. (Eds.), Social Work Practice in Africa. Indigenous and Innovative Approaches. Fountain, Kampala, pp. 1–19.

Twikirize, J.M., & Spitzer, H. (Eds.), (2019b). Social Work Practice in Africa. Indigenous and Innovative Approaches. Fountain, Kampala.

Ulriksen M.S. (2016) The development of social protection policies in Tanzania, 2000-2015: CSSR Working Paper No. 377. Published by the Centre for Social Science Research University of Cape Town, South Africa.

UNCHS (Habitat) (2000) Strategies to combat homelessness. UN-Habitat

UNCRPD- United Nations Convention on the Rights of Persons with Disabilities (2006). Department of Economic and Social Affairs Disability. New York.

UNDP (2019) Human Development Report: Gender Inequality Index.

UNICEF (2009) United Republic of Tanzania – Child Protection.

United Nations Children's Fund (UNICEF). (2012) "Cities and Children: The Challenge of Urbanization in Tanzania." Tanzania: UNICEF.

United Republic of Tanzania (URT). (2000) The Tanzania Development Vision 2025. Dar es Salaam: Planning Commission.

United Republic of Tanzania –The National Policy on non-governmental Organisation-NGOs, (2001).

United Republic of Tanzania (2003) National Ageing Policy: Ministry of Labour, Youth Development, and Sport.

United Republic of Tanzania: Poverty Eradication and Economic Empowerment Division, (2010) 'Tanzania Gender Indicators Booklet' Dar es Salaam, Tanzania.

United Nations (2016) DP/DCP/TZA/2 (Executive Board of the United Nations Development Programme, the United Nations Population Fund and the United Nations Office for Project Services): Country programme document for the United Republic of Tanzania (2016-2021) 25-29 January 2016, New York.

United Nations Children's Fund, (2011) World health Organization and World Bank workshop in Tanzania. WHO report on disability.

Uromi, S. M. & Mazagwa, M. I. (2014) Challenges Facing People with Disabilities and Possible Solutions in Tanzania, *Journal of Educational Policy and Entrepreneurial Research,* Volume 1, No 2.

USAID | Health Policy Initiative Task Order 1 (2008) Gender-Based Violence in Tanzania: An Assessment of Policies, Services, and Promising Interventions. *Initiative U.S. President's Emergency Plan for AIDS Relief.*

Vaismoradi, M., Turunen, H. & Bondas, T. (2013). Content analysis and thematic analysis: Implications for conducting a qualitative descriptive study. *Nursing & Health Sciences, 15*(3), 398-405.

Vaismoradi, M., Jacqueline, J., Hannele, T. & Snelgrove, S. (2016). Theme development in qualitative content analysis and thematic analysis. *Journal of Nursing Education and Practice, 6*(5), 100-110.

Vaismoradi, M. & Snelgrove, S. (2019). Theme in Qualitative Content Analysis and Thematic Analysis. *Forum Qualitative Sozialforschung / Forum: Qualitative Social Research, 20*(3), Art. 23, http://dx.doi.org/10.17169/fqs-20.3.3376.

Van Doren, J.W. (1988) Death African style: The Case of S.M Otieno, in The American Journal of Comparative Law, Volume36, Issue2 Spring1988: pp329-350, https://doi.org/10.2307/840412.

Van Nes, F., Abma, T., Jonsson, H. & Deeg, D. (2010) Language Differences in Qualitative Research: Is Meaning Lost in Translation? *European Journal of Ageing,* (7) 313-316. http://dx.doi.org/10.1007/s10433-010-0168-y.

Vanobbberghen, F., Letang, E., Gamell, A., Mnzava, D. K., Faini, D. & Luwanda, L. B. (2017) A decade of HIV care in rural Tanzania: Trends in clinical outcomes and impact of clinic optimisation in an open, prospective cohort. *PLoS ONE* 12(7): e0180983. https://doi.org/10.1371/journal.

Van Staden, A. M., & Weich, D. J. V. (2007). Profile of the geriatric patient hospitalised at Universitas Hospital, South Africa. SA Family Practitioner, 49(2), 14–14c.

Vuckovic, M., Altvater A., Sekei, L. H. & Kloss, K. (2017) Sexual harassment and gender-based violence in Tanzania's public service: A study among employees in Mtwara Region and Dar es Salaam, in *International Journal of Workplace Health Management* Vol. 10 No. 2, 2017 pp. 116-133. Emerald Publishing Limited 1753-8351 DOI 10.1108.

Vyas, S., Jansen, H.A.F.M. (2018) Unequal power relations and partner violence against women in Tanzania: a cross-sectional analysis. *BMC Women's Health* 18, 185 (2018). https://doi.org/10.1186/s12905-018-0675-0.

Wade, L. (2009) The social construction of social problems- Society Pages-, accessed at https://thesocietypages.org/, on 10 Dec. 2020.

Wagao, J.H. (1992) Adjustment Policies in Tanzania, 1981–9: The Impact on Growth, Structure and Human Welfare. Palgrave Macmillan, London.

Wamara, F.M.A. (1997) Magu District Livelihood Security Project-baseline survey report. Magu, Tanzania: CARE International.

Wangwe, S.M. & Rweyemamu, D. C. (2001) The state of Tanzania's social sector in the development context – Economic and Social Research Foundation (ESRF), Dar es Salaam.

Watkins, J. M., Mohr, B. J. & Kelly, R. (2011). Appreciative inquiry: Change at the speed of imagination (2nd ed.). New York, NY: John Wiley.

Weisbrod, B.A. (1975) Toward a theory of the voluntary non-profit sector in a three-sector economy, Russell Sage Foundation, New York.

Wellington, J., Bathmaker, A., Hunt, C., McCulloch, G. & Sikes, P. (2005). Succeeding with your doctorate. London: Sage.

West, J. & Watson, D. (2006) Social Work process and practice: Approaches, knowledge and skills, Palgrave: Macmillan.

White, V. (2006). *The state of feminist social work*. London, UK: Routledge.

Whitmarsh, L. (2008). Are flood victims more concerned about climate change than other people? The role of direct experience in risk perception and behavioural response. *Journal of Risk Research* 11: 351–374.

Wilkins, D. & Boahen, G. (2013) Critical Analysis Skills for Social Workers, McGraw-Hill Education: Open University.

Wisner B. (2016) Vulnerability as Concept, Model, Metric, and Tool. Published online: 31 August: https://doi.org/10.1093/acrefore/9780199389407.013.25

Women's empowerment, Accessed on 23 January 2021, at https://en.wikipedia.org/wiki/Women%27s_empowerment).

World Health Organisation (WHO) (2009) Violence Prevention – the evidence: Promoting gender equality to prevent violence against women. JMU-Centre for Public Health/WHO Press, New York/Switzerland.

World Health Organisation (WHO) (2012) Understanding and Addressing Violence against Women; WHO: Geneva, Switzerland.

World Bank, (2003). Gender Equality and the Millennium Development Goal.
World Population Review (https://worldpopulationreview.com/world-cities/dar-es-salaam-population accessed July 2020).

Woodroofe, K. (1974) From Charity to Social Work in England and the United States, Routledge, London.

Wright E.O (2007) A framework for Emancipatory social science, University of Wisconsin-Madison. Accessedat http://www.ssc.wisc.edu/~wright/Emancipatory-social-Science-Berkeley-talk.pdf, December 2020.

Yakushko, O., Badiee, M., Mallory, A. & Wang S. (2011) Insider Outsider: Reflections on Working with One's Own Communities, Women & Therapy, 34:3, 279-292, DOI: 10.1080/02703149.2011.580685.

Young, R & Collin, A. (2004). Introduction: constructivism and social constructionism in the career field. Journal of Vocational Behaviour 64(3), 373-388.

Yangwe M. D. (2014) Street Children in Tanzania: Are the International NGOs Making a Difference? A Case Study Approach: Examining the Issues of Street Children in Tanzania Politics | Policies | Funding from the UK International NGOs Perspectives. doi:10.13140/RG.2.2.31358.18241. ResearchGate.

Yount, K.M. (2005) The Patriarchal Bargain and Intergenerational Coresidence in Egypt. *The Sociological Quarterly*, Volume 46, Issue 1, 137-164.

Yount, K.M., VanderEnde, K. E., Dodell, S., & Cheong, Y. F. (2016). Measurement of women's agency in Egypt: A national validation study. Social Indicators Research, 128(3), 1171–1192. https://doi.org/10.1007/s11205-015-1074-7.

Yount, K., Crandall, A., & Cheong, Y.F. (2018). Women Age at First Marriage and Long-term Economic Empowerment in Egypt. *World development*, (102), 124-134.

Zambelli, E., Roelen, K., Hossain, N., Chopra D. & Musoke, J.T. (2017) My Mother Does a Lot of Work': Women Balancing Paid and Unpaid Care Work in Tanzania: *National Report for Women's Economic Empowerment Policy and Programming*. BRAC Research and Evaluation Unit. Accessed on 2nd April 2021, at https://opendocs.ids.ac.uk/opendocs/bitstream/handle/123456789/13283/Tanzania%20v2.1%20 SCREEN.pdf?sequence=2.

Zu Selhausen, F.M (2019) Missions, Education and Conversion in Colonial Africa: *African Economic History Working Paper Series No. 48/2019*, ResearchGate.

HERZ FÜR AUTOREN A HEART FOR AUTHORS À L'ÉCOUTE DES AUTEURS MIA KAPΔIA ΓIA ΣΥΓΓΡ
JÄRTA FÖR FÖRFATTARE UN CORAZÓN POR LOS AUTORES YAZARLARIMIZA GÖNÜL VERELIM SZ
ORE PER AUTORI ET HJERTE FOR FORFATTERE EEN HART VOOR SCHRIJVERS TEMOS OS AUTC
RZÖINKÉRT SERCE DLA AUTORÓW EIN HERZ FÜR AUTOREN A HEART FOR AUTHORS À L'ÉCOU
AÇÃO ВСЕЙ ДУШОЙ К АВТОРАМ ETT HJÄRTA FÖR FÖRFATTARE Á LA ESCUCHA DE LOS AUTOI
TEURS MIA KAPΔIA ΓIA ΣΥΓΓΡΑΦΕΙΣ UN CUORE PER AUTORI ET HJERTE FOR FORFATTERE EEN
ARLARIMIZA GO   ZÖINKÉRT SERCE DLA AUTORÓW EIN HERZ FÜ
OR SCHRIJVERS   AÇÃO ВСЕЙ ДУШОЙ К АВТОРАМ ETT HJÄRTA FÖ

The author

Dr David Henry Kanyumi is a lecturer in social welfare and social work in a global context. He is publishing a book for the first time because he has always been troubled by the social problems in his home country and wants to contribute to finding a solution. He has a PhD in Social Work and Social Policy and is a teaching associate at the University of Strathclyde, Glasgow.